The
Emergence
of Greece

The Making of the Past

The Emergence of Greece

by Alan Johnston

ELSEVIER · PHAIDON

Advisory Board for The Making of the Past

Frontispiece: Metope from a temple of Hera at Foce del Sele near Paestum. Late 6th century BC.

ISBN 0 7290 0043 5

Elsevier Phaidon, an imprint of Phaidon Press Ltd.
Published in the United States by E.P. Dutton & Co. Inc., 201, Park Avenue South, New York, N.Y. 10003

Origination by Art Color Offset, Rome, Italy
Filmset by Keyspools Limited, Golborne, Lancs.
Printed and bound by Brepols, Turnhout - Belgium

Contents

Maps

Preface to the series

This book is a volume in the Making of the Past, a series describing the early history of the world as revealed by archaeology and related disciplines. The series is written by experts under the guidance of a distinguished panel of advisers and is designed for the layman, for young people, the student, the armchair traveler and the tourist. Its subject is a new history – the making of a new past, uncovered and reconstructed in recent years by skilled specialists. Since many of the authors of these volumes are themselves practicing archaeologists, leaders in a rapidly changing field, the series is completely authoritative and up-to-date. Each volume covers a specific period and region of the world and combines a detailed survey of the modern archaeology and sites of the area with an account of the early explorers, travelers, and archaeologists concerned with it. Later chapters of each book are devoted to a reconstruction in text and pictures of the newly revealed cultures and civilizations that make up the new history of the area.

Titles already published in the series

The Egyptian Kingdoms   **Biblical Lands**
The Aegean Civilizations   **The New World**

Titles to appear in 1976

The Spread of Islam   **Man before History**
The Emergence of Greece   **The Greek World**
Barbarian Europe   **The Rise of Civilization**

Future titles

The First Empires   **The Kingdoms of Africa**
The Roman World   **Rome and Byzantium**
Ancient Japan   **Prehistoric Europe**
The Persian Revival   **India and Southeast Asia**
Ancient China   **Archaeology Today**

Introduction

The transition from the Bronze to the Iron Age in Greece was followed by two colonization movements and an Orientalizing period. Visions of verdigris changing to rust? Portly administrators lording it over normally subservient natives? Mummies and hieroglyphs at Athens? Illusions that may only be fostered by the frequent use of the word "Archaic" in this volume.

Such archaeological shorthand attempts to state over-concisely what happened between the Lion Gate and the Parthenon – something clearly of significance to change Greece from a palace-centered network of petty kingdoms into a politically experienced collection of autonomous city-states whose individual members were capable of producing work in the fields of literature and all the arts still regarded with admiration and deference today.

"Iron Age" is a convenient phrase indicating that iron and not bronze is now the basic metal used for artifacts; though not wholly inappropriate, it is a misleading title for the years we shall cover – 1100 to 500 BC. "Archaic" covers the period preceding the "Classical" age – words originally coined to describe the development of Greek art down to its "flowering" in the 5th century. "Colonization" is our word for what the Greeks called "setting up home abroad," and we shall see that many of these settlements first set up in our period became famous cities, responsible for the dissemination of Greek art, ideas and life-style over much of the Mediterranean world – first eastward across the Aegean to Miletus, Ephesus, even Troy, then west to Sicily and southern Italy (the area soon dubbed "Great Greece" whose history we shall survey down to the years of Roman expansion), also north to Byzantium and the Black Sea and south to Cyrene and Libya, near neighbors of Carthage.

We cannot ignore a return traffic – during this period Greece made renewed and fruitful contact with the old, and some new, civilizations of the Near East, resulting in our "Orientalizing period," the eager acceptance of ideas and iconography into many aspects of Greek life.

Another name given to the Iron Age is the "historical period," which may mislead even more. Only during the last 250 years of our period was writing used by the Greeks, and not until its very end do we find mention of any form of historical writing – not too long before our earliest preserved historical texts, of Herodotus from Halicarnassus and the Athenian Thucydides. The poets of an earlier age may tell us something of the conditions of their times – Homer, Hesiod, Pindar among them – but they wrote for their contemporaries and not for us.

Thus in the "historical period" a great deal of our knowledge must still be derived from archaeology. Here there may be little to impress on the scale of Mycenae or the Acropolis, but let it be noted that an early Greek temple was erected on the ruins of Agamemnon's palace, while the Parthenon is built on the foundations of an earlier temple. As at England's York Minster or France's Notre Dame, we would hesitate before removing the offending building to extend our knowledge of earlier times. The archaeology of "Archaic" Greece has often been hampered by such tenacious rebuilding – it is easier to strike gold than to reach the early levels of Naples or Istanbul!

While the buildings in such levels are often of slight construction, ruined, robbed or rotted away, and the archaeological sites of our period may often disappoint the visitor, the objects found in such excavations are regularly of far more intrinsic and historical value than those found elsewhere and a visit to the museum will without doubt repay the visitor's curiosity.

Chronological Table

DATE	POTTERY STYLE	EVENTS IN GREECE	EVENTS IN THE EAST	EVENTS IN THE WEST	ART AND ARCHITECTURE
1100 –		Mycenae burned			
		First burials in Kerameikos	Miletus colonized		
	Submycenaean				Silver-working at Argos and Thorikos
1050 –	Protogeometric	Sparta occupied			
900 –	Early Geometric				Leukandi centaur
850 –			Greek traders at al Mina		
800 –	Middle Geometric			Carthage founded?	
		Olympic games, 776		Euboeans found Pithekoussai	
750 –		Aristocracies flourish			Dipylon master / Olympia tripods
	Late Geometric			Corinth founds Syracuse / Foundation of Sybaris and Taras	Homer
		Spartans take Messenia / Lelantine war			Hesiod
700 –	Orientalizing		Cimmerians take Gordion		
650 –		Pheidon king of Argos / Cypselus becomes tyrant of Corinth		Zaleucus, law-giver at Locri	First stone temples at Corinth and Isthmia
			and attack Sardis	Himera founded	Chigi vase
		Cylon's attempted coup at Athens	and the Ionian cities	Cyrene and Selinus founded. First Greeks in Spain.	Nikandre statue
		Draco's law code?	Greek traders at Naucratis. Milesian expansion into Black Sea.		
			Thrasybulus tyrant of Miletus. Alcaeus and Pittakos vie at Mitylene		
600 –		Solon's reforms / Sacred war over Delphi / End of tyranny at Corinth		Foundation of Acragas	Sappho
				Greek traders at Gravisca	
	Archaic (black-figure)	Pisistratus' first attempt at tyranny of Athens		Phalaris tyrant of Acragas / Camarina destroyed by Syracusans	François vase / Corfu temple
			Croesus king of Lydia 561–546		Vix crater
550 –		War between Sparta and Tegea	Cyrus takes Sardis and then Ionian cities	Malcho campaigns in Sicily	Temple of Artemis at Ephesus
			Polycrates tyrant of Samos	Siris destroyed by Achaean colonies	Exekias / Siphnian treasury / Peplos kore
525 –		Death of Pisistratus			
		Cleomenes king of Sparta (519–488?)	Darius king of Persia 521–486. Campaign in Thrace		Euphronios
	(red-figure)	End of tyranny at Athens / Reforms of Cleisthenes		Sybaris destroyed	Birth of Phidias?
500 –			Ionian revolt / Burning of Sardis		Temple of Aphaea, Aegina
		Argives defeated by Sparta at Sepeia	Battle of Lade and sack of Miletus	Campaigns of Hippocrates, tyrant of Gela	Berlin painter
490 –		Persians sack Eretria, Battle of Marathon			
		Ostracisms at Athens	Xerxes king of Persia (485–465)	Gelon takes Syracuse	First Parthenon begun
480 –		Xerxes' invasion		Carthaginians defeated at Himera	First victory for Aeschylus' tragedies
			Battle of Mycale		

The country. Man's way of life has always been conditioned by his environment, and we should bear this in mind when we consider the civilization of Greece. The country is a tangle of mountains punctuated by fertile plains, few of any large extent; about three-quarters of the land would have been uncultivatable in antiquity, and except for the very richest plains the soil is full of stones. There is little to suggest that Greece's appearance was much different in the period with which this book is concerned. Perhaps there were larger forests on the mountains and the climate may have been a little damper, but basically the long hot Mediterranean summer would still have determined agricultural production, with the main corn crop ripening during May, beans, lentils and chick-peas harvested through the summer, grapes nearer its end and olives in the autumn. At a period when individual communities had to be self-sufficient there could be no question of abandoning the basic necessity of a grain crop for a more economic use of the land. "If a man has not got a year's supplies stored in his house he will have precious time for arguing and debate," writes Hesiod in about 700 BC from his unloved home in Boeotia. Stock-rearing was by no means neglected in our period, and the seas doubtless provided quantities of fish.

Inland communication was a tiresome, though not impossible, business; the mountain passes were high, no navigable rivers existed and in times of hardship road-building was not considered. The sea afforded an easier journey between most points, though we should not underestimate the sudden fury of the Mediterranean winds at any time of year; wind and sea clearly account

Black-figure Athenian vase of about 525 BC, found in Etruria, showing women at a fountain house. All the women (and the lion-spouted fountain) are named on the vase.

for the majority of the metaphors introduced by early poets into their writing. One benefit provided by the mountainous terrain was an abundance of naturally fortified acropolis sites on which to settle or take refuge; many were supplied with water, but the Greeks were used to storing rainwater in cisterns or to walking down to the

Previous page: typical sparse countryside of mainland Greece – the plain of Plataea where the Persians were decisively defeated by the Greeks in 479 BC.

Below: air view of Samos showing the site of the ancient city. The terrain is typical of the Aegean islands.

nearest spring for their daily requirements. The indented coast of the mainland and islands offered many little sandy bays on which smaller craft could be beached, and land-locked harbors where boats could ride, but there were also long stretches of rocky shore ready to receive the storm-caught ship whose oars could not save her.

The particular drawbacks and merits of different areas should not be forgotten; some of the finest harbors are in infertile surroundings, and some of the richest plains contain swamps which, although not malarial in our period, were far from healthy. The Mycenaeans had drained Lake Copaïs in Boeotia, but it was again under water in the Iron Age. Hilltop sites sometimes became too small for a growing city or were too large to be defended in comfort. The enemy could easily poison a water supply outside the city walls, and a town set near an important sea-lane could get easy pickings from piracy.

After the fall of Mycenae. Archaeological studies have shown that the palace-based Mycenaean civilization of Greece slid into an ignominious decline during the 12th century BC, although the reasons for this decline are obscure. Citadels were burned, large areas abandoned and in particular overseas contacts were almost wholly lost, after a vigorous trade had been carried on with Italy and the Near East for several centuries.

During the 12th century two waves of settlers from Greece, perhaps even Mycenae itself, came to Cyprus. It will be useful to ask how we know this, for the answer will reveal the kind of evidence on which we must build our picture of the Dark Ages of Greece which followed.

Archaeological discoveries have contributed to this conclusion, especially in distinguishing the two separate periods of migration, but it is only in recent years that any quantity of material closely akin to Mycenaean products of the 12th century has been found on Cypriot sites. It consists mainly of fragments of pottery, and we shall see that, in Greece too, much of the archaeological material relevant to the history of the early Iron Age is limited to pottery of recent discovery.

The migration to Cyprus had long been posited by philologists, who noted that the dialect of Greek later spoken in Cyprus was closely related to that of Arcadia, the mountainous heart of the Peloponnese, and rather less closely to that of Attica and the central part of the Aegean and Asia Minor. The decipherment of the Linear B script suggests that these were the main dialects of the Bronze Age Greeks, and that the migration to Cyprus occurred during that period; those left behind retreated to the hills, where we find them in the Iron Age surrounded by Dorian Greeks with their lisping "*th*" and broad "*a.*" These Dorians replaced the rulers of Mycenae, but their origin is most difficult to detect; since a related dialect was spoken to the northwest they may have come from that area, but it is also possible that they had always been in Greece, but were earlier subservient to Mycenaean rulers.

Olive groves in modern Greece and the olive harvest in antiquity pictured on an Attic vase of about 520 BC found in Etruria. Greeks probably introduced olive-growing to the Etruscans.

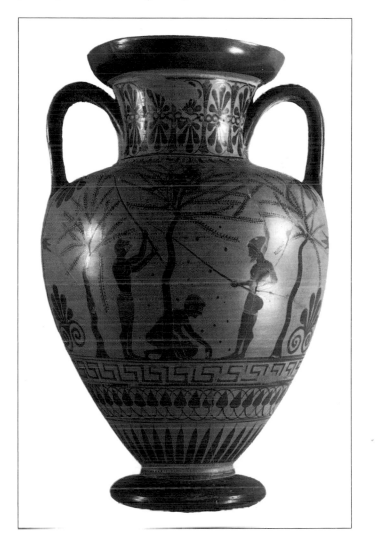

The Mediterranean.

Sources of our knowledge. Here we might ask what the Greeks themselves said about their past, but we have to confront one most important fact: Greece was illiterate between the end of the Bronze Age and the 8th century, and all our written records date from long after the events of the Dark Ages. Furthermore, writing was not extensively practiced before the 6th century, and the surviving literature of the years 750 to 450 includes nothing of great historical value. Most of it consists of verse, ranging in subject-matter from epic poetry to scurrility via tragic plays and cosmic musings. The Dark Ages are recalled in legendary terms – Thucydides, the Athenian general and historian, writing in the later 5th century, prefaces his account of the great Peloponnesian War, in which he took part, with a survey of the development of Greece in which he attempts to divest the remote past of its heroic trappings. However we must remember that he only had access to material used by previous writers and could do no more than rationalize their versions. He speaks with some uncertainty of the years following the Trojan War, an event generally accepted as historical:

"Greece remained in a state of ferment and migration preventing peaceful growth. The return from Troy was a lengthy business and caused many upsets; most cities saw feuds and revolution, with exiles departing to new foundations elsewhere. . . . In the eightieth year after the fall of Troy the Dorians took over the Peloponnese in company with the descendants of Heracles."

The question of how much reliance we can place on such assessments depends not so much on the scrupulousness of the author as on that of his sources; and all sources go back to an oral tradition bridging over 400 years. There is indeed a wealth of information relating to the period preserved in the works of later writers, not least the compilers of Greek dictionaries during the Christian era. Stories of the founding of cities by heroes and their sons abound, but the recurrence of stock themes and the discrepancies between different versions of a single alleged episode cannot command our confidence.

The earliest and the longest of the written sources is provided by Homer, that enigmatic figure from Ionia whose 28,000 lines of verse in the *Iliad* and *Odyssey* describe so many facets of his heroes' lives. But where did his ideas come from? Were they the product of a fertile imagination, centuries-old tradition or personal observation? We shall see that his basic material comes from all three sources, and in any given case the particular source can only be deduced from external evidence. Homer can contribute only incidentally to a history of the Dark Ages.

Early colonies. In the chapter just quoted Thucydides goes on to talk of the colonization of Ionia by the Athenians. This eastward move was a major event of the early Dark Ages, resulting in the foundation of such towns as Miletus and Ephesus. Finds at Miletus suggest a short gap between Mycenaean departure and the arrival of new settlers, but only at a very few other sites on this coast has excavation revealed a similarly early Greek presence, which preserved traditions would lead us to expect. Again the dialect map can tell us much; in the central section of the coast together with the offshore island of Samos we find cities using the Ionic dialect, which is akin to Attic. We may doubt whether Athens could have supplied all the settlers, as Thucydides claims, but he was influenced by later Athenian propaganda, whereas Herodotus of Halicarnassus, writing a little earlier, talks of migrations of Ionians from other parts of Greece. The social structure of Athens did have points of similarity with that of the Ionic cities, and the boast of Athens to have survived the end of the Bronze Age unscathed seems confirmed by excavation.

North of the Ionians were the Aeolic colonies who were linked by their dialect to Boeotia and Thessaly on the mainland. The inhabitants may have moved east as a result of pressure exerted by Dorian invaders or settlers, since substantial Dorian elements are present in the later mainland dialects. They settled on the island of Lesbos and the mainland as far south as Smyrna and Chios, though they were soon replaced in the latter two areas by Ionians, probably by the end of the 9th century at the latest. Troy

was also reinhabited by Aeolian Greeks from Lesbos, but not till the 8th century.

The southern coastal areas and the islands of the Dodecanese were eventually settled by Dorian Greeks, including three towns on the island of Rhodes, Ialysos, Camiros and Lindos (the present city was founded in 407), as well as Cos, Cnidos and perhaps Halicarnassus.

Accounts of the founding of these towns were largely legendary and cannot be correlated with the limited archaeological material available. How to identify Dorians archaeologically has long been a disputed question; they were once thought to be recognizable as northern invaders using long dress pins and stronger slashing swords than the Mycenaean rapier, and cremating their dead; but much of this evidence comes from the cemeteries of Athens, where no Dorian is known or alleged to have settled. Evidence drawn from dialect tells us that Dorians also colonized the southern Cyclades, Melos and Thera, and Crete. Here again we face difficulties in interpretation of evidence – later Cretans spoke with a Dorian accent, save for some non-Greek speakers in the eastern part of the island, but in the archaeological record there is no clear break between the last Minoan period and the early Iron Age. There are signs of a decline in standards and a marked retreat to remote and secure sites, but no abrupt change. The unedifying conclusion that the Dorians are not to be recognized by archaeology is becoming increasingly likely.

We can assert with more confidence that life in the early Dark Ages was carried on at subsistence level. Graves are piously but poorly equipped, any form of artifact other than pottery is rare and architectural remains are of the most meager kind.

Dating. It is the study of pottery which has produced the basic chronological scheme of the period. From changes in the shapes and style of decoration as well as the examination of stratified sequences (not common yet for the earliest years), we can build up a background picture and with a certain amount of confidence place new finds within the framework thus obtained. Further changes can then be detected, for example in the comparative richness or poverty of burials, in artistic standards, in typology and use of utensils and weapons. It is more difficult to put calendar dates to the sequence. During the Bronze Age imported Egyptian objects or Mycenaean exports found in the Near East helped align civilization in Greece with known Pharaoh dates, but in the early Iron Age Greece stood almost isolated. Not until the later 9th century do we find any Greek objects in an archaeological context which can be given a calendar date, and even then dispute can arise. From that period a trickle of Greek vases found their way to sites in the Near East whose building and destruction are recorded in the archives of the Assyrian kings or the Old Testament. In between the two fixed extremes we can do little more than date our sequences by

The dialects of mainland Greece and the islands.

Doric
Ionic
Aeolic
Achaean
Northwest Greek
Aeolic and Northwest Greek

0   150 km
0   100 mi

MACEDONIA
Thasos
CHALCIDICE
Samothrace
Imbros
EPIRUS
THESSALY
Lemnos
AEOLIS
CORCYRA
PHTHIOTIS
Lesbos
Leucas
AETOLIA
LOCRIS
Scyros
ACARNANIA
PHOCIS
Euboea
AEGEAN
Chios
IONIAN SEA
ACHAEA
BOEOTIA
ATTICA
ELIS
ARCADIA
ARGOLIS
Samos
IONIA
SEA
MESSENIA
LACONIA
Naxos
CYCLADES
SPORADES
Rhodes
Crete
Cyprus

probable length of the subdivisions which we can isolate.

The style of painted pottery used in the major sites has given names to these archaeological periods. We use the terms Protogeometric, Geometric and Archaic as shorthand for "about 1050 to 900," and so on, though it should be stressed that they basically describe styles of decoration which did not change simultaneously throughout the Greek world.

Expansion to the west. Thucydides finishes the paragraph quoted above by telling us that the Peloponnesians founded most of the colonies in Sicily and Italy, but bypasses the 200 years or so which elapsed between the end of the retreat to Ionia and the more purposive push west. It is a telescoping of time for which we may forgive him, since at the beginning of his sixth book he gives us precious details of the foundation dates of some of the Sicilian settlements – 733 for Syracuse in Sicily, 728 for Megara Hyblaea and 688 for Gela among others. These dates have become the cornerstone of archaeological chronology for the 8th and 7th centuries, despite the fact that historians have distrusted them on a number of grounds, for example because they are based merely on a count of generations from foundation to the time of Thucydides' own source. However each new excavation at these sites seems to confirm his text.

What determined the dispatch and destination of this wave of colonies? At about this time Hesiod stresses the difficulties of making a living from the land in Boeotia, yet sees worse troubles in setting sail and indulging in trade. He confesses himself a landlubber, but his father had taken up trading from Cyme, an Aeolian colony in Asia Minor; however he had failed and migrated to Ascra in Boeotia. Hesiod implies (and archaeology has confirmed the fact) that by this period a fair number of Greeks were living by trade and had been doing so for some time. It is just possible that contact between Greece and the Near East had never been completely broken in the Dark Ages, though it must have been very limited in the years around 1000. A small trickle of eastern artifacts, jewelry, ivories and metalwork, reached Greek sites in the 10th and 9th centuries BC, becoming a stream but never a flood by the end of the 8th. The pioneers in this renewal of trade were probably mainly Greeks, and perhaps Phoenicians too (a term which to a Greek meant anybody of Semitic race from the eastern Mediterranean). The Greeks included men from the Cyclades and Rhodes, but especially from Euboea and her two main towns Eretria and Chalcis. A trading post was set up before 800 at the mouth of the Orontes river in Syria and Euboeans had also established themselves by 760 on the island of Ischia in the bay of Naples – in both these places they had their eyes on a trade coming from further afield in the Near East and central Italy respectively.

Ischia is not mentioned by Thucydides. His records for Greek seapower in the Iron Age go back only as far as the Corinthians, who on the trading front at least succeeded the Euboeans at the end of the 8th century. The reasons for the Euboean demise may have been various, but a contributing factor was undoubtedly a war waged between Chalcis and Eretria concerning possession of the Lelantine plain which lay between them. This is one of the few historical episodes to emerge clearly from later literary sources, though even so we are given no specific dates for the war nor are we told who was the victor. Another such episode of the same period was the first war between Sparta and her western neighbor in the Peloponnese, Messenia; it lasted 19 years and resulted in the Messenians becoming slaves or helots on Laconian estates, where they were a source of constant worry for the true-born Spartans for centuries to come.

A persistent story has it that bastard sons born to Spartan women while their husbands were away at war were sent off to settle in Italy at Taras (Taranto), the only Spartan colony founded during these years. This colony, like many others, was on a site of a type dear to the Greeks – an easily defended hill surrounded, in this case on three sides, by the sea and with an enclosed harbor, the best in southern Italy. Syracuse was founded on a similar site, while other settlements on hills were protected on one side only from the sea – for instance Gela and Locri. The purpose of many of these colonies was to ease pressure of population at home, hinted at by Hesiod, and for the most part the settlers chose coastal and fertile areas in the climatically similar regions of southern Italy. This was most certainly the case with the colonies along the instep of the "foot" of Italy, between Taras and Locri – colonies founded for the most part by Achaeans from the narrow coastal strip along the north coast of the Peloponnese. Two of the most successful, Metapontum and Sybaris, were placed in very rich agricultural land, though neither had a convenient acropolis on which to seek refuge.

Knowledge of these sites undoubtedly came from the earlier traders, but there is also a probability that folk memory stretched back to the Greek activities in the area during the Bronze Age, and persistent stories of Greek settlement here by refugees from the Trojan War may not be wholly without foundation.

These foundations paid nominal respect to the mother city and often established cults in honor of their founders, but most were so far from home that their affairs could be conducted independently. To our knowledge it was not often that the affairs of the homeland and of the west impinged closely on each other before the later 5th century. Groups of exiles continued to seek homes in the west, rarely found without tribulation, and Sardinia was twice mooted by the Ionians as a haven of refuge when they were under pressure from Persia. However, in the realm of commercial contact east and west were closely linked. In all this, we should admit the very fragmentary nature of the evidence at our disposal for the early history of virtually all the colonies, while excavation has only

Ivory figure of Syrian "Astarte" type but Greek workmanship – one of six found in a grave of the Dipylon cemetery in Athens, c. 730 BC.

andom information about their architectural and
chievements.

The evolving state. The 7th century brought important
changes in many spheres of life on the mainland – some
would claim that subsequent years merely saw a con-
solidation of these. Many were inspired by new contacts
with the east and were already under way in the later 8th
century. In the field of pictorial arts the development of
narrative representations and the range of subjects
portrayed owed much to the east, as did the appearance
of lifesized sculpture in stone and many of the themes
chosen by the early poets of Ionia and the Cyclades.

Social changes were probably even more dramatic,
though our picture of them is dulled by a dearth of direct
evidence. Wealth continued to increase, as physical remains attest, but this wealth was not equally distributed
and tensions arose among individual communities as a
result of the excesses of the ruling classes. Up to this period
authority within these communities was mainly in the
hands of the noble families, though occasionally we find a
single person retaining overall rule. Specific posts of an
administrative nature, religious, judicial and military, had
been created, and could be inherited or held for a given
term from one year to life; but our knowledge of these is
scanty in the extreme. In Athens the "king" was concerned mainly with cult affairs, while the "archon" was
the chief executive. At Sparta a unique form of government had emerged by the end of the first Messenian war
under two kings of equal stature, an assembly of 28 elders
and five ephors (overseers), whose origins may have been
as tribal leaders representing their people.

What happened in this situation of increasing wealth,
especially commercial, and traditional landowning aristocracy, was the promotion in many towns of unconstitutional rulers – "tyrant" being the non-Greek word
often used to describe them at the time. Though found
widely throughout the years 650–500, the causes of their
usurpation seem to have varied considerably. We have a
certain number of contemporary verses written by people
much concerned with the political situation and the tyrants,
though rarely do they give us specific insights into
individual situations. Alcaeus of Mytilene, contemporary
of Sappho, was an embittered rival of more than one
successful candidate for leadership in the years around 600,
and in 593 Solon was given special powers to solve an
acute agrarian problem in Attica; he writes that people
were disappointed with his middle-of-the-road solution
and surprised that he did not make himself tyrant. At
Megara Theognis uttered many platitudes extolling the
purity of mind of those of noble birth.

The cause of the unrest at Athens was the plight of small
farmers who had mortgaged their land, families and
themselves to the richer classes. An abortive attempt to
seize power had been made in 632 by Cylon, but even
earlier than this Cypselus became tyrant at Corinth,

Orthagoras at Sicyon and Pheidon at Argos, though the
latter's exact dates are hotly disputed. We are told that
Cypselus and his son Periander extended Corinth's commercial interests, but we cannot detect any substantial
changes in her fortunes from the archaeological evidence
either at the beginning or at the end of the tyranny. We have
little information about the status of traders at this period,
and so it is dangerous to think in terms of Cypselus
supporting middle-class merchants against aristocratic
landowners, though he certainly did topple a hereditary
oligarchy. At Sicyon a racial element crept in when
Cleisthenes imposed abusive names on the three Dorian
tribes and banned Homer's songs of "Argive" Greeks. In
about 580 he gave his daughter in marriage to a leading
Athenian aristocrat, Megacles, who was then a serious
contender for power. Such dynastic marriages were
frequent, their ostensible purpose being to prop up
relations between individual tyrannies, though few lasted
beyond a third generation.

We can be a little more specific about the last tyranny of
consequence on the mainland – that of Pisistratus at
Athens. Solon had reinstated smallholders and given them
further legal protection, as well as basing the class structure
on wealth not birth, but dissension continued. Three sets
of interests were at odds, each led by a prominent
aristocrat and each based on a particular part of Attica. The
least known of the aristocrats, Pisistratus, succeeded in
establishing himself as tyrant in 546 at the third attempt.
He owed his success to silver from mines he controlled
in northern Greece and the mercenary soldiers he hired
with it. The use of mercenaries was rare on the mainland
before the 4th century, but was common in the east, where
Greeks and Carians had served from a very early date.

Thucydides attributes to the tyrants a lack of initiative
and an inactive foreign policy. He was more impressed by
the militarism of the later Sicilian tyrants, but probably
had in mind Pisistratus and his sons Hippias and Hipparchus, who are not known to have gone to war while in
power. Yet their social achievements were greater than
Thucydides allows, especially in encouraging craftsmen
and builders. The same is true of Polycrates, tyrant of
Samos at this period, although he was expansionist in
extending his rule over neighboring islands and building
up the first powerful naval force in Greece. Herodotus
mentions his other achievements: a huge temple of Hera, a
long mole to protect the harbor essential to his navy and a
water-conduit cut through the rock above the town. We
may add to this list the extensive fortification wall and
ditch, the latter cut by prisoners of war. Pisistratus too
improved the water supply at Athens. He centralized the
administration of Attica at Athens, having previously
wrested the island of Salamis from the Megarians. The
earlier tyrant of Megara, Theagenes, is best remembered
for the fountain-house he had built – virtually the only
relic of antiquity to be found in the town.

We have to be cautious in interpreting our sources

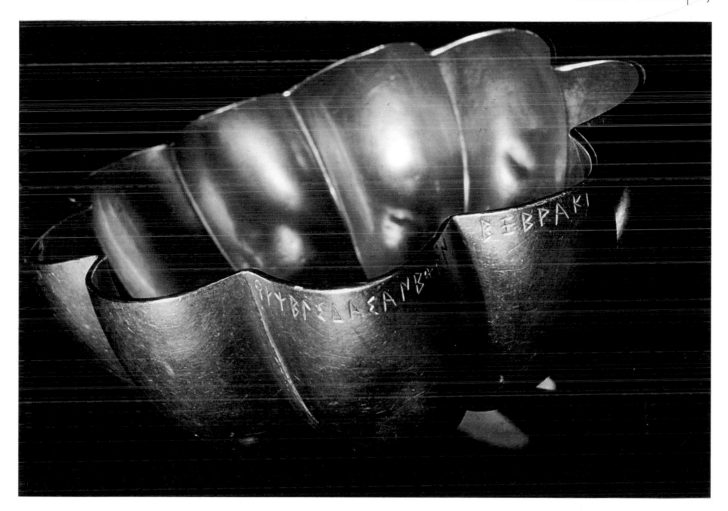

A hammered gold bowl dedicated by the sons of Cypselus, tyrant of Corinth, at Olympia. About 600 BC.

concerning the tyrants, since they attracted many fables and legends as well as a flotsam of genuine information, as do all major historical figures. For example Solon is said to have reformed the Athenian monetary system, and earlier Pheidon was considered to have introduced coinage to Greece. However, as we shall see, they lived before money was known in mainland Greece and long before it became an everyday commodity.

Ionians and Persians. Coinage was one of the ideas borrowed by the eastern Greeks from their neighbors, in this case the Lydians. During the 7th century the whole of Asia Minor suffered from incursions of warlike nomadic tribes from the north, especially the Cimmerians and Treres, who burned the Phrygian capital Gordion in the early 7th century and Lydian Sardis about 650 as well as harassing the Greek colonies and sacking one of them, Magnesia on the Maeander. Some of these colonies had themselves started to send out offshoots around 700 in the area of the Dardanelles and Propontis, but the tempo of their advances was set back by the Cimmerians and picked up only late in the century, when Miletus in particular pushed far up into the Black Sea, beyond the Bosporus, where the Megarians had planted the twin settlements of Chalcedon and Byzantium in the meantime.

Thucydides mentions Ionian naval power after that of Corinth, during the reign of Cyrus in Persia (550–528), but we cannot doubt that Ionian traders had been very active since around the turn of the century. Their pottery, the surviving part of a trade that must have included textiles and the other traditional exports of the Orient, is found in many of the Greek colonies, not only to the north, but also in Sicily, Italy, France and Spain, as well as the trading posts established in the Near East – al Mina, Tell Sukas further south and Naucratis on the Nile Delta. The Corinthian tyrants were on friendly terms with Thrasybulus of Miletus early in the 6th century, and at its end the Milesians went into mourning for the destruction of her ally Sybaris.

The Lydian kings were generally favorably disposed towards the Greeks, although Miletus was repeatedly attacked and Smyrna taken by siege late in the 7th century. Croesus plied the oracle of Delphi with gifts, but its prediction that he would destroy a great empire by attacking Cyrus came only too true in 546 when his own kingdom fell to the Persian. Cyrus was less tolerant of the Greeks, capturing all the coastal towns save Miletus and installing vassal tyrants. Many Greeks fled, notably those

Seated male figure dedicated at the
sanctuary of Apollo at Didyma on the
coast of Asia Minor. About 580 BC.

of Teos, who settled at Abdera in Thrace, and also the Phocaeans, whom Thucydides thought worthy of a special mention. They had already founded Massilia (Marseilles) in about 600 and played a leading role in trade with the west, especially France and Spain. They also had a settlement at Alalia on Corsica, whither the exiles from Ionia now fled. They were rapidly ousted by the combined fleet of the Etruscans and Carthaginians, who did not take kindly to their buccaneering methods, and eventually found a home at Velia, south of Paestum.

Eastern influences on the art of the east Greeks are naturally strong, though not to be exaggerated. The so called Egyptian avenue lined by statues at the sanctuary of Apollo at Didyma, south of Miletus, was not an original feature of the 6th century, though the figures dedicated there, seated dignitaries and recumbent lions, are eastern in style. On Rhodes it is probable that there were some Phoenician glassmakers at work at least as early as the 7th century, while the large numbers of Cypriot imports and other eastern influences on Samos and the Halicarnassus peninsula indicate particularly close contacts. Architecture borrows many details from the Near East, though often translating into monumental form moldings and decorative designs used more modestly there. In Crete too there were very strong eastern influences at work in the 8th and 7th centuries, suggesting actual settlement of artists and refugees, though we may prefer to think of the Cretans as being avid borrowers but poor adaptors of outside ideas. At any rate Crete becomes very much a backwater after 600, although we should not overlook the early and persistent Cretan habit of publishing their laws on stone (another eastern borrowing). These laws dealt with a large range of topics including land tenure and inheritance – the main problems of Archaic Greek society.

Spartan ascendancy. Though the female of a Cretan household had more generous rights of inheritance than women in the rest of Greece, the Dorians in Crete kept to their tribal tradition of all-male messes, membership of which alone entitled one to full citizenship. The same system operated at Sparta, and is often regarded as a peculiarly Spartan institution designed merely with military training in view. Indeed during the 7th and 6th centuries it became necessary for Sparta to be ever ready for war. In 663 she suffered defeat from the Argives, and this encouraged the subservient Messenians to revolt, engendering a period of considerable unease at Sparta itself. In the 6th century Tegea in Arcadia was eventually defeated, but instead of enslaving the captive city, which had been regular policy up to this point, the Spartans more wisely enrolled them into a confederate alliance of which Sparta was *de facto* and probably *de jure* head. By the end of the 6th century this alliance, which we call the Peloponnesian League, had become the major force in mainland Greek affairs. For a period the Spartans even had pre-

tensions to becoming a naval power in the league's crusade against the remaining tyrants. It was not the first such confederation in Iron Age Greece; others, from our slight knowledge of them, were founded with a common religious bond. For example the Panionion, sited south of Ephesus on a hill now lugubriously called Machine Gun Height, was a focal point for the religious and social celebrations of the Ionian Greeks. A federated system, of which we know few details, arose during the later 6th century among the Boeotians, with Thebes at their head.

We should note the Spartans' manipulation of racial propaganda to boost the new league, which stressed that the Dorians had merely returned to the Peloponnese to claim their inheritance as descendants of Heracles, the Bronze Age ruler of Tiryns, rather than as simple invaders. The Argive hero Orestes was also turned into a local Spartan prince – politics and mythology readily mixed.

By the mid-6th century the Spartan constitution was fossilized, though we are told of an increase in the powers of the ephors. This may have been merely an increase in influence, not constitutional power. One particular ephor of the period, Chilon, is alleged to have had a hold over the kings, and in about 540 the ephors showed their concern for the succession in one of the royal houses by together persuading the king Anaxandridas to take a second wife after his first appeared infertile. Herodotus takes particular delight in relating the sequel: the second wife bore Cleomenes, whereupon the first produced three further sons – Dorieus, Leonidas (the hero of Thermopylae) and Cleombrotus (the victor at Plataea).

Dorieus and Cleomenes contested the succession, but Dorieus was out-maneuvered and left Sparta to seek his fortune, unsuccessfully, in Africa and Sicily. Cleomenes, as king of what was at the time the dominant house, led Sparta to yet greater strengths, deposing the remaining tyrants of Greece. The Spartan constitution was liberal when compared superficially with the tyrannies, but citizenship of Sparta was confined to an ever-decreasing group of true-born Spartans.

Democracy at Athens. The final tyranny removed by Sparta was that of Hippias at Athens. His brother Hipparchus had been assassinated in 514, though apparently not for political motives (despite the fact that the murderers, Harmodius and Aristogiton, were soon made into folk heroes as destroyers of the tyranny). The tyranny lasted till 510 under an increasingly embittered Hippias. He was removed by the Spartans in concert with the Alcmeonids, who had already made one unsuccessful attempt a little earlier. This family had come under a curse for killing Cylon and his henchmen when they sought sanctuary after their coup failed back in 632, had amassed wealth in Lydia and were alternately in and out of favor with the tyrants.

The sequel to the liberation of Athens was not what the Spartans had expected. A power struggle between the

Harmodius and the bearded Aristogiton assassinated Hipparchus, brother of the tyrant of Athens, in 514 BC. Their statues, of which these are Roman copies, were reerected in the Agora in 477 BC after the Persian sack.

leading families resulted in the Alcmeonid Cleisthenes, grandson of the tyrant of Sicyon, turning to the common people for support, promising them democratic reforms and so beating off an initially successful intervention by Cleomenes on his opponent's behalf.

The reforms passed by Cleisthenes in 507 are often represented as a mile-stone along the road to democracy, although true conservatives at Athens in later years would prefer the constitution of Solon. The essence of Cleisthenes' measures was a new tribal structure and elective council based on it. Neither idea was entirely new to Greece – we shall note a broadly based council on Chios, and at some point in her Archaic history Sparta adopted six new tribes instead of the original three Dorian divisions. Yet the format of Cleisthenes' tribal reforms seems novel; it was based on existing local communities, but he created ten new tribes out of the old four. In so doing he broke the very close links between family, cult and political power and influence that were the basis of Archaic society, and gave a much larger proportion of the population an opportunity to debate the city's business.

It was a turning point in Athenian history, but in 506, before the reforms could be implemented, Sparta once

more intervened in an attempt this time to put the oligarchs back in power, acting in concert with the Boeotians and Chalcidians. Only disagreement in the Spartan camp saved Athens. Herodotus is brief:

"First the Corinthians (allies of the Spartans) agreed that this was not the right course of action, about turned and departed; then Demaratus, the other Spartan king, in joint command, followed suit, though he had not previously had any differences with Cleomenes. As a result of the disagreement a law was passed at Sparta forbidding both kings to accompany a military expedition."

The seriousness of the situation led some Athenians to request aid from Persia; indeed Herodotus reports that Athenian envoys gave Darius the customary tokens of submission, earth and water, but were "severely rebuked" on returning home. Cleisthenes may have been involved – at any rate he disappears from the scene at this point. His opponent Cleomenes later rose to an almost autocratic position at Sparta, engineering the removal of the recalcitrant king of the other house, Demaratus, and later winning a crushing victory over Argos in 493. Soon afterwards he became deranged and took his life, but probably not before stirring up the helots once more in revolt.

The Persian threat. Persia and the Greek states never had very cordial relations, and the antipathy was to last with varying degrees of intensity until Alexander conquered Persia in 331. The Persian king Darius campaigned in northern Greece and the Danube basin in 512, and had difficulty securing the full cooperation of the Ionian Greek leaders he took with him. When the Persians made an unsuccessful attack on Naxos in 500 the Ionians decided on open revolt; the pro-Persian tyrants stepped down and a unified command was set up. Athens and Eretria sent help to their fellow Ionians, and an expedition in 499 succeeded in firing the provincial capital of Sardis. Darius was not amused and bade his servant tell him three times before dinner every evening, "Remember the Athenians." However, he first had to overcome the Ionians, who added the Cypriots and Carians to their cause. It was a stubborn stand, not finally quashed until dissension and treachery in the confederate ranks lost them the vital naval battle in front of Miletus in 494; the city was captured and burned, and excavation has since revealed its ashes. Phrynicus, an Athenian dramatist, was fined for presenting the *Fall of Miletus* on the stage soon after. Herodotus makes the whole revolt more the personal affair of the sinister tyrants of Miletus, Histiaeus and his nephew Aristagoras; however the selfish double-dealing which he (from Halicarnassus) presents could scarcely have inspired the tenacity which some of the Ionians showed.

Darius prepared to take his revenge on Eretria and Athens. They had good warning of his attempt, for in 492 he had already set out, only to have his fleet wrecked on Mount Athos. In 490 his generals sailed directly across the Aegean and sacked Eretria, with its fine new temple of Apollo; they landed in the north of Attica in Marathon bay. Hippias, the old tyrant, was with them, hoping to be reinstalled. However he had to watch a humiliating defeat for the Persians, as the Athenian hoplite force attacked them at the double across the plain, led by the polemarch Callimachus and by Miltiades, one of the generals. The Persians were unable to deploy their cavalry – an arm in which Athens was weak – and were forced back to their ships or into the coastal marsh.

The men of Plataea alone aided Athens on the day. The Spartans made polite and perhaps valid excuses about being unable to leave their borders during the celebration of the festival of Hyacinthus, but they later visited the battlefield in awe. Miltiades was awarded the crown of victory; he had had experience of the Persians, who had ousted him from his little principality at Gallipoli in 494. However, his success was short-lived, and he died soon afterwards from injuries sustained in an abortive attack on Paros. He was heavily fined for this latter action and his son Cimon had to pay. We may note that his accuser was Xanthippus, the father of Pericles.

Individuals loom large in the following decade at Athens, for in 487 the law of ostracism was first implemented, under which it was possible for the citizens to vote into a ten-year exile any public figure whose conduct

One of a series of silver coins struck at Clazomenae for the various Ionian cities united in revolt against Persia after 500 BC.

displeased them. The first choices were alleged Persian sympathizers, but later on other politicians became candidates, including Cimon. Xanthippus was the "successful" candidate in 484. Themistocles emerged as a leading figure during these years, avoiding the ostracism he is said to have engineered for others. It was he who persuaded the Athenians to devote the proceeds of a rich new silver find in the Laurion mines in 483 to building up a fleet instead of making a general distribution. First in his thoughts may

Weapons from the field of Marathon – only one bone-hilted sword belongs to the heavy infantry. Arrowheads and a lead sling bullet attest the presence of light-armed troops.

have been the war in progress against the old enemy in the Saronic Gulf, Aegina, but Persia was surely not forgotten.

Xerxes had a revolt in Egypt to attend to first, but then began preparations to avenge his father. A channel was cut through the neck of the Athos peninsula and a vast land and naval force assembled. In the full tradition of epic narrative, Herodotus spares nothing in exaggerating the size and ferocity of the host. They arrived in Greece in the autumn of 480, to find awaiting them, for the first time since the Bronze Age, an almost united Hellas, with defensive plans well laid. A council of the Greeks had been set up in 481 and Sparta made commander-in-chief; local quarrels were forgotten, although Sparta's traditional enemy, Argos, remained neutral and a worried oracle at Delphi counseled despair.

The outcome of the invasion is well known. The Persians took the important pass at Thermopylae from the rear, guided by renegade local Greeks, and Leonidas and his band of 300 Spartans were wiped out. At sea the Persians once more misjudged the Aegean, despite having large numbers of Ionian triremes in the fleet, and storms reduced its size to near parity with the Greeks. Boreas, the north wind, soon became a popular cult figure. But the Persians proceeded south and occupied Athens, overcoming with

Above: a Corinthian helmet dedicated to Zeus at Olympia by one Miltiades, who is presumed to be the victor of Marathon.

Opposite page: the peninsula of Athos, the most easterly of the three prongs of the Chalcidice. In 480 BC Xerxes dug a channel across the neck of the peninsula.

little difficulty a small garrison left on the Acropolis, and then thoroughly wrecked its buildings and offerings.

In September 480 battle was joined in the straits between the Attic coast and the island of Salamis. The Athenians and Aeginetans bore the brunt of the fighting, to a large extent against fellow Greeks, although not a few of the Ionians came over to the Greek side during the battle. The eventual Greek victory, together with the flight of Xerxes to Asia, put heart into the land forces, and the following spring they advanced beyond the isthmus of Corinth to inflict a further thorough defeat on the rump of the Persian army at Plataea. Greece was freed and the myth of Persian invincibility (if it actually existed) was destroyed.

Tyrants and traders in the west. The Sicilians had been invited by the council to join in the defense of their motherland, but were not without their own troubles in

480. Our sources for the history of the colonies are very meager and only few glimpses of 6th-century events are preserved for us. During the century tyrants came to power in a number of cities. Early in the history of Acragas, founded in 588, Phalaris seized power and became a byword for cruelty. He allegedly roasted his opponents alive in the belly of a bronze bull, and their screams were said to have echoed forth like the lowing of the beast. But all these accounts contain a very large element of later embroidery. At the end of the century a tyranny emerged at Gela; it passed to Hippocrates in the 490s and he rapidly expanded the territory under his control, capturing the Chalcidian colonies of Naxos, Leontini and Zancle and forcing Syracuse to hand over Camarina. His successor, Gelon, took Megara Hyblaea and eventually Syracuse, where he transferred the seat of power. Anaxilas became tyrant of Rhegion, probably in 494, but was defeated in his attempts to capture Zancle by some adroit moves executed by a body of Samian exiles whom he had hoped to use in the attempt. However, they could only keep Zancle for themselves for a few years before Anaxilas captured it and installed refugees from Messenia, and thenceforth Zancle was known as Messana.

In 489 a third tyranny arose, at Acragas, under Theron. He quickly formed a marriage alliance with Gelon of Syracuse, and advancing north took Himera in 482, removing the tyrant Terillus. The Acragantines had already begun the program of temple-building of which such striking remains are left today, and which must have brought great prestige to the city. Her neighbor Selinus, also under a tyranny in the years before 515, had been engaged even earlier in architectural self-advertisement, and during the 5th century the two cities vied in the number, size and magnificence of the temples they erected.

The wealth required for these works came largely from further west, from trade conducted with the Phoenician settlements at the western end of the island, Motya, Panormus and Solous, as well as with Carthage across the water. Selinus was founded about 100 years later than Motya, in 628. She was one of the first Sicilian colonies to issue coins, using silver brought from Spain, as no doubt did her counterpart on the north coast, Himera, founded by Chalcidians and exiles from Syracuse in 632.

Relations between the Greeks and Phoenicians were not always friendly. Thucydides states that the Phoenicians already had trading posts on the east coast of Sicily before the Greeks arrived, though there is no archaeological evidence to support him. The presumed foundation date of Carthage, a colony of Tyre, is also embarrassingly earlier than the earliest material yet found, 814 as against the later 8th century. Around the middle of the 6th century a Carthaginian general, Malcho, campaigned in Sicily and Sardinia, and Greeks and Phoenicians clashed on two occasions when exiles from Greece tried to settle in the far west of the island – Cnidians around 580 and Dorieus the Spartan king in 510. In 480 Terillus of Himera, together with the Selinuntines and Anaxilas, asked for Carthaginian assistance against attacks from Acragas and Syracuse. An army was sent and laid siege to Himera, but Gelon infiltrated its lines and inflicted a heavy defeat – on the very same day, Greek historians insist, as the Persian fleet was put to flight at Salamis.

On his way to Sicily Dorieus had aided Croton in southern Italy in a war with Sybaris; at least that was the Sybarite version recounted by Herodotus who, as often, adds and comments on an alternative story – that of the Crotoniates, who denied any outside assistance. This war between Achaean colonies was the culmination of a series of upheavals. At first the Achaeans sought to drive other Greeks from the area, and succeeded against Siris, an Ionic colony from Colophon, in about 530; but a few years later little Locri, assisted by Rhegium, stood against them. Sybaris and Croton emerged as the strongest and most flourishing powers, owing much of their prosperity to trade with the inhabitants of the hinterland and also across the toe of Italy to the Tyrrhenian sea, where they planted subsidiary colonies. After her destruction by Croton in 510, the wealth of Sybaris became legendary. This fabled luxury has yet to appear from excavations, which are at least revealing the devastation caused by the diverting of the rivers through the town by the Crotoniates.

Life in most of the western colonies was based as much on agriculture as on trade. Many families lived in scattered farmsteads, and Demeter was one of the deities particularly favored, though never accorded a showpiece temple. Syracuse and other Dorian colonies did not come to terms with the local inhabitants, but built fortified posts to protect their borders and outlying communities. Contact with the motherland was maintained in particular through the national games, at Delphi and notably Olympia, where Italian athletes had resounding successes. The tyrants later sent their chariot teams to carry off many a prestigious victory, yet their many thankofferings had always to be commissioned from sculptors and bronze-workers of the mainland or Ionia.

Our guide of the previous chapter, Thucydides, may also be regarded as the first Classical archaeologist; for in Book I of his *History of the Peloponnesian War* he has a record of excavated material and an interpretation of it:

"During the war the Athenians purified Delos, removing the tombs of all those buried on the island. Over half of these turned out to be Carians, recognizable by the range of weapons interred with them, and by the manner of burial – still followed in Caria."

In 1898 Greek archaeologists discovered the pit on the neighboring island of Rheneia in which the Athenians had deposited all these remains, and although much of the material first mentioned in this excavation report of about 420 is still unpublished, we can be sure that Thucydides was wrong. None of the finds are non-Greek, and it is inconceivable that all the "Carian" material mentioned by Thucydides should have escaped the Greek excavators. Thucydides was an army man and makes typology of weapons the basis of his judgment. Forms of weapons and armor developed little over the years in which the Delos cemetery was in use, though the custom of burying such objects in graves was outmoded long before Thucydides' day.

If we cannot satisfactorily explain Thucydides' interpretations this is mainly because of lack of information. He gives no drawings of graves or objects, no stratigraphical sections, no record of whether cremation or inhumation was practiced; he was not able to ascertain cause of death or way of life from bone analyses; he does not individually describe any of the objects found, including pottery, which would provide us with the best evidence for the date of the Delian graves, the nationality of their occupants, and to a lesser extent the circumstances of burial. As in so many other ancient civilizations, by their vases shall you know them!

To be fair to Thucydides, it was not until 2,300 years later that many of these principles began to be adopted by excavators. Throughout the rest of antiquity historians and travelers often noted visible remains of earlier ages, but they usually contented themselves with accepting the explanations purveyed by local inhabitants in which any plausible folk memories were swamped under a superstructure of myth and legend.

After the reawakening of interest in the Classical past in the Middle Ages, Archaic Greece (the period spanning the ill- or non-defined gap between the Trojan War and the 5th century) had long to sit in the shade of her Classical offspring. A few Archaic monuments were known from an early date, but even when recognized as such, were normally dismissed as not being works of the "golden era." The colossal statue of Apollo on Delos was seen by an Italian visitor as early as 1445, and in the 17th century was sawn up for transport to Venice, but the pieces were abandoned and lie there still, save for three toes which reached the British Museum. Copies of the statues of the Athenian tyrant-slayers Harmodius and Aristogiton

were discovered in the early 16th century in Italy, but were not correctly identified. In any case they were just near enough the Classical ideal to serve as models for Renaissance artists.

While the 17th and 18th centuries saw a considerable increase in the number of travelers bold enough to go to south Italy, Greece and Turkey from Western Europe, their interests were still primarily the Classical and later periods of Greek civilization. They sketched architectural fragments and copied inscriptions, but only dug to free what was already visible on the surface, and that was rarely of the Archaic period.

Italian noble families collected gems, coins and vases, but few were recognized Archaic pieces. The vases came mainly from the cemeteries of Campania and Sicily, areas from which Sir William Hamilton, plenipotentiary to the King of the Two Sicilies at Naples from 1764 to 1800, assembled his two successive collections, the first of which was sold to the British Museum in 1772. The origin of these vases was, very fairly, assumed to be that of their most frequent place of discovery, so that what we now term 5th-century Attic red-figure was dubbed "Nolan," and the less common Attic black-figure "Sicilian." Earlier pieces, mainly our Corinthian, assumed a number of disguises, often simply "Primitive." The legacy of such terms lived on until 1896, when the British Museum vase catalog of Attic red-figure included the words "of the finest style" in its title.

Archaic art recognized. With the baroque Laocoön and simpering Apollo of the Belvedere setting the standard of true taste in the antique, it was perhaps not surprising that in 1816 Elgin could only persuade the British government to part with a niggling sum in return for the marbles he had removed from the Parthenon. Yet by 1812 the Trustees of the British Museum were already willing to spend far more to acquire the first set of readily recognized Archaic sculptures discovered – the pedimental decoration of the temple of Aphaea on Aegina. The English and German travelers had mixed feelings about their enterprise, "owing to the privations and dangers which attend such labours, including sickness, death from exposure to malaria and the attacks of a lawless population. Full of these bright anticipations, a party of four . . .

Previous page: a marble kouros and kore of the finest workmanship, dating to the 530s, as excavated in a field near Merenda, Attica. The inscribed base of the kore, found elsewhere, reads: "The memorial of Phrasicleia: I shall be called 'maiden' forever, for this is the name that the gods have decreed instead of 'bride.' Aristion of Paros made me."

Opposite page, above: one of the best-preserved temples in Greece is that of Aphaea, beautifully situated on a hill in the northeast part of Aegina. It was built in about 510, after fire had destroyed its predecessor.

Opposite page, below: the English and German expedition encamped with their spoil and helpers in front of the temple of Aphaea on Aegina in 1811.

having spent the evening with Lord Byron in pouring out libations in propitiation of his homeward voyage to England . . . left the Peiraeus just after midnight and arrived at break of day under the Panhellenian mount."

To ensure safety from the French fleet, the marbles they found were sent to Malta, but the auction was held as arranged on Zante, much to the annoyance of the English representatives who went to Malta and learned there that Ludwig of Bavaria had put in a successful bid. The Museum also failed to remove to England in the next decade the even earlier metopes from the massive temple C at Selinus in southwest Sicily. On these were to be seen obvious traces of painted decoration, unequivocally confirming observations from the Aegina and Elgin marbles that all Greek sculpture carried much painted detail. A nasty taste must have been left in the mouths of those who belonged to the purist school.

Etruscan urns. During the early years of the 19th century more and more vases were being excavated in Greece. One such find should have led to a reappraisal of the whole question of dating and origins of Greek vases, but the excavator's interpretations were long resisted. In 1815 Thomas Burgon unearthed some amphoras outside the walls of Athens, containing cremated ashes. He washed the dirt off one and to his surprise found painted decoration, clearly indicating by its explanatory inscription that this was one of the vases awarded to the winners in the Panathenaic games. The inscription was very archaic and Burgon placed the piece in about 600, far earlier than the traditional date for such "Sicilian vases." In 1847 he was the first to put forward a scheme of development of Greek pottery between the Mycenaean period and his own amphora, a scheme substantially verified by all later work and discoveries.

Burgon's painted amphora is now in the British Museum, as are many of the vast quantity of vases which were to revolutionize the study of Archaic Greece when they were hauled out of the earth on the Tuscan estate of Napoleon's brother Lucien in 1828–30 – the first rich Etruscan cemetery had been tapped, at historically insignificant Vulci. Fortunately for posterity the "excavations" were observed by Edouard Gerhard, who was a founder member of the Istituto della Corrispondenza in Rome in 1831, and in the pages of its *Bulletin* and *Annual* the progress towards a correct interpretation and dating of primitive, Sicilian and Nolan vases can be traced. Partisan Italians persisted in ignoring the full implication of the Greek inscriptions often to be found on these vases. For example, the signature of Exekias on a certain cup was read as Ezekiel, and the scene interpreted as the story of Noah! By 1854, when Otto Jahn published the first full museum catalog of Greek vases, in Ludwig's cabinet, the main lines had been drawn. "Primitive" was recognized as Corinthian, though it still harbored other waifs, and both Sicilian and Nolan were described as Attic, notwithstand-

The earliest intact prize amphora from the Panathenaic games, perhaps of 566 or 562 BC, excavated in Athens by Thomas Burgon in 1813. The reverse shows a mule cart. "From the games at Athens" is the inscription painted beside the figure of Athena Promachos.

ing the strong objections of the eminent sculptural expert who was director of the German Institute at Rome, Emil Braun.

The rediscovery of Athens. The most fruitful of the Acropolis excavations took place under the auspices of the Greek Archaeological Society and the casual observation of other archaeologists in 1885–89. Around the Parthenon, especially in the deep filling on the south side, were found many objects shattered by the Persian invaders of 480. One of the walls brought to light was readily recognized as the Cyclopean Mycenaean fortification wall, yet others were less recognizable and the great complexities of the site desperately needed an accurate and full recording, which was not carried out. A few photographs, some sketches of sections and many unlabeled finds remain. The drawing of architectural fragments and listing of tomb groups was an easy task compared with the demands for accurate recording of excavations which were now being attempted.

Exploration continued in the graveyards of Athens, mainly to the west of the city. In 1871 a particularly rich

Above: large-scale excavation on the Acropolis at Athens in June 1886 was carried out south of the Parthenon, revealing debris from the Persian invasion and old column drums built into a wall.

Below: column drums from the temple of Athena destroyed in 480 were defiantly built into the outer walls of the Acropolis.

area was found, close to the modern Plateia Eleutherias, north of the Dipylon gate. Among other rich graves were a large number containing objects of the Geometric period. The grave markers set above were the finest pieces – huge amphoras and kraters with their all-over patterned ornament admitting figured panels with scenes of mourning and fighting. The Austrian Emil Conze, following up the work of Burgon, soon set these new finds in their correct place in the early Iron Age, though it was to be some time before it was fully demonstrated how these styles linked up with those of the 6th century. All the same, it was by now clear that the beginnings of Greek art stretched far back beyond the lifetime of the early artists recorded in literary texts.

Confirmation for the result of the Acropolis excavations came in 1890–91 when Stais sampled the large mound in the plain of Marathon, universally accepted as covering the mass burial of the Athenians who fell in 490. The burials were found accompanied by mainly second-rate vases, especially *lekythoi* in the black-figure technique. On the Acropolis were found many sherds of red-figure vases, clearly burned in the fires of 480, whereas only one red-figure vase came from the Marathon mound. It was some time before the conclusion was generally accepted that these two styles of vase-painting must have coexisted for more than 50 years in the period 530–460. Once this fact was established the dating of levels in excavations throughout the Mediterranean world was put on a firmer footing, and Attic pottery became the yardstick for the chronology of the period.

The major sanctuaries. Olympia and Delphi both became objects of excavation during the 19th century. A French expedition had tested the soil around the temple of Zeus at Olympia in 1829, and removed some fragments of sculpture to the Louvre, but little Archaic material was found before the commencement of full-scale excavations by the German Institute in 1875. In the second season there came to light in the Altis, the sacred enclosure, the remains of the early temple of Hera, in which Pausanias, Boeotian travel writer of the 2nd century AD, had noted one wooden column still in place. Columns and capitals of a wide range of dates were found, but the absence of other remains of superstructure brought home the fact that mudbrick and wood were important materials in early Greek architecture. One of the excavators was Wilhelm Dörpfeld, Schliemann's assistant at Troy soon afterwards, and it was probably partly his desire to link the remains of Troy with Dorians entering the Peloponnese that led him to champion a very early date for the temple of Hera, despite strenuous opposition from the acutely observant Adolf Furtwängler. There was indeed some cult activity at Olympia as early as the 10th century, but no building can be associated with the offerings of that period.

The Germans also cast eager eyes on Delphi, high in the mountains behind the plain of Amphissa. Here the poet

Byron and his friends had already placed their signatures on one of the blocks of the Roman gymnasium. It was the French School at Athens that eventually won permission to excavate in 1891, but first they had to move the village of Kastri from above the site to a new position around the corner, where it still stands. Once again Pausanias was a guide for the excavators, who soon brought to light a number of the buildings he mentions. Who could blame the action of the local prefect at Amphissa in trying to intercept for the impoverished Greek exchequer the "Trésor des Athéniens," whose discovery was announced in a telegram to Paris sent from his town?

The excavations were very poorly recorded and published. All finer points were disregarded, and more interest was shown in the unearthing of architectural fragments and inscriptions. Despite the remoteness of the site it had suffered heavily at the hands of stone-robbers, or more particularly lead-collectors who found hacking out the lead clamps of the ancient walls easier than mining for the metal in the centuries after the fall of paganism. Yet the slope of the site did mean that there were many retaining walls in whose lee substantial remains had been preserved, especially Archaic and Classical sculpture hidden from the grasp of Roman collectors.

The Greek east: gunboats and spades. Few Archaic monuments stood preserved in the east. The most notable were the seated figures and the lions flanking the route between temple and harbor at Didyma, south of Miletus, which were eventually brought to the British Museum in 1857 aboard the naval vessel *Supply*. The Museum was active in this area at the time, largely under the influence of Charles Newton. In particular two of the seven wonders of the ancient world were sought – the Mausoleum at Halicarnassus, of 4th-century date, and the temple of Diana of the Ephesians, also best known as a temple of the 4th century, although Herodotus writes of an earlier building when he states that Croesus, king of Lydia, dedicated most of the columns during his reign of 561–546. The first expedition located this temple immediately under later remains, but the high water table prevented thorough investigation. When Hogarth (archaeologist and intelligence officer) came out under naval escort in 1904, he had traction engines to pump away the water. Further excavations in the central area recovered even earlier structures, in and around which were found large numbers of small ivories, gold ornaments and, most important, primitive coins; but conditions in the oozing mud were appalling. Hogarth's report for 3 December noted "little in the sieves and men's fingers too cold almost to get that little out." "Mud larks" appear five days before. Current work by Austrian archaeologists may clear up problems of dating these earliest phases.

In 1886 an Egyptologist and pioneer in scientific method in archaeology, William Flinders Petrie, turned his attention to a Greek site on the western branch of the Nile Delta, Naucratis. Herodotus tells us it was granted to Greek traders by King Amasis of Egypt in about 565. Petrie found workshops turning out trinkets and also shrines, poorly preserved, but yielding quantities of votive offerings – mostly vases, much broken, but many bearing incised dedicatory inscriptions in Ionic letters to Apollo or Aphrodite. The pottery for the most part was not Attic, and Petrie concluded that it was the produce of those cities who shared in the foundation of the post – all, save Aegina, eastern Greek cities. The literary evidence provided by Herodotus gave further opportunity for the dating of such pottery, though Petrie surmised that the settlement must have existed for at least 50 years before Amasis came to the throne. Rather too high a dating of such material from Ionian sites led to a vogue of "Panionianism," in which the cities of Asia Minor were seen as the source of almost all that was splendid in Greek civilization.

Towards a precise chronology. Petrie's publication was somewhat selective, and his enthusiasm for stratigraphy excessive in trying to isolate levels in the temple dump. Far more fully published, indeed ahead of its time, was the set of near-contemporary volumes which discussed the results of the excavations of the American School at Athens at the sanctuary of Hera across the plain from Argos, much closer to Mycenae and other Bronze Age sites than Argos itself. This factor, together with other legendary stories of the foundation of the cult, led the excavator Charles Waldstein to propose an extremely high chronology, which most scholars at the time considered grossly inaccurate. Most of the material belonged in fact to the 8th and 7th centuries, and if Waldstein had looked west he would have realized his mistake.

For it was during this period that the first satisfactorily conducted excavations were undertaken in Italy, in the Greek colonies, to contrast with the tomb-opening sessions in Etruria and in Campania. We should note in particular the long series of campaigns conducted from the late 19th century onward by Paolo Orsi, for example at Selinus, Megara Hyblaea and Locri. It was clear by the turn of the century that certain types of vase often found in Greece were also in regular use in the early days of the western colonies, whose dates could be fixed by Thucydides' invaluable statements. These dates have been the faithful prop of the archaeological chronology of the 8th and 7th centuries ever since.

Most of the excavations already mentioned could be carried out in open ground not covered by urban expansion. In Athens the building of King Otho's new capital had brought to light many ancient remains, a particular case being the building of the Piraeus electric railway in 1896 which cut through the northwest corner of the ancient Agora. In the same year the American School opened their excavations at Corinth, having first to remove some modern Turkish buildings. The Romans had made such a good job of destroying the city in 196 BC

An admiring group surrounds the unearthed torso of the early 6th-century kouros at Delphi in May 1894. We can appreciate here the slope of the precinct of Apollo.

that it is only recently that full-scale excavation of the shattered early levels has been undertaken, though cemeteries, the potters' quarter and the Archaic temple of Apollo were investigated in the 1930s.

Into the 20th century. Many hundreds of excavations carried out this century around the Mediterranean have yielded material of the Archaic period, and the need to excavate sites threatened by the bulldozer increases annually, in step with the growing concern of archaeologists over the neglect of the past and the apparent condoning of its destruction. Techniques of excavation have of course improved immensely, if unevenly, over the years, and the duty of telling the public exactly what they have destroyed is accepted by most archaeologists. The soil is treated as carefully as the objects found in it, the recording of find-spots and gridding of sites are taken for granted, the finest of brushes are employed increasingly frequently to clean surfaces and objects *in situ*, and financial allowance is made for the reservation of finds as well as their thorough publication. There is a growing tendency to store finds as near the site as security and finance will allow, thereby facilitating study and providing the visitor to the area with the key which is so often missing from archaeological wastelands – the finds made there.

It may be true that the Classical archaeologist has not been among the first to apply new techniques, perhaps because his dating can be carried out far more precisely than any scientific method would allow. Yet there is now no lack of consultation with scientists of every field, from geologist to nuclear physicist, in the examination and treatment of sites and objects. There has been a definite shift towards the excavation of living quarters rather than sanctuaries and cemeteries, in search of day-to-day life rather than art, though this cannot hide the fact that for the earliest part of our period archaeological evidence comes almost exclusively from cemeteries.

Mainland Greece. Two areas in Athens have been the object of extensive excavation this century, and both have yielded important Archaic material. Since 1926 the German Institute has scrupulously investigated the area around the Dipylon and Sacred gates, where a very full range of graves from the 11th to 6th centuries has been uncovered, and further into the city the American School has been working in the Agora and adjacent areas since 1932 with spectacular results, though the flattened site may suggest otherwise. Finds, together with excavation notebooks and filed catalogs, are stored on the site in the handsomely rebuilt stoa of the 2nd century BC, named after its donor, King Attalus of Pergamum.

Other sites in the capital have hit Archaic levels, but many were dug in difficult circumstances and over very restricted areas. Important pieces of relief sculpture were found in 1922 built into the city wall, which had been hastily erected under the inspiration of Themistocles in 479, as Thucydides relates:

"The speed of building is clear to this day; the foundations are a patchwork, including unworked stones, laid down as they were brought to the site, and many tombstones and architectural blocks were pressed into service."

In Attica the major cult center of Eleusis was summarily excavated in the late 19th century and also in the 1930s and 1950s. In 1906 the famous "Apollo" statues of the early 6th century were found at Cape Sounion, deliberately buried in a pit beside the temple of Poseidon. More recently many graves of the Geometric and Archaic periods have been uncovered in the inland plain to the southeast of Athens, as well as the two most finely preserved of all Archaic statues found near modern Merenda, again deliberately buried near the presumed grave mounds they once marked. At Thorikos to the south a series of campaigns by a Belgian mission has been concerned with seeking traces of industrial activity in this center of the Attic silver-mining region.

To the north Boeotia suffers constantly from tomb-robbing, though some burials were left for the archae-

The east front of the temple of Hera within the Altis at Olympia. Built in about 590, it originally had wooden columns which were replaced over the following centuries.

ologist, notably that of a very wealthy woman of the late Geometric period found recently at Paralimni, and a large number of later graves at Rhitsona, ancient Mycalessus, excavated by British scholars in 1904–05. These contained vast numbers of second-rate vases and figurines, and have been important in establishing the chronology of these cheaper, and therefore more common, products.

In the mountains to the west excavation continues at Delphi. It is clear that in the 8th and 7th centuries Corinthian influence was strong at the sanctuary, as it was west of Delphi, an unsettled area still in Thucydides' day:

"They regularly plundered each other's territory, and this way of life is still led in much of Greece – Locris, Aetolia, Acarnania, all that part of the mainland."

At Calydon (the scene of a famous legendary boar hunt), excavated in 1926–28, and at Thermon, excavated in 1896–97, Archaic temples much influenced by Corinthian precedent have been found. At Thermon it has been tempting to see an architectural link between a Bronze Age apsidal megaron structure just beyond the temple site and a similarly shaped, perhaps 9th-century, building under the temple itself, though the connection cannot be as close as many handbooks state.

Spectacular finds of Archaic material, notably armor and weapons, have been discovered in the renewed German excavations at Olympia in 1936–42 and 1952–66, much of it coming from disused wells and the banking

Royalty on Corfu. Kaiser Wilhelm seen in an open-air "study" at the "Achilleion," his summer retreat set high above the ancient city, itself largely situated within the Greek king's summer villa.

around the Classical stadium. More precision has been brought to the early period of the sanctuary's history, not least the discovery of Bronze Age material during work on the foundations of the new museum, not a rare hazard for site planners.

Treasure-hunters of previous centuries were no doubt put off by Thucydides' words about Sparta:

"If the town of the Spartans were deserted, the temples and foundations of the buildings left bare, I reckon that people in the distant future would have strong reservations about Sparta's vaunted power."

A series of campaigns was conducted between 1906 and 1927 by the British School at Athens at various sites in and around the modern town, set between the towering granite range of Taygetus and the ascending sandstone ridges of Parnon. The principal discovery was the sanctuary of Artemis Orthia, where the curious initiatory rites so excited the Romans that a theater was built around the temple and altar. As so often happened the earliest period of use was fixed too far back, but the vast quantity of small finds, many indeed small and cheap votive objects, threw much light on the early history of Laconian art. To this day there remains a large gap in the archaeological record of Laconia in the earliest Iron Age, a gap originally filled by the high dating of later material.

In the Argolid a number of sites have yielded abundant material dating from the 11th century onward. From the picture that emerges from Argos on the one hand and Tiryns and Mycenae on the other, it is clear that their relative importance was reversed in the Iron Age. We can piece together more evidence for the years immediately

following the demise of Mycenae than in any other area apart from Attica, yet it is still remarkably difficult to isolate the arrival of the Dorian people who made up the bulk of the Iron Age population. Current work at Asine, near the modern resort of Tolon, adds to this evidence. The excavations here were originally inspired by the late King Gustaf VI Adolf of Sweden, not the last of the royal patrons of antiquarianism, but a leading archaeologist in his own right.

Such a description would not suit Kaiser Bill, yet between 1911 and 1914 he took an enthusiastic interest in the uncovering of an early 6th-century temple while staying in his summer residence on the fashionable island of Corfu. The temple was utterly ruined and is scarcely identifiable today, but there did survive the earliest known set of stone pedimental sculpture, centered on one of the most impressive Medusas of Greek art. A second smaller but equally interesting pediment was found nearby during foundation digging in 1974.

To the south the island of Ithaca was an obvious target for investigation, though Dörpfeld firmly believed that Odysseus' island was to be equated with modern Leucas, where he built his own villa. British excavations at two sites in the 1930s proved that Ithaca flourished in the 9th to 7th centuries, attracting very rich dedications at its shrines; one belonged to Odysseus in the 3rd century BC, but we cannot say if that was the case earlier.

The Aegean. The Aegean islands have attracted a large, ever-increasing number of expeditions. Of those nearest the mainland, Euboea and Andros deserve note. On Euboea, Eretria was excavated by the Americans in 1891–95 and later by Greeks, but only recently have Swiss excavations reached the lower levels. During the same period the British School dug at Leukandi, a promontory site near Chalcis, finding that it was continuously occupied from the Bronze Age till the 8th century. However, at Chalcis modern building impedes investigation considerably.

Supplementary work on the temple of Aphaea at Aegina by Furtwängler in 1901–02 and more recently by the German Institute has revealed an earlier temple whose painted details are particularly well preserved, together with an inscription recording its construction in the mid-6th century. Furtwängler hit on an enigmatic set of heads, deliberately buried, and clearly belonging to a third set of pedimental figures similar to those bought by Ludwig. They belonged to an original east pediment, for some reason replaced after a decade or so on the building. In the town of Aegina stands the sole surviving column of a temple of Apollo of late Archaic date among a maze of remains dating from early Bronze Age to Roman. From here and from a cemetery nearby come some of the best, if fragmentary, works of Corinthian and Athenian vase-painters of the 7th century, a period which had long been poorly represented by excavations elsewhere.

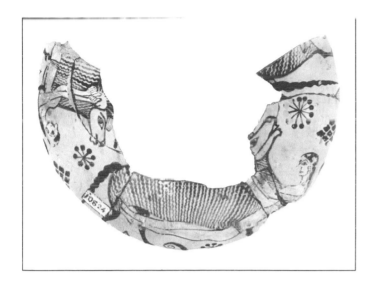

Top: Odysseus clings to a ram in the escape of his party from the cave of Polyphemus (Homer, *Odyssey*, Book 9). This fragmentary jug was painted largely in outline technique, and was found under the temple of Apollo at Aegina in 1895. It dates from the mid-7th century.

Above: elaborately carved floral patternwork on a marble block from an Ionic temple in southern Chios, of the late Archaic period.

Right: wooden artifacts have been found in the swampy ground of the Samian Heraion, among them this statuette of Hera. She wears a long belted dress and tall backless crown. The statuette dates from around 630.

Many of the ancient towns in the Cyclades lie directly under their modern successors. Such is the case on Naxos and Paros – in the latter at least the rich architectural remnants built into medieval structures can be studied above ground. On Siphnos too the British School had to excavate among the houses to find a shrine and plain living quarters of the 6th century in the years 1935–37.

The relative prosperity of the Cyclades in the late Geometric period has been underlined by Greek excavations at Xombourgo on the island of Tenos between 1952 and 1953, with the discovery of houses and many fragments of the large, local storage jars decorated with molded figures and often telling a mythological story. Similar finds have been made by the first Australian mission in Greece at Zagora on the inhospitable southwest coast of Andros, where a housing complex built in the 8th century was found on a remote and high headland. The headland is defended by a stout crosswall, and this, like Xombourgo, recalls Thucydides' words about towns of a day much earlier than his:

"Older foundations were set well back from the sea because of the piracy and brigandage which was deep-rooted and rife; we find them in the mountains to this day, both on the mainland and in the islands."

On all three of the large islands off the coast of Asia Minor (Lesbos, Chios and Samos) the ancient town lies under the modern capital, and thus little of Archaic Chios and Mytilene is known, while on Samos only the famous tunnel of Eupalinus and the vast defensive enceinte, both originally the work of Polycrates, have been investigated. However, across the plain to the west lay the site of the sanctuary of Hera, traditionally founded where a wooden image of the goddess was washed ashore. Much excavation here in the 1930s and since World War II by the German Institute has demonstrated that this was another site where a succession of temples was erected, starting from a temple-less sacred precinct and passing through three intermediate stages before Polycrates' final building arose. Unusual finds have been wooden objects, figurines and furniture, preserved in the waterlogged ground of the plain.

On Chios a site unknown from literary sources was excavated in 1955–57 by the British School at Emporio, in the southeast of the island – a hilltop village of the Archaic period was moved down to the harbor in the course of the 6th century where a fine new temple was later built, incorporating elaborate moldings of peculiarly Chiot type.

To the south, on Rhodes, Lindos was excavated by the Swede Christian Blinkenberg in 1902–05, the sanctuary of Athena producing a modest amount of Archaic material before Italian concrete turned it into its present unhappy state. In a nearby cemetery at Exochi, excavations by Friis Johansen yielded early pottery which brought precision to the study of east Greek Geometric styles. His publication appeared after the ten-volume *Clara Rhodos*, which gave the results of intensive research and excavation by an Italian mission in the 1920s and 1930s, including important material from the cemeteries of Ialysos and Camiros, thoroughly (if a little unprofessionally) dug and published.

Surprisingly little from our period has been excavated in Asia Minor. At places such as Miletus and Ephesus the overlying later levels considerably hamper investigations, while sites excavated before 1914 suffered much damage in the ensuing years – for example the small finds from the German excavations at Didyma withstood bombing by the Royal Flying Corps in 1916, but largely succumbed in a fire caused by negligence on the part of Italian armistice observers in 1919, and were further reduced by the burning down of a second home in the campaigns of 1922–23.

To the south two lesser sites have recently yielded very early graves of the Sub-Mycenean and Protogeometric

Travelers entering Smyrna. The Archaic city lay at the very head of the bay in the background.

periods; Iasus and Dirmil on the Halicarnassus peninsula add very considerably to our knowledge of the earliest Greek settlement in this section of the coast.

But the most important site of the period is undoubtedly Old Smyrna, a little north of the modern city which covers the remains of the Classical town. From 1948 to 1951 a joint Anglo-Turkish expedition worked here, and since 1966 Ekrem Akurgal has continued his investigations for Ankara University. Though the site was occupied in the 3rd millennium, the most extensive remains date from the Iron Age. Now standing half a kilometer from the sea, it was once a seagirt promontory which has recalled to many Homer's description of the city of the Phaeacians in the *Odyssey*.

"High walls surround the town, which is reached by a narrow causeway; on each side is an excellent harbour, and the smooth-running boats hem in the road. Nearby, next to a fine shrine of Poseidon, is the market-place, paved with close-fitting quarried stone."

Apart from houses dating back to the 9th century (rare finds indeed), most striking were the massive fortification walls of later years. But they did not save the city from attacks by Alyattes of Lydia, as Herodotus relates; his siege mound and his men's arrows were found, and pottery in the destruction levels placed the attack early in the king's reign. All the same, the 6th century saw a substantial revival, and it is worth noting that excavation often brings to light continued occupation in towns taken in war, when we might otherwise have expected some considerable gap.

Much excavation carried out in Crete has been aimed primarily at Minoan levels, though both Knossos and Phaestos were inhabited in the Iron Age. Yet even early in this century it was clear from finds that Crete was a significant area in the development of Classical Greek civilization.

Among significant excavations are those in the cave on Mount Ida, where Zeus was believed to have been hidden by the Kouretes. The excellence of all the metalwork dedicated here was confirmed in 1937, when Spyridon Marinatos excavated on the hillside at Dreros and discovered a temple of Apollo in which remained not only the depository box of the horns of sacrificed animals, but also the three sheet-bronze cult statues of Apollo, Artemis and Leto. Recent illicit excavations at Arcades to the south unearthed richly engraved panoplies of armor dedicated by the local population after being taken from some neighboring enemies.

The rather idiosyncratic architecture of the Dreros shrine is similar to that of a hilltop temple at Gortys, the true successor of Phaestos, and one of two buildings excavated by the Italian School in 1907–08 at Prinias on the route between Knossos and Phaestos. All have internal sacrificial hearths, but at Prinias were also discovered good remains of sculptural decoration of about 630, which for a long time were the major textbook illustrations of early Greek architectural sculpture, despite their uncertain

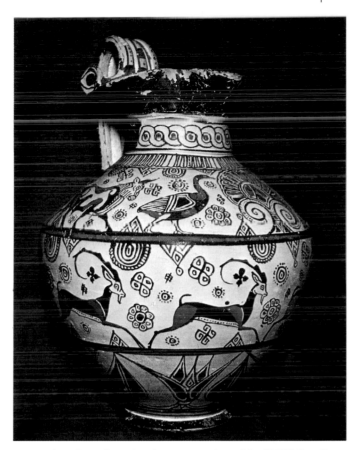

A typical product of east Greek potters – a jug of the "Wild Goat" style, dating from about 610. Animals parade against a tapestry of patternwork on a brilliant white ground.

placing on the building and lack of connection with mainland work.

The northern colonies. The present century has not been the most settled period for archaeological research in northern Greece. Only on the island of Thasos has a full program of excavation been carried out by the French School. Local marble encouraged sculptors, but more important resources were the gold and silver mines around Mount Pangaion, tapped from an early period by the native tribes.

During World War I, trenching of a more pressing nature turned up a number of finds in the area around Salonica and on the Gallipoli peninsula. Despite the lack of time for leisured study, the latter site gave clear evidence of a particular Athenian interest of the 6th century. Little major work has been undertaken between the two areas, though three fairly important colonies, Torone, Abdera and Maroneia, are now being dug. The same applies to the area between the Dardanelles and Bosporus, the site of several major colonies, notably Cyzicus, and at Istanbul foundation trenches for a museum extension have recently brought to light for the first time material stretching back to the early years of the colony in the 7th century.

The excavations of the Imperial Archaeological Commission of St Petersburg had revealed the contents of many of the *kurgans*, burial tumuli of the Crimea and neighboring areas, and the richness of the local Scythian culture; yet little of this was earlier than the mid-5th century, and it is only in the last 40 years that excavations have tested the lower levels of the Greek colonies in the countries around the Black Sea. Nothing earlier than 650 has been found, and indeed much of the earliest material comes not from the colonies but from local sites usually further inland. When finds do become frequent, after 600, the proportion of east Greek material clearly supports the written records of the part played by Miletus in this colonization – at Histria near the Danube delta, Berezan and Olbia (Ovid's icy abode in exile) on the Bug estuary, and Phanagoreia and Panticapaeum in the Crimea.

Greeks in the Near East. There were no Greek colonies in the eastern Mediterranean, but excavation has revealed several settlements of merchants and mercenaries, of which Naucratis has been mentioned. In the short-lived Hatay republic in the north, Sir Leonard Woolley sampled the remains at al Mina at the mouth of the Orontes. He found Greek material dating from the late 9th century. Greek mercenaries left behind their broken pottery in two historically datable forts still further south – Mesad Hashavyahu, north of Ashdod, a Judaean outpost of the 610s, and Tell Defenneh (Daphnae in Herodotus) on the eastern branch of the Nile Delta, taken by Cambyses of Persia in 525.

Cemeteries provide most of our knowledge of the Archaic period on Cyprus. In recent years Vassos Karageorghis has excavated several impressive tombs of Mycenaean type with broad entrance passages or *dromoi* at Salamis; in the dromos of one he found good remains of the owner's chariot and horses. We should also note his discovery of a 10th-century Phoenician presence at Kition in the southwest of the island.

The west. In Sicily work has been carried out at most of the Greek colonies in recent years and the results have been cumulatively impressive, if individually unspectacular. Particular attention has been paid to the habitation areas and the development of town planning, such as at Selinus and Himera and in the excavations of the French School at Rome at Megara Hyblaea. Investigations at lesser shrines have brought to light thousands of offerings, in particular terracotta figurines; the series from Acragas for example runs from the earliest years of the colony on into the Hellenistic period. Thousands of small pious dedications were found in a sanctuary of Demeter beyond the walls of Gela, while at the other end of the city what must rank as the best-preserved section of Greek fortifications found anywhere was rescued from the drifting sands in the years following 1951. Here one can truly appreciate the crisp cutting of the blocks and the use of mudbrick in the upper works, up to four meters above ground.

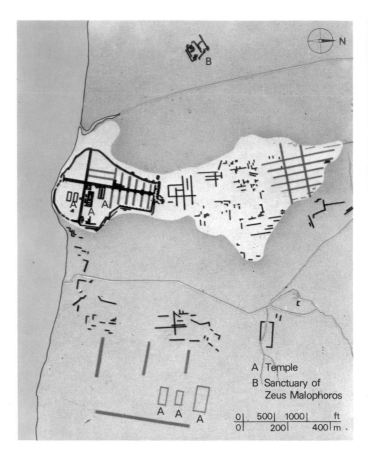

Selinus in Sicily. The plan shows the axial arrangement of the streets within the walls as well as the three temple precincts in the city and beyond the two rivers.

A Temple
B Sanctuary of Zeus Malophoros

Not to be overlooked are the good number of non-Greek settlements of the period which have been excavated to reveal the pace and extent of the Hellenization of the island. Orsi dug at many, and more recently sites such as Morgantina and Vassallaggi have yielded valuable results.

To the west, beyond Selinus and Himera, was the Carthaginian area of settlement. Much work has been carried out, and continues, at Motya, the principal settlement, with its still unexplained enclosed "harbor," while Panormus (Palermo) and Solous are beginning to yield Archaic material. The lofty citadel of Eryx, with its famous shrine of Venus, has been shown to have become Phoenician in the course of the 6th century. Earlier it belonged to the independent Elymians of nearby Segesta, where there is an unfinished Doric temple of the late 5th century, a monument to that city's dubious part in persuading Athens to assist her in 415, when Athens' envoys, says Thucydides, "made a persuasive report, though rather inaccurate with respect to the large sums of money said to be lying in the temples and public treasury."

The language of the Elymians is amply attested in the terse graffiti they cut on imported Attic vases excavated in recent campaigns, too terse for any decipherment as yet.

Above: the temples at Paestum seen in a print of the late 18th century. The two temples of Hera are in the foreground, that of Athena beyond the huntsmen.

Right: Sisyphus' punishment in Hades, pictured on a mid-6th-century metope from Foce del Sele, near Paestum. His endless efforts to roll a boulder uphill are aggravated by the bearded demon on his back.

In mainland Italy, too, great strides have been made in recent years. One of the pioneering expeditions took place at the mouth of the river Sele, north of Paestum, in 1934 and following years under the personal sponsorship of Paola Zancani-Montoro and Umberto Zanotti-Bianco. Here they found a remarkable building of sandstone, mudbrick and, we assume, timber, dating to the mid-6th century, which was quite probably a temple of Hera. At Paestum itself in 1954 excavations around the altars of the "Basilica" and the neighboring temples of "Ceres" and "Neptune" demonstrated that their true deities were Athena and Hera respectively. Two further discoveries of the late Archaic period are of considerable significance: on the road between the temples was found a crypt-like structure of modest size, complete with a number of fine bronze jars and Attic vases, perhaps the tomb of a hero, while among the tombs found outside the walls one painted on the inside with banquet scenes and a plunging diver is of unique interest.

In Campania to the north excavation at several sites has served to elucidate the history of the Greek settlements and their relationships with the Etruscans and other Italic peoples, though the investigations at Pithekoussai on the island of Ischia conducted by Giorgio Buchner and the University of Pennsylvania since 1952 take pride of place. They are described elsewhere, but as an archaeological addendum with contemporary significance we may note the observation that the teeth of the inhabitants probably owed their excellent state of preservation to the fluoride in the local water sources.

At Velia, south of Paestum, excavations have brought to light remains of the earliest Greek settlement on the attractive acropolis site. It was settled by Phocaeans from Ionia in about 540 after they had abandoned a post at Alalia on the island of Corsica. At Alalia so far only Etruscan settlement from the 5th century onward has been found, but at Massilia (modern Marseilles) material of

On the lip of an Attic black-figure cup of about 550 we see Zeus wielding a thunderbolt in each hand. Painted by Eucheiros, it was found in a grave at Medellin in central Spain in 1968.

Opposite page: foundations of two mudbrick kilns of the 4th century, excavated at Metapontum in 1972, showing the firing tunnel and round chamber. Among the finds here were numbers of painted vases executed by a known hand, including the hydria shown here, warped during firing and discarded.

undoubted Ionian origin from the earliest 6th century has confirmed the literary tradition of the Phocaeans' interest in this area. Along the south coast of France and the Rhône valley a number of native sites have yielded similar finds as well as Etruscan ware. Far up the Rhône, near the river Saône at Vix, a historic discovery was made in 1952 when the largest Greek bronze vessel to be found intact was dug up in the burial mound of a local princess; a single handle of the 600-gallon Vix krater weighs over 1 cwt. Important too are the Greek sherds of the 6th century and the unparalleled Greek influence in the fortifications on the Heuneberg, again north of the Alps, on the north bank of the Upper Danube.

In Spain literary evidence for Greek settlement is sparse and tallies ill with the excavated material. Only at Ampurias, near Barcelona, have extensive early remains been found, akin to those at Marseilles. Elsewhere most earlier material is scattered among the native sites and Phoenician posts, such as a 7th-century helmet from Jerez, Attic storage jars from a Phoenician colony at the mouth of the Malaga river and a fine Attic 6th-century cup from Medellin, in the region of the silver mines which attracted traders to southwest Spain.

Excavations of varying intensity and type have been carried out at four important sites on the "instep" of Italy

– viz. Sybaris, Heraclea, Metapontum and Taranto. The modern city of Taranto allows only occasional rescue work, but results are often spectacular, whatever the date of the remains found. They include good-quality imports of the 6th and 5th centuries, local pottery of the 4th, funerary relief sculpture, rich Classical and Hellenistic jewelry and a wide range of terracottas. Most striking perhaps are the sarcophagus of an athlete buried in the family vault with the prize vases he won at Athens, and the seated "Taranto goddess," probably a cult statue of about 480, found buried in a pit and smuggled out of the country to Berlin in 1915.

Metapontum possesses another romantically named temple, "the Knights' Table," in fact dedicated to Hera. A row of temples, whose foundations have been brought to light in excavations in the central part of the scattered site, seem to belong to Apollo Lycius, Athena and perhaps Aphrodite, while the most recently discovered, an Ionic temple of about 500, remains unallotted. Regular planning has been revealed by aerial photography and excavation not only in the town but also in the allotments of agricultural land for the settlers. Just as important was the discovery in 1973 of potters' kilns, yielding among many other things fragments of the works of a known artist of the early 4th century; they are the first sizable kilns of the

Classical period to have been found in any reasonable condition.

Fine vases illustrating the tragedies of Sophocles and Euripides and possibly made at Metapontum were illegally unearthed in 1963 from a tomb along the coast at Heraclea – perhaps the resting-place of a homesick Attic actor. Subsequently German and Italian archaeologists have uncovered sizable parts of the planned settlement of Heraclea dating from 432 into the Roman period, and in addition material going back to the 7th century, notably from a cemetery in which both Greeks and natives seem to have been buried, one in an amphora bearing a name in Cypriot script. The remains of Sybaris lay deep under the alluvial plain, but with the assistance of the protonmagnetometers of the Lerici Foundation (a modern survey technique) they were located in 1962, largely below the water table. Test drilling brought up sherds going back to the 8th century, but an elaborate and expensive drainage system had to be prepared before full scale excavation could begin. Results so far have been modest, but we can say that the renowned Sybarites seem to have lived in accommodation of slight pretension, whatever their life-style may have been.

Three excavations at sites of basically Etruscan nature have thrown important light on Greek matters. At the port by Cerveteri north of Rome the doyen of modern Etruscologists, Massimo Pallottino, discovered two temples, one with terracotta pedimental sculpture in late Archaic Greek style. Between the two temples a shallow pit contained three gold plaques inscribed in Etruscan and Punic, relating to the affairs of the temple of Astarte (Uni in Etruscan) under the official Thefarie Veluinas.

Not far north is Tarquinia and its port Gravisca. Rescue excavations have revealed here, since 1970, the first Greek site on Etruscan soil. Shrines of a commercial settlement dating from about 580 into the 3rd century were found, yielding fine pottery and dedicatory inscriptions to Hera, Apollo, Aphrodite and Demeter, together with an inscribed stone set up by an Aeginetan Sostratus, a trader known for his wealth by Herodotus. The finds demand that we reconsider our ideas about the trade routes of the western Mediterranean.

The Etruscans moved over the Apennines in the 6th century into the Po valley, and as ever they imported much Greek pottery. This has been discovered in such quantities and of such high quality (admittedly together with the dregs of the kiln) at Spina on the delta that it is tempting to see a part-Greek settlement there, though evidence for this is slight.

The major Greek colony in north Africa was Cyrene, founded in 632 from Thera. According to one version given by Herodotus the first party could find nowhere to settle and went back to Thera, but the Therans attacked them as they came ashore and would not let them land, ordering them to sail back again.

Parts of the Archaic city have been found in Italian excavations, notably a shrine to the founder Battus and a temple of Apollo. In 1966 a cache of Archaic sculpture came to light, buried perhaps during the Persian attacks of the 520s, and including two female figures and a sphinx column. The cult associated with the deposit was probably that of Demeter, as at Taucheira, itself a colony of Cyrene along the coast, where rich votive deposits were found by the British School at Athens in 1964–66. The stratigraphist and farsighted historian will appreciate the full description of the upper level, which yielded "Italian cap badges, various fragments of wine bottles – one stamped 'Unione militare Torino' cartridge cases, part of a gramophone record."

Euboea and Greek Expansion

The island of Euboea sprawls off the east coast of central Greece, affording a safe passage on its inside for shipping passing north and south. At the Euripus narrows the city of Chalkis stands only yards from the mainland, separated by this curious and fast-flowing tidal passage; the modern buildings have severely limited excavation of its predecessors. The island is largely mountainous, but to the south of Chalkis lies the fertile Lelantine plain and further south again the small coastal plain in which Eretria was settled around 800 BC. In between, on the southern edge of the Lelantine plain, a high mound about 250 × 100 yards stands right by the sea. Excavation has shown that this mound of Leukandi was first inhabited in the early Bronze Age, and the levels were built up impressively until the site was abandoned around 700 BC.

From literary and archaeological evidence we can piece together the first pioneering voyages in the 9th century onward by sailors from these towns, to reawaken Greek contacts with the Near East and then explore western waters. Eastward they visited Cyprus and joined with other Greeks to found a trading post of first importance in a Syrian settlement at the mouth of the Orontes river at al Mina. Prewar excavations revealed storerooms and ivory tusks waiting for export, as well as much pottery from the Cyclades, Euboea, Cyprus and local Greek workshops. Westward they continued their search for minerals to add to Cypriot copper; the iron of central Italy in particular attracted them. In about 760 a settlement was placed on the north coast of the island of Ischia in Italy called Pithekoussai, and soon after followed colonies at Cumae nearby and at Naxos in Sicily, more agricultural than commercial in character.

Only a small area of the large mound of Leukandi (*below*) has been excavated. It possesses small harbors at each end and the modern brickworks demonstrate the suitability of local clay for bricks and pottery.

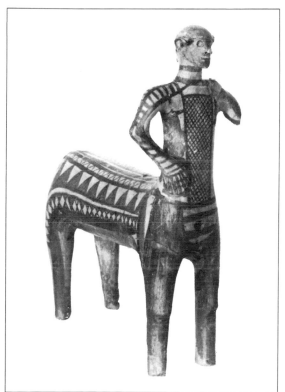

Pithekoussai (*above*) also commands two harbors, from a greater height; between them the cemetery was placed. The other harbor is now the flourishing resort of Lacco Ameno. The settlement was placed with an eye to trade with Italy to the north, but the graves have revealed many connections with Greece and the traders of al Mina. The drawing of a sealstone of red serpentine (*right*), found in a baby's grave, depicts a two-headed, tailed monster and was cut perhaps at Tarsus in Turkey around 720 BC.

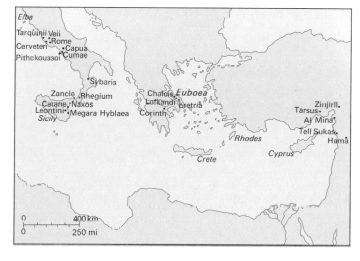

A unique terracotta centaur (*above*) from a 10th-century tomb at Leukandi, a creature otherwise unknown in Dark Age art. Related vases are known from Cyprus and Athens, places with which Euboeans traded through these centuries. The map (*right*) shows sites where Euboean pottery of the 9th and 8th centuries has been found as well as the Italian and Sicilian colonies.

Euboea (Greece)

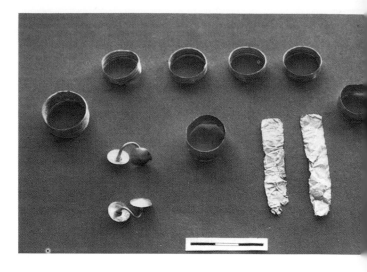

The perfunctory small pot (*below*) from an early 9th-century tomb at Leukandi is also a milestone in Greek art history; it is the earliest known Iron Age representation of humans on a vase, and the archers confirm the importance of this arm of Dark Age warfare suggested by later depictions. The style may owe much to Cyprus, and objects imported from the east are frequent finds in the tombs; one of the 8th century even had a bronze belt made in Etruria. The wealth of Leukandi is attested by the comparatively large amount of gold found in the tombs; illustrated (*right*) are a number of rings and bands as well as a pair of earrings from a single burial of the mid-9th century. The simple technique of the work is akin to that of most contemporary jewelry in Greece.

Rare finds from the excavations are fragments of clay molds for decorated bronze tripod legs of the 10th century, while the cup with pendant semicircle design is almost a trademark of the Euboeans, from Palestine to Italy, in the period 900–750.

Eretria

Eretria, founded to the south of Leukandi, perhaps in the late 9th century, quickly flourished. The acropolis had a plateau at its foot which served as the site of the town till the Roman period; on either side there was marshy land, particularly by the sea on the south. Here we see the slopes of the acropolis, the Classical theater, and in the foreground the leveled remains of 4th-century palatial buildings. In the earliest period a stream was diverted to protect the houses at the foot of the acropolis and across it, excavated immediately below the foundations of the "Palace," was a small cemetery of warriors and their families, revered and heroized for many years after their burial in the years around 700. Here we see one of the cremation urns of bronze during excavation, with its stone lid removed. Buried with it were the deceased's sword and spears, and many weapons accompanied the other male burials, including a bronze spearhead of Mycenaean origin.

In the aerial view of Eretria we see again the Classical theater and west gate with other buildings. The sanctuary of Apollo Daphnephoros, "laurel bearer," lay nearer the coast. Here a fascinating series of temples has been brought to light by recent Swiss excavations: an original apsidal temple was replaced by a more modern-style building in about 650, which in turn gave way to a stone Doric temple, not long before Eretria was sacked by the Persians in 490 – in revenge for the help rendered to the Ionians in their revolt against Darius in 499. One of the marble pediments depicted Athena (*far left*) in the center, among battling Greeks and Amazons; the best-preserved figures (*left*) show Theseus carrying their Queen, Antiope, on to his chariot and out of the fray.

Ischia (Pithekoussai)

The hazards faced by the merchant venturers of Pithekoussai are vividly demonstrated in the scene on a locally made krater of about 700. The variety of fish, including a man-eater, betrays long acquaintance with the sea on the part of the painter. Despite this the merchants brought to Ischia quantities of objects from many parts of the Mediterranean world

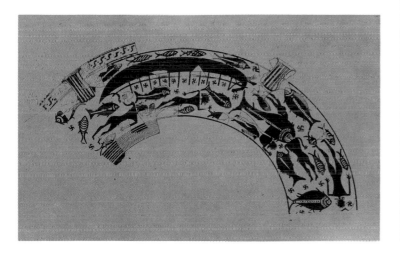

One such object is a cup from Rhodes of about 725, inscribed at Pithekoussai with three lines of verse, written backwards – "I am the bibulous cup of Nestor; whoso drains this jar shall soon enough be possessed of beribboned Aphrodite's passion" – an echo of the *Iliad* which suggests local knowledge of Homer's work, as well as of writing itself, which is attested from many lesser graffiti of these years.

Most of these finds come from tombs cut in the volcanic soil which corrodes and warps many of the objects deposited. Clusters of tombs were built up, family groups of stone cairns, one still unexcavated in this photograph. A striking import (*below*) from the Near East is a Syrian face flask, from the same mold as examples found at Tarsus and Zinjirli, north of al Mina.

The Pithekoussans soon plucked up courage to settle on the Italian mainland opposite, at Cumae, close to a native town; they named the site after the Euboean town of Kyme. The earliest Greek levels seem not to have come to light in the excavations, conducted mainly before World War I, but the colony clearly flourished in the 7th and 6th centuries to the detriment of Pithekoussai which declined rapidly after 675. Euboean vases appear in the earliest graves, but the bulk of imported pottery then becomes Corinthian, with local imitations soon appearing in numbers, as in Etruria to the north. A particularly interesting Protocorinthian vase from Cumae is a little flask of about 660, inscribed with a warning in sharp contrast to that on Nestor's cup – "If anybody steals Tateie's jar he (or she) will go blind." This aryballos, as we call the shape, would have contained perfume, perhaps of a kind imported from the Near East, like the trinkets in many of the Cumae graves. Regrettably, no sanctuary of the period has been excavated on the acropolis of Cumae; only terracotta revetments of early buildings have come to light. A more prosaic view of Cumaean life is given by the constant symbol of the city on her coins, the simple mussel shell.

A coin of Naxos on Sicily, a Chalcidian colony, also advertises local products, for on the reverse is a cluster of grapes to underline the relevance of Dionysus' head on the obverse. It dates to about 510. The god was also highly revered on the Cycladic island of Naxos, the home of some of the earliest colonists in Sicily who, with the Euboeans, settled on a promontory below the fertile slopes of Etna.

3. The Dark Centuries

The catchplate of a bronze fibula (safety pin) engraved in about 700 in Boeotia. It shows a battle on board a ship whose ram and steering oar are typical features.

To appreciate correctly the history and culture of Archaic Greece, it is essential to ignore preconceptions based on a later age. This is not an easy task, since much of our evidence for the period comes from Athenian writers and Attic pottery, and it is of course Athens that achieved so much so brilliantly in the 5th century. Six hundred years passed between the demise of Mycenae and the Athenian empire; we must be prepared to see many different aspects of the face of Greece during those centuries, and must be even more alert in this respect when our evidence is at its most scanty. When literary and archaeological evidence is silent we have no right to assume that there were no power struggles, no emigrations, no wars. The evidence we do have should at least indicate the mood of each period, and during the darkest of these periods it so happens that our preconception regarding the dominant position of Athens turns out to be not far wide of the mark.

In reconstructing a picture of Archaic Greece we shall for the first 400 years or so rely heavily on the evidence of archaeology, especially pottery, after which the emphasis will gradually shift in favor of written sources; for by the 5th century we have virtually contemporary accounts available, and so archaeological remains become the prop, not the edifice itself. Not that we should exaggerate the extremes – in some areas archaeology still plays a major role in the 5th century, while the reliance we place on literary sources for the early period may be disputed, as we have seen, but will be far from minimal.

Pottery can be of crucial importance in forming a chronological framework, but can do little to help us piece together a social, let alone political, history of any period. Except for part of the 7th century, Attic pottery is superior to most of its rivals, but we may note that only one Greek writer, and he a Boeotian, Pindar, ever goes out of his way to praise the work of the Athenian Kerameikos.

Literary evidence for the Dark Ages on the other hand can only have an oral origin, since Greece did not become literate till the 8th century. Long after this it is likely that most "historical" records were retained in the memories of officials, usually priests, rather than in any more (or less?) permanent form. Exaggeration and error, not to mention fictional elaboration, can easily creep into oral tradition. The handing down of family trees was a major aspect of such traditions, and any respectable family would trace back its origins not only to the legendary period of the heroes of Troy, but also a couple of generations further to the gods themselves, and in so doing they invariably condense the Dark Ages into the briefest span instead of recognizing the centuries they actually occupied. It is no easy task to see exactly where truth shades into fiction in such a progression.

Homer. The poems of Homer are a prime example of this oral tradition. It is true to say that for centuries they were taken as gospel, reflecting the history of about 1200 BC. The date of Homer himself was disputed, though modern

An Attic red-figure stamnos of about 480 depicting the sirens tempting Odysseus and his men – one of the rare depictions in art of Homer's tale.

opinion has hardened at about 700 for the final fashioning of his works. So are those works set in 700 BC, the period of the fall of Troy, or some time in between? As so often happens, the answer seems to be now one, now the other; we must use Homer extremely carefully as evidence for any single period, and we must also allow him the poetic licence that is his due. A few examples may illustrate the many-sided nature of his works. While the heroes fight with bronze weapons (inconsistent with the practice of Homer's day), the laborers use iron tools (impossible in the Bronze Age). Agamemnon has the title "anax," which was unknown in Iron Age society, though the political meetings which Homer records seem more at home in the period of the petty aristocracies than the Mycenaean monarchies. The architectural complexities of the palaces of Homer's heroes recall Bronze Age buildings, but he knows of none of their rich trappings.

Even here we are talking mainly of literary evidence which may be of relevance to the 8th century. Go back 200–300 years and that evidence is reduced largely to plausible stories of disorder and migration in suspiciously legendary wrappings.

The aftermath of the Mycenaean collapse. So the history of the Greek world from 1100 to after 750 has to be written mainly from archaeological evidence, and compared with earlier and later periods this does not amount to a great deal. Only one site, the Kerameikos cemetery in Athens, has yielded reasonable quantities of material covering this whole span, and even in this instance the total number of vases of the Protogeometric period is only a little over 200, and apart from pins and finger-rings fewer than 20 other objects have survived. A similar picture comes from a large but poorly published cemetery in the northeast of Salamis, and it can be corroborated by finds at Leukandi, Mycenae and Argos. Virtually all our evidence for the Protogeometric period comes from tombs which are infrequently found at sites other than these, while in some areas, notably the southern Peloponnese, there is a total gap in our knowledge.

The Kerameikos cemetery is a new foundation of about 1075. Athens was already populated and prosperous, but as elsewhere the sub-Mycenaean graves appear in new areas, and for the first and only time graves were dug on the Acropolis. At the same time the Mycenaean life style lingered on in some parts of Greece, even on the east coast of Attica at Perati.

It is extremely difficult to say who these "new" Athenians were, and what happened to the Mycenaean inhabitants. A recent writer has resorted to the conclusion that "save in Central Greece the Mycenaeans melted away like the summer snows." Some lived on in Greece, either in remote areas, catching up later with developments in Attica and the Argolid, or with a changed way of life under the influence of new arrivals, perhaps from a variety of areas to the north and west. But we have to deduce most of this from the evidence of vase shapes and decoration and methods of burial. As we have noted, nowhere do the Dorians emerge clearly from any such considerations.

The most striking change to be found in the Kerameikos cemetery is the use of single pit graves instead of the communal family tombs so common in the Mycenaean world, and almost the whole of Greece (with Crete a clear exception) follows suit. At Athens cremation soon replaces interment, though this is little copied; Leukandi has many cremations, but they are very rare at Argos before 700. The body would be burned near the grave and the ashes collected up in a clay jar; offerings could be placed in the jar or in the pit beside it. This form of burial may have come from Asia Minor, but it is not clear whether single burials are a revival of the older Mycenaean practice or were introduced from more northern areas such as Thessaly and Epirus, where they were the more normal custom in the immediate past. In most cases children were inhumed, and the number of child burials suggests a very high rate of infant mortality.

A jug and a cup usually accompanied the dead, and occasionally a metallic object is included – rings, a pin, or later a sword or spear. Towards the end of the sub-Mycenaean period at Athens and Argos some of these objects are made of iron rather than the bronze common up to this date, and indeed for a time around 1000 bronze becomes something of a rarity, resuming popularity in the

A selection of the types of bronze fastenings (both plain and "safety" pins) used in Greece during the Dark Ages, showing the development from the simple sub-Mycenaean to the elegant Late Geometric. The pins can measure up to 47 cm.

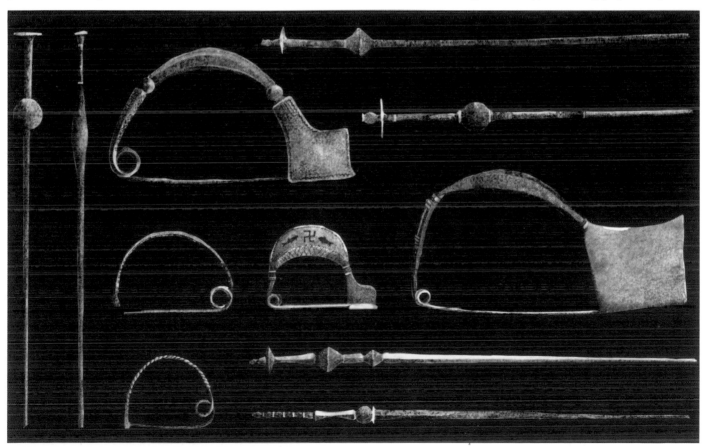

later 10th century. We should remember that iron is only used in "Iron Age" Greece for cutting weapons and tools, bronze being retained for armor, decorative work and a good proportion of spear- and arrowheads. Iron only becomes superior to bronze when expertly puddled and tempered, and is not reworked as easily as bronze; but at least ironstone was available in many parts of Greece, while most copper and all tin had to be imported. Supplies of copper came mainly from Cyprus, whence knowledge of ironworking also came to Greece in about 1050. The extensive use of iron in the following years suggests that exports from the island were severely restricted for a period, though at Tiryns unusual iron pins are topped by heads made of imported ivory.

At all events little metal was left for luxuries once pins for clothing and weapons for defense (and no doubt offense) were provided. The situation was already picking up by the 10th century – traces of silver-refining installations have been found at Argos and at Thorikos in Attica, while at Leukandi many gold trinkets and fragments of molds for the legs of large bronze tripods are of 10th-century date. Such three-legged cauldrons are of a type well known later from the Acropolis, Olympia and Ithaca, and were used as prizes in the games and as dedications to the gods.

The attention paid to pots and pins cannot conceal the fact that we know very little of the buildings of Protogeometric Greece. Mycenaean architectural techniques, both the large-scale Cyclopean masonry and the domestic timber and stone construction, had disappeared; only at Iolcus in Thessaly is a Dark Age structure of well-cut stone found. Elsewhere we are lucky to discover the flimsiest foundations. Where permanent residence was taken up, mudbrick must have been the main material, though a few rough stone buildings are known from places where stone is plentiful; one such building near modern Naxos seems to have been of the Mycenaean porched hall type. An apsed house has been found at Asine in the Argolid, and at Smyrna a free-standing house of the later 10th century is of oval shape, some three by five meters, and was made of mudbrick. It probably also had a thatched roof – a minor indication, along with a more robust type of dress pin, that the climate of the period was rather cooler and wetter than before. The oval and apse recur later, and it is not impossible that the latter harks back to the pre-Mycenaean tradition of the mainland. At one of the few sites in Messenia known from this period, Nichoria, we even find small chamber tombs of a horseshoe shape.

In such circumstances there could have been little demand for highly artistic objects, yet it is clear that in the more progressive areas craftsmen could find a living. We see this particularly in the pottery, but smiths would also have been kept busy enough. It is in the vases too that we first see the beginnings of a new confidence and self-assertion. In the latest Mycenaean period vases were increasingly sloppily made and decorated, with a narrow range of linear patterns and inherited shapes. Then, with no clean break, and not uninfluenced by Cypriot work, shapes begin to tauten as the vases are thrown on a faster wheel, the various parts are given individual attention and carefully related to each other, and decoration, though still limited in scope, is carefully applied, again with due consideration of its place on the vase. In particular we may note that the motif of concentric circles or semicircles, in vogue earlier, is now drawn with the aid of a compass and multiple brush, bringing a crisp precision to Attic Protogeometric work which has immediate imitators in other parts of Greece, for instance in Argos and Thessaly.

Although the decoration of vases is nearly wholly linear, exceptions should be noted: a horse tucked under the handle of a Kerameikos amphora and two rather lifeless

Ground plan and restoration of a mudbrick house at Smyrna, dating from about 900. It is a freestanding construction, oval in shape, measuring 5 m × 3 m. Such houses sometimes had flat roofs, but were more often thatched before the invention of tiles in the late 8th century.

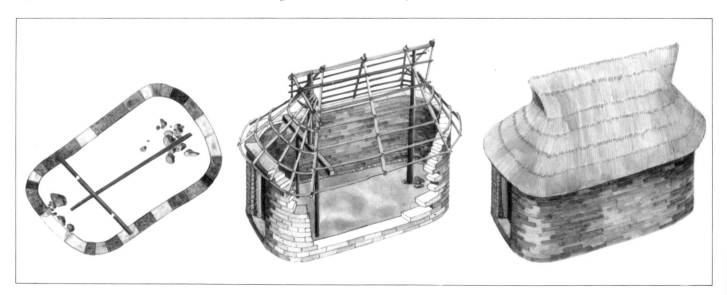

archers facing each other on a very mean hydria from Leukandi. Painted terracotta animals are occasionally found – a fine stag from the Kerameikos, bulls on Samos and a toy horse on wheels from near the Kerameikos.

Few sites have produced Protogeometric material, and the population of Greece could not have been large. There is no definite confirmation of material further west than Ithaca, where a strong local culture continued unbroken from the Mycenaean period; nothing from Laconia, but again full continuity of occupation on Crete. Here we may note in particular relatively rich burials at Knossos, with silver and gold in modest but still noticeable amounts and a thriving but bleak mountain-top village at Karphi to the east, inexplicably abandoned in about 1000. In Asia Minor Miletus was reoccupied by people using sub-Mycenaean pottery of a type close to that of Athens, as did settlers at Assarlik, close to later Halicarnassus to the south. Protogeometric pottery is reported from Sardis, and graves have recently been excavated at Iasus in which there is a proportion of handmade vases suggestive of local Carian participation in the settlement, such as is reported in literary sources for Miletus and elsewhere. A more substantial break between Bronze and Iron Age habitation occurred on Cos and Rhodes, where the earliest material is later Protogeometric; on Cos it is akin to Argive, suggesting the origin of the settlers.

Most of these sites, including those in Asia Minor, were inhabited in the Bronze Age, and so folk memory may have played a part in the reoccupation. Yet we may demand a more substantial reason for such distant migration to Ionia, and we should note that the need for easily defended, well-watered sites made many choices inevitable; the existing Cyclopean walls of Mycenae and Athens afforded welcome places of refuge for the people and animals of Protogeometric communities, who are not known to have had the resources to erect any new defenses of their own.

For many aspects of life we have virtually no information, and religion is one of these. At a few sanctuaries which later became famous a handful of Protogeometric sherds have been found, but nowhere outside Crete is continuity of worship securely attested. However, the basic conservatism of most religions encourages us to override archaeological evidence in this instance, and to suggest that the holy places were kept alive in however modest a way, even if some of their Mycenaean deities were imperfectly remembered or new gods took over at their expense.

Revival. There is a certain amount of truth in the seemingly naive judgment that the Geometric period was the same as the Protogeometric, only more so. There was a general and sustained growth in population, wealth and artistic invention, during an era which archaeological evidence at any rate suggests was relatively peaceful. Two changes deserve particular attention as being not without

A typical amphora of the Protogeometric period with funnel mouth, rounded body and simple linear decoration.

impact on subsequent history – the adoption of the alphabet and the westward movement of the Greeks. But let us first consider developments in those aspects which we have already examined in the Protogeometric period.

Much of our material still comes from tombs, but tombs of increasing number and richness. The old sites remain and mostly flourish – Athens, Corinth, Argos, Cos – but many more can be added, some with signs of habitation in the latest Protogeometric phase.

In Attica numerous villages spring up outside Athens, some of which almost outshine the city for magnificence of burials. In Athens itself the increase in the number of wells dug in the Agora in the 8th century is a clear indication of a growing population, as is the increasing pace of burials in one well-used family vault in Knossos. The general character of burials shows no striking changes apart from their growing wealth – over 50 vases were found in single tombs at Eleusis, Anavysos and Athens, and quantities of jewelry buried with the aristocratic Boeotian lady at Paralimni. At Athens in particular ostentatiously large amphoras and kraters are set up as grave markers. A similar trend towards monumentality of expression is seen in the man-sized bronze tripod cauldrons dedicated at many sanctuaries in the 8th century. Here material suddenly becomes more abundant, and by the later 8th century architectural remains are found relatively frequently, for instance at Delphi, and Olympia, and the shrines of Hera on Samos and in the Argive plain, of Apollo at Corinth and Thebes, of Athena at Tegea and Athens, and many more.

While vases remain the most common finds, there is a very obvious increase in supplies of metal and imports of finished metal products; in both categories we can place decorated bronzework and gold jewelry. Towards the end of the period armor reappears in metallic form, and gradually the Greeks again take up gem-engraving, ivory-carving, the techniques of filigree, granulation and hollow-casting in metalwork, and it is probable that large-scale sculpture in wood was attempted, followed by limestone carving in the early 7th century.

Settlements and sanctuaries. Recent excavations have begun to shed much light on the architecture of the period, in particular its diversity of style. Hesiod tells his readers to construct their homes of timbers stripped of their bark, to discourage crows from roosting, and we may thus assume a widespread use of wood despite the lack of traces of it in archaeological contexts. The materials which do survive are mudbrick and stone, the latter still used only for foundations save in naturally rocky regions, and rarely more than roughly squared. The shapes of buildings and their arrangements are very varied – at Smyrna in the 9th century one area was laid out with rows of small rectangular cabins of mudbrick on stone foundations, though later there was a return to less regularly arranged apsidal buildings. A few of these houses had more than one room, and buildings consisting of clusters of rooms have been found at Eleusis and in the sanctuary of Hecademus (later the Academy), once in the countryside beyond the walls of Athens. Nowhere are there certain remains of any upper story.

At Zagora on Andros the houses of the settlement abut one another, with the exception of one structure at the highest point, which is reminiscent of a Mycenaean palace in its general plan, though in few details. It was laid out in about 750 with a large central room with wooden columns, a hearth, porch and subsidiary rooms. Stone benches serve as sleeping platforms, as in many other houses of the Archaic period, but at Zagora they were soon converted to hold large storage jars for corn and oil, and further conversions indicate a rapidly growing population. The neck of the promontory was cut off by a stout fortification wall against which simpler houses abutted. A similar arrangement has been found on the hill of Aghios Andreas on Siphnos to the south, where a Mycenaean defense wall was refurbished in the late Geometric period. Elsewhere at this date fortifications are rare, a striking exception being the massive circuit at Smyrna, clearly designed to protect the colony, already spilling out from its original site, from attacks by various enemies from the hinterland.

Zagora may have been within the influence of the Euboean towns; the geographer Strabo tells us of an early Euboean "empire" embracing the northern Cyclades. However the architecture so far revealed at Eretria and Leukandi has few similarities; the predominant form is the

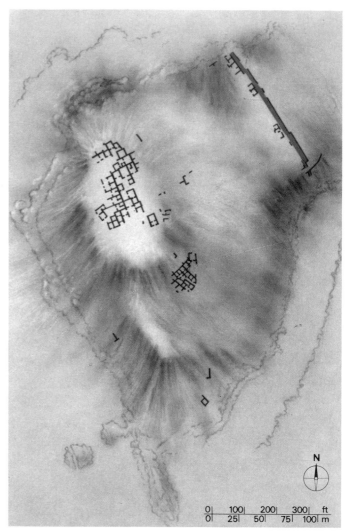

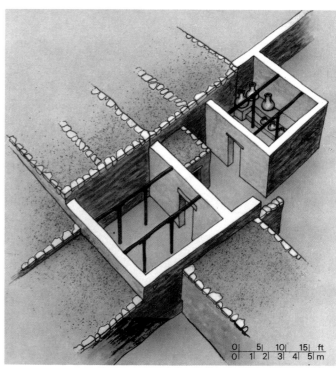

isolated apsidal building with porch and living room, which is perhaps the commonest type of structure of the period. It was certainly this form which most influenced the development of the Greek temple, and in the ensuing period we shall see that most of the architectural efforts of the Greeks were expended on religious buildings. In the 8th century it is not easy to distinguish sacred structures from profane, and conclusions have rather to be drawn from the character of the finds and the subsequent history of the site: that is, whether it became a sanctuary or not.

Opposite page: plan of the excavated areas of the headland site of Zagora on Andros, dating from around 700 BC, and a visualization of a typical Zagoran house. Note the houses built up against the fortification wall, the benches for storage jars in many of the rooms, and the isolated temple, in use long after the site was abandoned.

Right: partly reconstructed model of a temple dedicated at the Argive Heraion in the late 8th century. The temples of this period were undoubtedly decorated with murals as shown here.

Below: the gradual expansion of the temple of Hera in her precinct on Samos, from a narrow 100-foot shed in the 8th–7th century to an Ionic temple measuring 109 × 53m in the years of Polycrates' tyranny. This type of replacement is typical of Archaic sanctuaries.

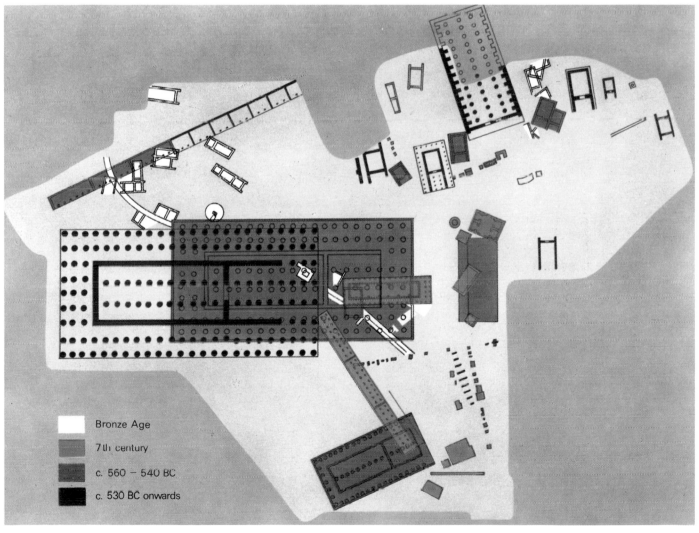

Bronze Age

7th century

c. 560 – 540 BC

c. 530 BC onwards

Minute but precious fragments of painted stucco panels (perhaps some 6 feet wide) which decorated the outer walls of the temple of Poseidon at Isthmia in the early 7th century. Here we see part of a horse's mane.

Most forms of worship were conducted at an open-air altar within a larger sanctuary in which any temple merely served as the shelter of the cult statue of the deity, and sometimes doubled as treasury and law court. As long as cult statues remained rare, the temples themselves were not very imposing structures. We should note, as so often, an exception in Crete and a few other areas where there is evidence of offerings being made at altars inside buildings which may have had both religious and secular functions.

Lack of expertise may have prevented the construction of wide buildings, but monumentality could be expressed in length, and there appear in the years after 750 a series of long, narrow temples, often 100 feet long (hecatompedon) and not more than 15 feet wide, for example at Eretria, Corinth and Samos More orthodox and earlier short temples with apses are known from the Corinthia and Argos, while terracotta models from the same area show porches, high, triangular windows (like those at Zagora) and steep, presumably thatched roofs. These models are decorated with patternwork like vases, but we should note that at the early 7th-century temple of Poseidon at Isthmia shattered fragments of painted blocks have been found, proving that the outside walls carried panels with figured compositions. Squared stone was largely used for this structure, and the roof was tiled. Clay tiles were traditionally a Corinthian invention, but were far heavier than thatch and demanded stouter walls to support them. The walls of the contemporary temple of Apollo at Corinth were inscribed with sacral laws.

The temples at Eretria are discussed elsewhere in this book, but the sequence on Samos deserves mention here. The first temple of Hera replaced a small shed used as a shelter for the cult image. It was a long building with a row of posts down the middle supporting the roof, requiring that the statue be moved to one side to enjoy a clear view of proceedings outside (at Ephesus and elsewhere it was permissible to move the statue to a good vantage point). A little later a colonnade of wooden posts was built, probably veranda-style, around the outside. Then a flood in about 660 destroyed the temple, and it was rebuilt with two rows of internal posts and an integral colonnade. At Isthmia and probably Corinth there were also colonnades, that at Isthmia perhaps being made of fluted wooden columns. Such colonnades were probably intended as shaded areas in which the inhabitants could walk and talk – an extension of the simple porch. On Samos the sanctuary was equipped after the flood with a long, freestanding, open-fronted shed, the first of the stoas which were to become a basic and magnificent feature of Hellenistic town centers.

The heart of the *temenos* or precinct remained the altar towards which the temple faced, usually east. A particularly common type of altar was a long and low platform, sometimes of considerable size, as at the sanctuary of Artemis Orthia at Sparta. At Olympia the ashes of the sacrificial animals were concreted with the waters of the Alpheus, gradually building up the famous ash-altar of Zeus.

Reconstruction of a typical 6-foot bronze tripod dedicated at Olympia, having been won as a prize in the games. It dates from the late 8th century. The horses which form part of the plastic decoration represent those which gained the victory.

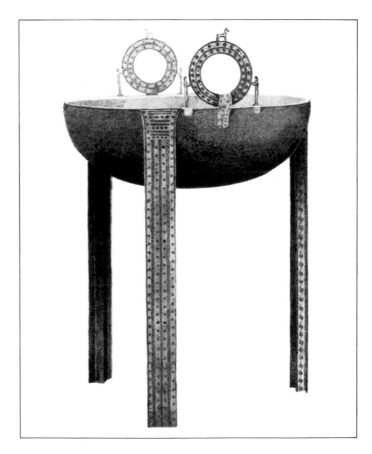

Mainland Greece.

Metalwork. As far as we know, there was as yet no temple in the Altis, nor at Delphi, though excavation has revealed plentiful traces of cult activity in the 9th and 8th centuries. The Olympic Games were traditionally founded in 776, a report which archaeological evidence cannot prove or disprove. However it is noticeable that the bronze tripods we have mentioned become far more frequent at this period, while the prevalence of bronze statuettes of horses (though one, of solid bronze, was nearly 2 feet high), whether free standing or as decoration for the tripod bowls, points to the chariot race as a major competition, even though later literary sources give the footrace priority. Hesiod tells us he was awarded a tripod for his victory in the Euboean song contest held at the funeral games of Amphidamas, a warrior who died in the course of the Lelantine War.

Much of the bronzework is in the Greek tradition – the tripods, swords, spears, perhaps arrows as well. Elsewhere foreign influences are at work. A pair of greaves from the Athenian Acropolis are of pure Danubian origin of the 9th century while on Crete, which had been more open to imports in the Protogeometric period, the late 9th and 8th centuries see very strong Near Eastern influences as well as imports. In particular we might mention a series of embossed shields dedicated to Zeus on Mount Ida together with decorated Phoenician bowls. The latter found their way to further Greek sites such as Olympia and Delphi.

The first set of armor that was to typify the Greek hoplite soldier appears in the late 8th century, though there is no proof that the tactic of massed infantry was employed till a later date. The warrior grave excavated at Argos in 1953 is one of the more eloquent finds of the period, even though much disturbed by Roman construction works. The young soldier was buried with the first breastplate and helmet known to us since the sub-Mycenaean period, and also found were gold rings and iron axes, spits and fire-dogs in the shape of warships. The helmet is of a type unknown later, but the linen-lined corselet has the bell shape with a muscular torso embossed on it which remains standard issue for over two centuries. Helmet and corselet may owe much to central European models.

The warrior was probably a foot soldier, but what was the role of the horse at this time? We have seen the part it played at Olympia, and many of the bronzes found there were probably made at Argos. Argive Geometric vases frequently depict the animal. A contemporary Attic vase portrays a horse ridden by a cuirassed warrior, and another shows a helmet plume held by a support in the shape of a horse's head. Yet there is no evidence to show that cavalry was used extensively on the mainland at this period or later, though in Ionia and Sicily the case was somewhat different. Similarly, the use of chariots for warfare rather than for racing or the transport of richer warriors is most unlikely outside Cyprus, where eastern influences were immeasurably stronger than in Greece. Bits found in graves show that the horse was used throughout the Dark Ages, but may not have been ridden extensively till the 8th century.

Pottery. We are led to some of these conclusions by archaeological finds and literary evidence, but representations which now begin to appear increasingly on artifacts, especially vases of the late Geometric period, are of considerable help. The largest collection of material is in the scenes on the big Attic grave markers, their style of figure decoration being inspired by the angularity of the Geometric ornament which invades an increasing area of the vase in the years between 900 and 700. Both human and animal figures are aggregates of parts, a profile head and legs separated by a triangular frontal torso. At first they are depicted in silhouette, with a dotted eye and no sex, though before long differentiation is introduced and the use of outline drawing extended to show details of shields and dress. The scenes are deceptively varied in detail, though the range of themes is narrow at first – processions of mourners to the bier, chariots and warriors in cortege, fights, sea-battles, hunting and some athletics. Perspective was attempted by showing even those aspects which could not really be seen, rendering these smaller and placing them above, below or beside the main feature seen in the foreground.

Most Greek states had their own, often distinctive schools, but few used figure-scenes as much as the Athenians. The Argives liked them, and Corinthians, Boeotians, Euboeans and Cretans painted them more than occasionally. Elsewhere it was mostly the generation of the meander and zig-zag, wheel and diamond – incipient stagnation.

Eastward ho! The welcome breeze stirred up by a renewal of contacts with the east, which revived the art of pottery, had already made its presence felt in the less conservative arts. Such a bald statement makes light of the

Bronze statuette of a warrior, perhaps Zeus, of the early 7th century, found under the temple of Hera at Olympia. The god's martial character is very evident from such "spear-brandishers."

Left: a mid-8th century bowl of the late Geometric period with a frieze of human and animal motifs, including warriors and sphinxes, imitating similar designs on Phoenician metal bowls.

Right: krater from the Dipylon cemetery, used as the tomb marker of an aristocratic Athens warrior. It shows the bier on the hearse, mourning men and women and a cortege of chariots in honor of the dead man.

Below: the earliest known full Greek inscription is found on this jug of about 730 from the Dipylon cemetery in Athens.

perils and excitement faced by the Greeks who made these eastward journeys and opened up the way for momentous changes at home. At al Mina in Syria the commercial area was in use for 500 years and reflects the vicissitudes of struggles for power in Syria during those years. The earliest material is Euboean and Cycladic, with a good proportion of Cypriot and local ware, while Corinthian and eastern Greek pottery predominates after about 700. These early travelers probably traded more than just clay vases, though we cannot be more specific; what they took back to Greece is a little easier to decide. As far back as the early Protogeometric period objects of imported faience are found at Leukandi, and ivory fragments at Athens and elsewhere. At al Mina Sir Leonard Woolley discovered elephant tusks ready to be shipped to Greece, and we have examples of 8th-century ivories of Greek workmanship, heavily dependent on Syrian and Phoenician originals. Scraps of imported ivories from Greek sanctuaries come from inlay work on furniture, such as a handsome throne and bed found in a tomb at Salamis on Cyprus. The decoration on these and on the metal bowls from Phoenicia consists mainly of friezes of real and mythical animals, most of them unknown to Greeks at home, together with rich floral patterns of palmettes, papyrus, lotus and the symbolic tree of life. All these elements find a home in Greek art of the later 8th century and are a major feature in the 7th; we may single out the lion, sphinx and griffin, as well as the floral chains replacing more geometric ornament in subsidiary positions.

Throne decorated with carved ivory panels, found in the dromos of a royal tomb at Salamis on Cyprus. Fragments of such panels have been found on Greek sites and may have belonged to similar impressive pieces of furniture imported from the eastern Mediterranean.

Also borrowed were many aspects of eastern myth and religion, but we can rarely be sure whether these often garbled and half-rationalized transfers took place in the Bronze Age or with this renewal of contacts – probably both. One such debated question is the introduction of Apollo to Greece – a latecomer in legend, was he of the late Mycenaean or early Geometric period?

However, we should not regard this "Orientalizing" period as a nine days' wonder; interchange of objects and ideas between Greece and the east was virtually uninterrupted, though reaching its peak of influence on Greek life in the period 750–650.

Literacy. It was by no means inevitable that writing should have been among these borrowings from the east. During the Dark Ages there is no evidence that any Greeks were literate. Homer mentions writing only in the story of Bellerophon, in which a written message plays an integral part – a story which could well have its roots in the Bronze Age. However, literacy survived in the Near East, though the evidence is not extensive, and we cannot easily judge the pace at which the Aramaic and Phoenician alphabets began to go their separate ways during these years.

The earliest known inscriptions from Greek sites are scratched on clay vases; few date to before 700 and there is little to encourage the idea that literacy was at all widespread in the following century. Many are mere fragments of an original text, and most of the complete pieces take the form "I am the possession of X," with the object always doing the talking. The earliest scrap may date to c. 760 and comes from Ischia, where there are a fair number of similar inscriptions of 8th-century date, including a three-line verse graffito of about 720 which is modeled in part on a Homeric text. Slightly earlier is a single verse line cut on an Attic jug, telling us that it was the prize in a dancing contest.

As inscriptions become more common we see that the Greek states used various forms of the alphabet, but that all of them adopted some innovations which more or less transformed the Phoenician script into a western alphabet from the outset. Most important was the general introduction of vowels (five in most states, seven in Ionia) by using otherwise useless Semitic signs. Also all the Greek states have confused the names and sounds of the four Semitic "s" signs, though some used Σ as their simple sibilant, others M. It would seem therefore that one ingenious Greek or group of Greeks made a deliberate attempt to adapt the Semitic alphabet to Greek use before passing it on to other Greeks who intentionally or otherwise changed some of the characters with which they were presented. The Cretans retained an alphabet closest to the Phoenician, but even the progressive Euboeans could retain ᛘ when most other states had made the simplification to ᛘ. It was the Euboeans, however, with their colonies at Ischia and Cumae, who taught the Etruscans their letters, whence the Romans learned them, with the result that the Euboean forms CDRS are found in the Roman and our own alphabets, rather than Ionic ΓΔΡΣ.

The written material of the Archaic period which we possess is executed almost wholly on stone, metal or clay. The bulk consists of owners' inscriptions, dedications to a wide range of deities, laws (mostly sacral), artists' signatures and epitaphs. Literacy varied from area to area and the range and character of preserved texts differ from place to place. One imponderable factor is the use of perishable materials – wood, wax, leather and papyrus; a cautious position is advisable since it is noticeable that the Greeks did not readily develop a cursive style of writing more suited to pen and ink or wet clay, but persevered with the straight and spindly lines of the graffito. We should not, however, deny that the poets of the 7th century committed their work to writing.

. . . and then west. We have seen a vital role played by Euboeans not only in reopening contacts with the east, but also in opening up the way west. Other Greeks are only dimly seen in these ventures, though they no doubt participated; tradition gave Rhodes a prominent part in early voyages west before the first Olympiad, according to Strabo. Archaeology tells us that the Rhodians did develop some export lines, but only later in the 8th century – a small container for scent, itself imported from the east, and drinking cups like the inscribed vase from Ischia, which were widely exported and imitated throughout the Mediterranean world for a century or more. However, far more significant during this period was the rise of Corinthian participation; her pottery begins to be found early in the 8th century at sites to her west, notably Delphi and Ithaca, then Vitsa up near the Albanian border by 750. After this the same two types of vase, perfume flask and drinking cup, begin to take over; Euboea fades away after 700 and Rhodes plays only a minor role to the finer wares of Corinth. Athens is represented by a single, though widespread, export – large oil-amphoras taking Attica's main product to Morocco, Spain, Egypt and the Black Sea by the end of the 7th century.

Corinth's commercial prosperity began at about the same time as the foundation of Syracuse in Sicily in 733, some time before the period of Corinthian ascendancy mentioned by Thucydides. The oldest colony in Sicily was not Syracuse, but another Euboean settlement, Naxos, below modern Taormina, which was founded together with men from the Aegean island of the same name. They erected an altar to Apollo the Leader at the point where they stepped ashore, and this became a center of Sicilian ritual in later years. Soon after Syracuse was founded came a spate of settlements around the rich plain of Catania, south of Etna; Naxos placed colonies at either end, Catane and Leontini, while colonists from Megara, after a series of difficulties, finally settled in 728 at a site some eight miles north of Syracuse on land given to them by a local chieftain, Hyblon. They had tried to settle at an old Mycenaean site even nearer Syracuse, Thapsos, where their leader Lamis died; a grave which was probably his has been found in a reused Sicel tomb, furnished with a couple of Corinthian cups. Nearer the end of the 8th century the Chalcidians from Cumae and Euboea ensured their passage through the straits of Messina by settlements on either coast at Rhegion and Zancle.

The reasons for this series of colonial foundations have been much discussed, and we have noted some of the problems already. Was it trade, pressure of population, or perhaps political tension at home that prompted them?

The fact that there was no single compelling reason is clear enough even from ancient sources, though they are of uneven value – pirates make their nest at Zancle, bastard sons settle at Taranto, drought forces Therans to Cyrene. It is difficult to estimate pressures at home which may have caused the departure of a section of the community, just as we cannot fairly appreciate why in the Dark Ages Ionia was settled rather than nearer areas of Greece. We have seen from Herodotus' account that the Theran settlers at Cyrene had to be forced to leave home – the tense situation he portrays may well have been caused by drought, which withers crops growing in Thera's fine, volcanic soil. A later decree of the Cyreneans embodies what is probably part of the original foundation charter – it requires each household to send one of its sons, on pain of death, and allows him to return to Thera only in absolute necessity. All those who disobeyed the terms (said to be those given by Apollo at Delphi) were put under a curse by which they were to melt away like the wax dolls which the whole population of Thera had to place in a fire. In other legal texts of a similar nature there is much concern about rights to possession of land and citizenship as well as inheritance in the city of origin or the colony.

Yet looking back to the 8th century we cannot doubt that it was trade that led the colonists from Euboea. The piles of slag by the site at Pithekoussai indicate the smelting of iron, and analysis has shown it to be iron from Elba. Bronze was also worked on Ischia. Therefore it was the search for more metals which brought the Greeks into contact with central Italy and the Etruscans. We may speculate about the name Chalcis, which means "the bronze one," though there are few clues as to when the town got its name.

The securing of the Straits of Messina was a logical progression, as more Greeks grew interested in trade as a means to wealth. Thucydides' description of Zancle as a pirates' base may owe as much to the anti-Chalcidian sentiments of his primary source for Sicilian affairs, Antiochus of Syracuse, as to the rough-and-ready nature of early trading ventures. Both before and after its foundation fair numbers of Corinthian vases were passing through the straits, and it is difficult to see how the Chalcidians could have been pursuing narrowly selfish and lawless policies. We should not forget a tradition that Eretrians founded a colony on Corfu at the same time as

Corinth founded Syracuse. Corfu was an avoidable but desirable staging point on the journey west, and together with other clues from Ithaca and Vitsa there begins to emerge a picture of Euboean and Corinthian cooperation during the second half of the 8th century.

Catane and Leontini fall into another category, the latter being inland, though once on a navigable river. Naxos needed the grain which could be grown in the plain of Catania far better than on the fertile but hilly ground around her. At both Naxos and Leontini recent excavations have yielded sherds of the later 8th century, while the first fortification wall at Leontini, of the earlier 7th century, was made of large well-cut blocks.

The case of Syracuse has been more extensively debated. It was founded by Archias, a member of the ruling Bacchiad family at Corinth, with settlers largely from the inland area of Tenea; one not too reliable source also gives a drought as the cause of their departure. Yet they settled at the finest harbor site in Sicily, with a copious supply of fresh water on the peninsula. The fact that they fought to win the site from native Sicel inhabitants shows that they

Opposite page: the Iron Age successor of the doomed Bronze Age Akrotiri settlement on Thera is set high on the island's main non-volcanic outcrop, near its only natural water source.

Below: aerial photography has revealed the lines of drainage channels separating colonial land-holdings at Metapontum in southern Italy. The town itself also had a regular plan as early as the 7th century, though the earliest Greek material has been found at Incoronata.

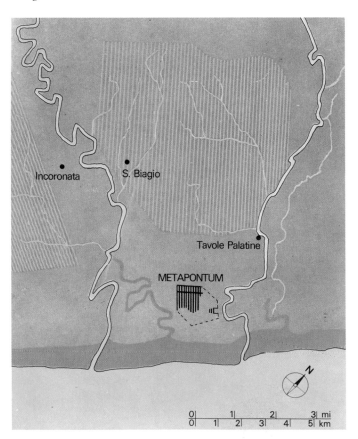

were little interested in trade and wished rather to gain territory for their own subsistence – an impression given further support by the delightful and possibly true story that one of the colonists gambled away his allotment of land on the outward voyage. Possession of such an area of land was of course a basic necessity for any colonist; one of Hesiod's main complaints was that his brother had cheated him of his share of inheritance, and we may imagine that it was a common cause of dispute in a period of increasing population.

Similar motives may be seen in the foundation of Gela by Rhodians and Cretans in 688, dominating a large plain on the south coast, and also that of her own colony to the west, Acragas, 108 years later.

In southern Italy agricultural considerations were even more important in founding colonies. The dates we have for the foundations come from sources later than Thucydides, notably the compilation of events written up by the church historian Eusebius of Caesarea, and preserved for us in extracts in even later writers – an annotated Latin translation by St Jerome and a garbled Armenian translation. What we have has to be treated very carefully, in particular since we regularly find the three versions varying slightly in their dates of the same events, as well as cheerfully including double dates for individual episodes.

The guiding hand of Corinth can be seen in the numbers of colonists from lands bordering the Corinthian Gulf who took part in these settlements, under the guidance of Apollo at Delphi. Thucydides says that on his way to Syracuse, Archias found Dorians already temporarily settled near Locri, and indeed there is evidence of Greek trade and potters at work among the local Sicels some time before Locri was founded in 673; after this the local settlement comes to an end. Of Croton, founded soon after Sybaris, little can be said owing to lack of research and excavation. Further north, in the instep, both Sybaris and Metapontum were founded in rich plains. At Sybaris the earliest structures so far found are small rectangular houses built of rough stones on a grid plan; they are probably not earlier than 600, and the same date can be given to the land division around Metapontum. There is little material earlier than about 650 here, though the Armenian version of Eusebius has 773 as a foundation date. While the settlers were no doubt content merely to get away from cramped conditions at home, their mentors from Corinth were quick to set up trading relations (and had perhaps already done so) with the inhabitants of native settlements inland.

Again despite the excellence of its harbor, we may also doubt the commercial aspirations of the Spartan colonists at Taranto in 706; at all events a plentiful and handy supply of fish was assured. We may note the later coin types of these colonies – a bull at Sybaris, a head of corn at Metapontum and a dolphin at Taras.

We are poorly informed on the early history of these colonies. We may note a mass grave of some hundreds of

bodies marking some disaster at the founding of Acragas. Long before this, Zancle and Syracuse had expanded, Zancle to obtain agricultural land at Mylae (modern Milazzo) before the end of the 8th century, and Syracuse to gain control of the southeastern corner of the island, placing strong outposts at Acrae and Casmenae in the hinterland in the first half of the 7th century and a larger colony at Camarina on the south coast in 598. The numbers involved in all these colonial ventures must have been small; counting tombs and trying to project death rate leads to very low figures, but is scarcely a reliable method. The area with traces of 8th-century occupation at Pithekoussai and Syracuse is large enough, while at Megara a central part of the town some 50 by 70 meters was left free for public buildings.

The system of government prevailing in the mother city seems generally to have been adopted, together with her cults and often her burial customs too. This accounts for the presence of a king at Taranto and the strong oligarchy at Syracuse, a landowning minority which emerged from whatever equal awards of land were made to the first settlers. The founder or oecist may have been given a cult in later years, but he and his descendants had no overriding political powers. When Thucydides tells us that the various colonies had an Ionian or a Dorian constitution he must be thinking primarily of his own day, and even then we can reconstruct little of his meaning. As time elapses it is the independence of the colonies that stands out; tyrants in mother cities did not or were not able to install favorites in colonies, save in the case of the possessions of Corinth in the northwest of Greece, which were probably not foundations on the same level as full colonies. Certainly mother and daughter did not always see eye-to-eye. The first naval battle known to Thucydides took place, he alleges, in 663 between Corinth and Corcyra, who were to cause the outbreak of the war which he himself saw and recorded; and when Camarina revolted from Syracuse in 552 she was defeated in battle.

Northern expansion. The early colonies in the west were matched by others to the northeast, but the evidence for these is shaky, coming from later sources, especially Eusebius, and few controlled excavations. The three-pronged peninsula of north Greece was and still is called Chalcidice – "the Chalcidian land," after the colonies planted there by the Euboean city, though dates are hard to find; the Eretrians on Corfu were replaced by Corinthians, perhaps in 706, were refused reentry to Eretria and settled at Methone. As both Chalcis and Eretria colonized here, as well as Andros, we may assume that the movement was under way before the Lelantine war, which seems to have broken the back of Eretria – a

conclusion, one should add, based more on half-hints in literature and a scarcity of known Eretrian activity after 700 than on firm evidence of any kind. We can be sure that the war was over possession of the plain which lay between Chalcis and Leukandi; less certain are the reports in Herodotus and Thucydides of the participation of many other Greeks in the conflict, including Corinth and the inveterate enemies Miletus and Samos, giving the dispute international importance. We ought to be cautious in rejecting this evidence now that we know of Euboean interest in trade from an early period and the pretensions of Corinth at the time in question. However we must also use the terms "international" and "commercial interests" with care, for we know little about the extent of organized trade and the relationship between traders and those in whom was invested the right to declare war.

To the east of Chalcidice, the island of Thasos has been extensively explored, though no material earlier than the later 7th century has come to light. The colony was founded some time in the early part of that century by the father of the poet Archilochus – the latter commented "the misery of all Greece rushed to join us on Thasos." He missed the easier life of his home on Paros, and had little interest in mainland expansion in the area of the rich silver and gold mines of Mount Pangaion, where he ran away in the course of battle against the Thracians. Most of the other colonies along the north coast of the Aegean are 6th-century foundations, except for Chiot Maroneia, and Abdera is said to have been refounded then. Although the coastal plains are broad and fertile, the Thracian tribes put constant pressure on Greeks in later centuries and probably discouraged settlement earlier.

Although 8th-century dates are given in our literary sources for the foundation of three colonies further north, Cyzicus in the Propontis and Sinope and Trapezus (Trebizond) on the north coast of Turkey, they receive no support from archaeological investigation. The areas may have been known to the Greeks (a potter from Smyrna signs himself in around 700 Istrokles – after the Ister or Danube) and settlement in the Propontis is possible by this date. Aristeas from Proconnesus, one of those settlements, wrote a chronicle of his journeys far to the east before 680. However, there is no indication that the Greeks were using a trade route along the south shore of the Black Sea, and it could hardly be that the Ionians planted agricultural settlements in those far-flung regions at this period, in view of the relatively inhospitable climate. Nor is it likely that the population of Ionia had increased enough to necessitate overspill settlements so far away, where there is nothing to suggest that the local inhabitants, "proto-Scythians," would have been any more welcoming than the Thracians to the west.

The Sanctuary of Delphi

Delphi lies on a steep hillside on the lower slopes of Mount Parnassus, high above the Corinthian Gulf. A town flourished in the Bronze Age lower down towards the plain, and it seems that Delphi ("Wombs") was a sacred site even then. Apollo was not its master, for he did not arrive until the end of the Bronze Age; he took over the oracle from Ge, the Earth, whose creature, Pytho, he slew beside the temple, earning the title Pythios. Lower down the slope was the sanctuary of Athena of Forethought (*Pronoia*), site of one of the earliest Doric temples known to us; it too has yielded Bronze Age material of a sacral character. Yet it was in the Archaic period that the sanctuary of Apollo (*below*) flourished, with its oracle being consulted by all Greek and many foreign states and individuals before they embarked on major undertakings.

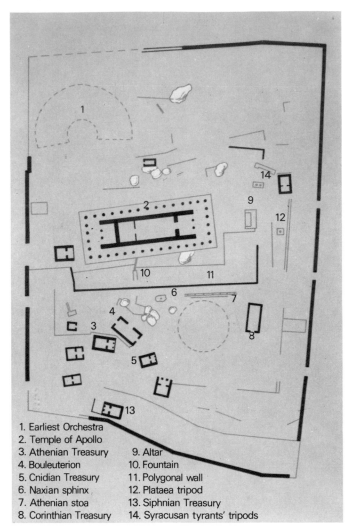

1. Earliest Orchestra
2. Temple of Apollo
3. Athenian Treasury
4. Bouleuterion
5. Cnidian Treasury
6. Naxian sphinx
7. Athenian stoa
8. Corinthian Treasury
9. Altar
10. Fountain
11. Polygonal wall
12. Plataea tripod
13. Siphnian Treasury
14. Syracusan tyrants' tripods

The sanctuary of Apollo (*left*) spread up and down the slope from the temple terrace. The temple was originally a simple structure, of which very little has been found; it was destroyed and rebuilt in the later 6th century when the Alcmeonids, exiled from Athens, curried the oracle's favor by contracting to build the east facade from Parian marble. One of the earliest buildings apart from the temple was the treasury, or storehouse, of the Corinthians in which were kept the rich offerings of the Lydian kings, including the gold and electrum bars dedicated by Croesus. Such storehouses increased in number and architectural pretension throughout the 6th and 5th centuries, most flanking the sacred way which wound up the hillside to the temple terrace. In front of the temple the Sicilian tyrants set up their costly offerings, and here too was the gold tripod held aloft on a six-meter-high bronze column of twisted snakes, dedicated by all the Greeks who had repulsed the Persians in 480–479.

Excavation began in earnest in 1892, but first the village which lay over the site, Kastri, had to be moved around the corner. In the photograph below we see the site before the removal. The archaeological world waited to hear of finds of buildings and sculpture, as detailed in the guide book to the site written by Pausanias in the 2nd century AD; but most of the statues had already been carried off to Rome, and what was discovered had been buried long before Pausanias' visit.

The bronze charioteer, part of a group dedicated by the tyrant of Gela, Polyzelos – as the inscription on the single block of the base found with it relates – was probably thrown down in the earthquake of 373 BC which submerged the town of Helike under the Corinthian Gulf. It was unearthed on 28 May 1896, and in the photograph (*right*) we can see the irregular methods of excavation; we note, too, the holes made in the feet when the piece was wrenched from the car. The statue was assembled from separately cast sections, carefully joined and polished.

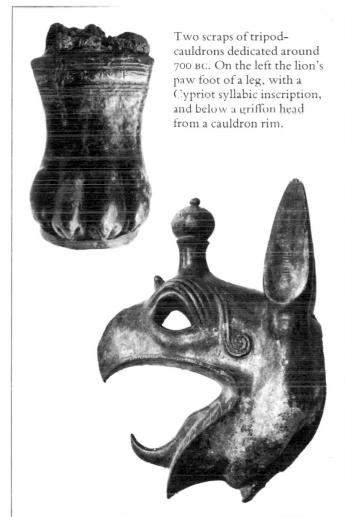

Two scraps of tripod-cauldrons dedicated around 700 BC. On the left the lion's paw foot of a leg, with a Cypriot syllabic inscription, and below a griffon head from a cauldron rim.

From the air we see the cliffs rising above the steeply sloping sanctuary and the olive-filled plain of Amphissa below. In the foreground is the temple of Apollo, the sacred way, and above, the theater and stadium of the Classical period.

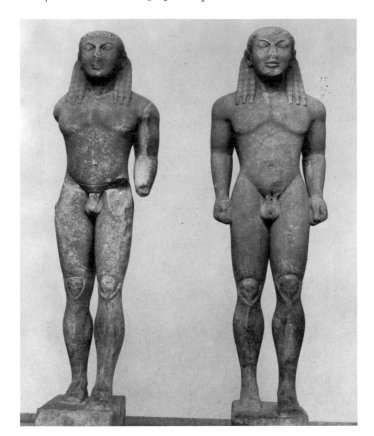

The treasuries, though small buildings, became increasingly luxurious. The Cnidians erected the first marble building known to us in about 550, but the men of Siphnos, in the Cyclades, outdid them later with a treasury whose elevation is seen restored above. Richly carved moldings accompany a full set of sculpture. Silver mines on Siphnos provided the revenue, but were flooded out in 525 – because, some said, of the Siphnians' failure to pay a full tithe to Apollo.

Two fine sets of free-standing sculpture of the Archaic period were discovered at Delphi.

Above (*left*) are the twin marble kouroi whom we may equate with Kleobis and Biton, sons of the priestess of Hera at Argos, whose story is related by Herodotus. They are among our earliest kouroi, carved in a powerful Peloponnesian style by an Argive whose name is only partly preserved.

Above is the Naxian sphinx set up on a 30-foot-high Ionic column just below the temple terrace by those pioneers of marble sculpture in about 570. Naxos dedicated another to Apollo on Delos, whose full significance yet escapes us.

The porch of the Siphnian treasury, like that of the Cnidian before it, was supported not by columns but by two symmetrically posed korai figures, supporting the architrave on high, decorated, crowns. We call them Caryatids and perhaps know the type best from the south porch of the Erechtheum on the Athenian Acropolis. The Siphnian caryatids were tricked out with much jewelry and wear *chiton* and *himation* in normal Ionic fashion. The sculptor may have come from the Cyclades; one of the artists carved his name on the north frieze, but it was carefully defaced in antiquity.

The north frieze of the treasury (*above, top*) depicts the battle of gods and giants. Here we see Cybele and Herakles in a lion-drawn car, following Apollo and Artemis.

The oracle of Delphi played a large part in the colonizing movement of the 8th to 7th centuries. Croton uses the Delphian tripod as the main type of her coins (*middle*) and in the late 5th century adds Apollo killing Pytho to it, and further mythologizes her history by calling the reclining Herakles on the reverse her founder.

On Delphi's own rare silver tridrachms (*immediately above*), issued around 480 BC, ram-headed metal drinking horns are accompanied by punning dolphins (*delphis*), while the reverse shows a coffered ceiling, perhaps that of Apollo's new temple.

The Athenians built their treasury at a date much disputed by scholars – perhaps after the battle of Marathon. It is a graceful Doric building, restored at the expense of the city of Athens in 1903–06. The metopes are sculpted and fairly well preserved. Although small, they are cut with skill and vigor and the advances made in the rendering of figures in action are particularly noticeable. Above the porch the traditional hero Herakles is joined by the Athenian Theseus in battle against the Amazons, probably symbolic of the invading Persians, while they each perform their individual tasks along the sides – Theseus on the south facing the visitor ascending the sacred way.

The finely fitted polygonal terrace wall of the temple of Apollo flanks the final stretch of the sacred way. It was built to support the extended terrace built up in the rebuilding program after 548, in which a number of earlier treasuries were dismantled. On the wall are carved countless inscriptions of the Hellenistic period recording the manumission of slaves to Apollo. In front we see the slender Ionic column bases of the Athenian stoa, built to house spoils from the Mede, as the inscription cut along the steps tells us.

The temple built in the later 6th century was in turn destroyed in the earthquake of 373 BC and what remains now is of a subsequent rebuilding, albeit on the original plan. The temple is longer than most Doric temples, in order to accommodate the shrine of the oracle. On specific occasions, save in the winter, when Apollo left Delphi, the priestess would go through an elaborate ritual, including drinking from the nearby spring of Cassotis and chewing laurel leaves. Seated on the holy tripod she would go into an inspired trance and her utterances would be interpreted by the priests to those who had paid the appropriate dues and made the correct sacrifices in order to consult the oracle. No trace of the oracular shrine has been found in excavation.

Opposite page: a magnificent bronze helmet embellished with horses, from Arkanes in Crete.

4. City-States
in Peace
and War

The 7th and 6th centuries in Greece passed amid power struggles in the city-states and an increase in interstate warfare. In Asia Minor successive waves of pressure from the hinterland had to be faced, waves which by the early 5th century also broke on the shores of continental Greece. A review of the tyrannies of Greece – how they arose, what they achieved and how they fell – will illustrate many facets of the development of Greek society, especially the various demands for constitutional and legal rights by its members.

Democracy is always regarded as the greatest product of the Archaic age of Greece, yet we shall see that rarely were the Greeks unanimous in wishing to avail themselves of this, despite the incentive afforded by the small size of their societies. The city-state or *polis* was well suited to the development of political systems in which each citizen could have his (not her) say in the running of affairs. The size of most states also meant that connections between its members would often have been close, and so personal relationships and feelings would have played an important part in the making of decisions. Attica, one of the largest states, is about the size of Kent, and the very maximum figure we could give to its population in around 500 would be some 150,000, women, children and slaves included.

Society and government. We have noted the decline of the Mycenaean royal houses and the leveling off of the families of better birth during the Dark Ages. In the literature of the 7th century we find ample references to squabbles and ill-feeling between and even within such families. Hesiod talks bluntly of the venality of the local chiefs, and at the end of the century Alcaeus bitterly remarks of the Mytileneans: "They thronged together, praised that guttersnipe Pittacus to the skies and made him tyrant of our hapless, gutless city." Alcaeus' brother Antimenidas may well have expected high office on Lesbos, but it is interesting to note that he went off to do a spell of mercenary duty with the Babylonians, and killed his own "Goliath."

In the 6th century and earlier a favorite political catchword was "eunomia" or "isonomia," implying a wish for stable, reliable government and fair and equal treatment for all; "demokratia" was its 5th-century successor. "Isonomia" meant the recognition of legal rights for all – an important step forward from a situation in which tribal leaders or magistrates could execute summary justice or retribution, leaving the weaker members of society at a disadvantage. The writing down of laws and especially the fixing of penalties (and by medieval standards they were by no means bloody) banished the religious and mystic element from many legal pronouncements. We hear of such law codes at Locri, Rhegion and Athens (that of Draco) in the 7th century, but few details seem reliably reported; scraps of actual examples survive from contemporary Crete.

"Nomos," law, is derived from a verb meaning "distribute" or "apportion," with particular reference to land. The land problem as we have seen resulted in the founding of many of the early colonies, and the struggle for possession of land by the poorer members of states remained a vital issue in the following centuries. The recognition of the rights of the individual in this respect contributed much to the structure of the Greek *polis* which emerged from the Archaic period, a structure in which the individual plays a far more prominent part than in any earlier civilization. Even in the Dark Ages the quarreling oligarchs had to rely at least in part on the support of their followers in order to maintain any advantage they gained, and as wealth increased such a situation could either stabilize or change, according to how that wealth was accumulated, distributed and used.

Dictatorship. The earliest tyrannies appeared in the Peloponnese, the first perhaps at Argos, a flourishing town in the Geometric period which, like Athens, found no need to send out colonies. Pheidon was a hereditary king who is said to have assumed absolute power; his dates are disputed (the later 8th century or more likely the mid-7th). He pursued an active policy of expansion especially to the south and west. In the former area he won a famous victory against the Spartans at Hysiae in 669, and for a brief period gained control of the Olympic Games in the west. We know little about the circumstances of his success, but it is at least plausible that he was the first to use the hoplite phalanx in battle with effect, a view which the Warrior Grave at Argos does nothing to damage. We know little about Argos after his death, but a broadly based constitution is seen later, in which "the king" was merely one official.

The archaeological record tells us that Cypselus took over a flourishing city at Corinth in 654. It had been run by the Bacchiads, a noble house who had fought with some success against the Megarians to the north, but had suffered the revolt of Corcyra in the 660s. Cypselus' father was a Bacchiad, but he is reliably said to have expelled his kinsmen; he may have held a military post as polemarch when he made his coup – it is specifically stated that he retained his position without the assistance of a bodyguard. He and his son Periander are said to have pursued active commercial policies. Evidence from pottery fragments shows that a slipway was constructed across the Isthmus before 625, facilitating travel between the east and Italy, although it is not clear to what extent it could accommodate merchant ships of the period as against smaller warships. A defense wall was also built to enclose the Acrocorinth and the town below, together with the potters' area. This was situated to the west of the town and was kept extremely busy, as we can judge from the vast numbers of Corinthian vases and terracottas, mostly of slight quality, found throughout the Mediterranean.

Periander was on friendly terms with Thrasybulus,

tyrant of Miletus, and married the daughter of the tyrant of neighboring Epidaurus. He arbitrated in a dispute over territory near Troy between Athenian and Mytilenean settlers – one of the earliest known records of arbitration. His widespread interests are also shown by the planting of Corinthian colonies at Potidaea in the Chalcidice, as well as in the northwestern areas; he sent 300 boys from Corcyra to Alyattes of Lydia to serve as court eunuchs, but the Samians rescued them; he gave his son the name Psammetichus after the Egyptian pharaoh, but he ruled only two years at Corinth before the tyranny was rejected in 582. We know little of subsequent events – the constitution seems to have been oligarchic, but as so often we cannot be sure how much power lay with a relatively small body of magistrates and how much with a broader assembly of the citizenry.

At neighboring Sicyon another dynastic tyranny flourished for much the same period, but lasted into the 550s before Aeschines was removed by the Spartans. We have noted the anti-Argive stance taken up by its most remembered ruler, Cleisthenes. Herodotus relates with gusto the marriage which he arranged for his daughter Agariste, in the true competitive spirit of the age; suitors were invited to Sicyon for selection and came from as far afield as Croton and Sybaris. The show was stolen by an Athenian, Hippocleides, who drank too much and nonchalantly danced on the table – an apparently unacceptable breach of etiquette, though similar aristocratic behavior seems well documented elsewhere. The hand of Agariste was won by another Athenian, Megacles, a leading contender for power at home.

Sicyon was also deeply involved with events at Delphi during the 590s. The men of Crisa, below Delphi, were exacting tolls from visitors to the sanctuary, and the Delphians also alleged that they had violated sacred land. They sought support throughout Greece and found it principally at Sicyon and the league of central Greek states convened at Thermopylae. Crisa was wiped off the map and Sicyon enjoyed a period of ascendancy at Delphi, probably at the expense of Corinth, who had had influence there for up to 200 years.

At Corinth the tyrants became as autocratic as kings and in this way lost the support of those whose interest had installed them. At Sicyon the Spartans performed the expulsion as they did elsewhere in Greece, never having a tyranny of their own. One cannot help feeling, uncharitably perhaps, that this was due more to the fact that any inspiring tyrant would have had to overthrow two kings, than to Sparta's apparent avoidance of internal dispute, as Spartans alleged. We have seen her difficulties – defeat at Hysiae, a subsequent revolt of the Messenians and in the 6th century defeat at the hands of Tegea. Dimly discernible in available sources can be descried internal problems, but those sources are difficult to interpret and date.

As so often is the case, one person in particular caught

A Greek lyre is shown in the hands of a satyr on this red-figure amphora of the early 5th century BC.

later historians' imagination, and a whole range of measures are attributed to him. At Sparta this man was Lycurgus, a reformer variously dated and made responsible for varying amounts, or the whole, of the curious Spartan constitution. There may have been such a man, and he may have been the initiator (perhaps in the later 8th century) of a reform which is quoted in the shape of an old document in Plutarch's *Life of Lycurgus*. Apollo of Delphi bids him reorganize the tribal structure, establish a council of elders and hold regular meetings of the people, at which their voice would be sovereign. Plutarch mentions that a rider was later added to this law, that the kings and elders were to be able to annul any pieces of "crooked" or "unsound" legislation passed by the people. Tyrtaeus, a hack producer of turgid martial verse during Sparta's struggle with Messenia in the mid-7th century, seems to paraphrase this document and places the people after the kings and elders; apparently the people could reject proposals laid before them, and may have had greater powers at an earlier period – a precious glimpse into the workings of an Archaic constitution. In all this there is no mention of the ephors, whose origins and constitutional position remain obscure.

We saw that Messenia had to be held down by force, and this demanded a high level of military preparedness. The true Spartiates had time to devote themselves to that end while the helots worked their land and the dependent but free *perioikoi* ("dwellers-around") supplied them with other necessities of life. At Sparta the Dorian way of life was pursued with the male population living in communal messes or *syssitia*, and giving their sons a strict athletic/military training, or at least those sons who appeared strong enough at birth not to be exposed on the mountainsides. As the Messenians began to haunt their lives, so the siege economy and life-style deepened, although it was no sudden change and was not fully effected till the later 6th century. We are told that Lycurgus forbade the use of money and luxury goods, but required the retention of the old currency of iron bars. However, tasteful architecture and bronzework were to be found in the town till the 5th century. Up to that point only Elis and Corinth of the Peloponnesian states issued silver coinage and we know that Argos and cities in Arcadia minted iron in the Classical period. Further, at some unspecified date before 550, the Samians gave Sparta help against the Messenians, and Laconian pottery is unusually common on Samos. All this suggests that Sparta had not closed her eyes to the world and was certainly more outward-looking than, for example, the Arcadians and Cretans.

When Sparta turned to a policy of alliances rather than conquest in the mid-6th century, she probably insisted from the start on inserting a clause in her treaties obliging the new ally to assist Sparta should the Messenians revolt, and to reject any Messenian exiles. We have also noted the brief extra-Peloponnesian activities of the Spartans, being approached by Croesus and the Ionians in revolt; some naval assistance was actually sent to a group of Samians exiled by Polycrates, though to slight effect. By the later 6th century the league included all the major Peloponnesian states save implacable Argos and unimportant Achaea.

The Corinthians' reluctance to attack Athens in 506 was not the only quarrel in the Peloponnese during these years. In 493 Cleomenes inflicted a savage defeat on the Argives at Sepeia, near Nauplion, and other warfare can be discerned from archaeological evidence; for example weapons were dedicated at Olympia and were often inscribed with the names of victor and vanquished. A number record a victory of the Argives over Corinth, presumably before 493; others tell of a victory of Sicyon, one of Psophis in Arcadia, and perhaps several by Achaeans, all in the later Archaic period.

One side of the base of a marble funerary monument of the late 6th century, found built into the city wall of Themistokles at Athens. It shows aristocratic Athenian youths playing a form of hockey. The sculptor has been experimenting with varied poses of the human body.

Tyrants arose also in many cities in Ionia and the Cyclades, though few are more than names to us. At Mytilene, perhaps Miletus too, individuals were given extraordinary mandates to solve social problems and held on to their position. The preserved verses of Alcaeus add spice, if little objective information, to the situation; one of his opponents, Pittacus, won praise from all other critics as a moderate ruler, though we would be unwise to accept all that is said of him. It would be pleasant to believe that he did indeed pass a law to the effect that offenses committed under the influence of alcohol should be punished by a fine double the normal amount!

Thrasybulus of Miletus brought the city through a long war of attrition waged by two successive Lydian kings, and won Lydian respect for it. Melas, tyrant of Ephesus, married the daughter of Alyattes, the second of those kings. Yet we do not know much about the achievements of these tyrannies; one is mentioned at Chios, but the most substantial information we have from the island is a document on stone, dating to about 575, found some ten miles south of Chios town. It is a legal text, mentioning a popular council with 50 selected members from each tribe and the right of the council or assembly to hear appeals against judgment.

After the fall of Lydia, the Persians set up their own tyrants in the captured Ionian cities, but were initially unable to conquer the offshore islands, and the Clazomenians even moved to a nearby peninsula site to try to preserve their independence. On Samos the tyranny of Polycrates flourished just at this period, down to 522. Polycrates was probably not the first Samian tyrant – we hear of the oligarchic Geomoroi (the same name was given to the Syracusan nobles) being replaced by a democracy in the earlier 6th century, a time of prosperity for the island judging from the preserved monuments of sculpture and architecture. This prosperity owed a lot to overseas trading, as did that of Samos' long-standing enemy Miletus.

Polycrates built up a strong navy and allied himself with

Amasis, the last pharaoh of Egypt, to strengthen his anti-Persian front. There is more than a hint of piratical activity on the part of his father Aeaces, who dedicated a statue in the city, perhaps on hanging up his rudder and cutlass. Polycrates was also on good terms with Lygdamis, tyrant of Naxos, who controlled the sanctuary of Apollo on Delos, long a center of Naxian influence; Lygdamis in turn had been helped by Pisistratus in securing power in the island. Polycrates survived a Spartan attempt to oust him but was crucified by a local Persian governor in 522, and soon after a Persian nominee was installed after a fearful bloodbath. Lygdamis did succumb to Sparta in 517, and a period of uneasy calm followed in the Aegean, to erupt into full revolt by the Ionians following an unsuccessful Persian attack on Naxos in 500.

Athenian society and constitution. Although we are much more fully informed about Athens at this period, we should not overestimate the extent of our knowledge. Herodotus, and Thucydides in some of his asides, tell us much; however they do not always agree with each other nor with another important text, the *Constitution of Athens*. This was probably compiled by Aristotle late in the 4th century, and is preserved for us in a single manuscript copy, discovered only in 1891, written on the back of a set of Egyptian farm accounts of the 1st century AD. It is a collection of political and constitutional information of great interest, but especially in the early chapters contains material of manifestly later fabrication; we must therefore be cautious in relying on the rest.

As in many other Ionian states there were originally

Laconian cup depicting King Arkesilas of Cyrene sitting under an awning to supervise the weighing and storing of a commodity of disputed identity. A masterpiece of observation fitted into a diameter of only 29 cm. About 560.

four "*gene*" or tribes, in Attica, composed of "phratries" or brotherhoods; these divisions go back beyond the Dark Ages, and their origins and functions in society are far from clear. The Dorians originally had three tribes, to which a fourth was added at Argos – the Pamphyloi ("all-sorts"), which presumably included all those of non-Dorian birth as well as newcomers. Tribal leaders had full religious responsibilities, which included many facets of what we term criminal law, especially the punishment of murderers. Even in the days when the laws began to be codified and written down, the paternal influence of the tribal leaders would have remained considerable.

The magistrates emerged above the tribal system. At Athens there were nine by the 7th century; the *archon* was the chief magistrate and gave his name to the year. His term was originally for life, then for ten years, and finally on an annual basis. The *archon basileus* retained the old royal title and dealt mainly with religious and judicial matters. The *polemarch* was the military commander, and six *thesmothetai* interpreted and administered the law in its broadest sense. On retirement from office all became ex officio members of the council or Areopagus. All such officials were drawn (probably by election) from the better families. Although our knowledge here is sketchy, we should note that the outlying towns of Attica probably had considerable independence in local affairs for most of the period down to Pisistratus.

We are given no motives for Cylon's attempted coup in 632, but we may suspect that circumstances had changed little when Solon was called upon to settle the problems of Attica in 593. He found freeborn Athenians heavily in debt, having mortgaged even their freedom away to the richer landlords. Preserved fragments of his own poems tell how he uprooted the stones which marked the mortgaged lands, freed many Athenians from slavery, both at home and abroad, and gave each section of the community no more than its due. He complains that by satisfying neither extreme, he incurred the displeasure of both. It was not his intention to make a radical re-distribution of land, nor to uphold all the privileges of the wealthy, but he makes it clear that he had no quarrel with wealth justly gained – the wealthy wrongdoer would be caught by Zeus in the end. Nonetheless, he did recognize that greed had brought civil unrest to Attica and had to be cured.

Apart from the reinstatement of the smallholders, Solon's main reform was to change the system of enrollment into social classes (and we should stress the importance of our knowledge of them here) from one based on birth to one based on wealth. This was calculated on the annual produce of a man's land in measures of corn (or the equivalent in oil or wine). Whether he extended the equation to income of other kinds, especially from trade, is a disputed point. Membership of a given class entitled a citizen to a varying degree of influence in the running of affairs. The qualification for the highest class,

Brother and sister commemorated on the most elegant and pretentious of Athenian grave monuments, found in the countryside of Attica in the family's burial lot. The inscription, though battered, suggests that the youth may have been Megacles, an Alcmeonid. About 530.

the Pentakosiomedimnoi, who monopolized a number of offices, was about 750 bushels of corn, and that of the lowest, Thetes, 150 bushels. In between came the Knights and the Yoke-men, named after a notional ability to own a pair of oxen. The first three classes were obliged to serve as hoplites, providing their own gear. The actual changes in class effected by these reforms would have been slight if the qualifiers remained the large landowners, but more substantial if wealthy traders were brought into the system. Also in the realm of agriculture Solon banned the export of much-needed corn and encouraged olive-growing.

Solon refused to make himself tyrant and left Athens, but his work did not last. We hear of anarchy (literally – "lack of archons") in the 580s, and afterwards rivalry between three factions led by members of aristocratic families, until Pisistratus made his first attempt to seize control in 560. The three groups had geographic names, and may well have had local economic interests at heart – the "plain-men" of Athens led by the blue-blooded Lycurgus being the traditional landowners, the "shore-men" under Megacles, the son-in-law of Cleisthenes of Sicyon, perhaps having commercial interests, and Pisistratus' "hill-men" from northern Attica, representing the interests of the towns in that area as well as the small crofter. We hear of experiments in which the archons were chosen from various social groups, but the full causes of dispute do not emerge clearly from the more obvious struggle for personal power.

We are told by Herodotus that in Pisistratus' final spell as tyrant from 546 to 528 he retained the existing constitution, though ensuring the election of his own nominees to key positions. Some of the measures attributed to Solon which may have survived then are the right of individuals to bring cases for judgment on behalf of an injured party, the right of appeal against judgment to the people sitting (in fact standing) as a court, and the establishment of a second council of 400 members (100 from each tribe) taking away some responsibilities from the Areopagus and working in liaison with the popular assembly.

It is to be regretted that our sources are poor or contradictory on these matters, since therein lie some of the seeds of democracy, in which each member of a community has access to the administration and judiciary through a free assembly. The extent of citizenship, and hence the right to join such an assembly, is also an important question; in many states there may have existed such an assembly with some legislative powers, but with membership restricted to only a proportion of the adult male members, as at Sparta and Syracuse. The workings of such constitutions are rarely seen; then as now measures were credited to their initiators, irrespective of whether they were discussed, emended or voted on. We may surmise that most tyrants were autocratic, while other forms of government owed what stability they had to the

A red-figure cup from the destruction deposits on the Acropolis shows a series of workshop scenes. On the left a painter is decorating a cup on the potter's wheel; in the center is a completed figure of a sitting Athena; on the right a smith crouches to tend his furnace, and his equipment and working cap can be seen hanging on the wall.

smooth running of the patron/client structure of aristocratic societies.

A fragment of a list of archons, published in the later 5th century and found in the Agora, shows that on assuming power after his father's death Hippias was eager to accommodate some of his rivals. We read the names of the tyrant's grandson, Pisistratus, of Miltiades (son of Pisistratus' enemy Cimon and future hero of Marathon), and another rival's son, Cleisthenes, whose father was Megacles. It was Cleisthenes' kin, the Alcmeonid family, who, as Hippias' rule grew ruthless, brought the period of tyranny to an end with Spartan help in 510.

We know little of what followed until 507, when a quarrel broke out between Cleisthenes and the archon Isagoras. Isagoras again called in the Spartans under Cleomenes to control the situation, perhaps under a treaty of accession to the Peloponnesian League, but Cleomenes was rejected. It is unfortunate that we cannot be sure of the sequence of events; was it Cleisthenes' program of sweeping reforms of the constitution which started the dispute, or did these only materialize when a Cleisthenic bid for power failed and he turned to the people for support? The first interpretation of events is probably the correct one, since Isagoras asked Cleomenes to help him send into exile many families who had no certain title to Athenian citizenship (enrollment in one of the tribes), and who would have been protected by the tribal reforms proposed by Cleisthenes. These people had been encouraged to settle in Attica by the Pisistratids, with their liberal policy of encouraging commerce and light industry at Athens.

Cleisthenes introduced ten entirely new tribes, artificially composed of three sets each of preexisting parishes or demes – one in the area of the city, one coastal and one inland. Some of the arrangements may have been gerrymandered to favor the Alcmeonids, but on the whole the radical changes served to weaken the hold of the old aristocracy. Cleisthenes' intention was that a man should no longer use his father's name in official circumstances, but that of his deme. At first the main role of the new tribes was to send 50 men each to a new council or "Boule" of 500 at Athens, and this council was to prepare business for the people. Additional legislation connected with this reform was probably intended by Cleisthenes, though passed after he had disappeared from the scene. The old tribal army chiefs were replaced by a board of ten generals, one per tribe, though overall command remained with the polemarch till after the battle of Marathon. From 501 onward, perhaps the first date at which the changes could be effected, the members of the council were required to take a stringent oath not to subvert the constitution.

The new tribes included all those whose citizenship had previously been suspect, and once a man had his allotment (parish and tribe) his descendants retained that allotment, whatever moves they made from the original home.

Cleisthenes retained Solon's class structure. There was probably no barrier to election to the Boule (and one reelection), but public service was not yet paid and this constituted an automatic barrier against the fully occupied country farmer. The archons had to belong to the upper two classes and some financial administrators to the first. The archons were directly elected from candidates, but a change in 487 introduced elections by lot from previously elected candidates. The lot was a decision-making principle much used in divination and other religious matters, and thus not a peculiar innovation; yet it certainly undermined the authority of the archons and subsequently the Areopagus as less able men joined its ranks.

A further control over the activities of political figures was introduced in 487, when the first ostracism took place. The *Constitution of Athens* considered it a Cleisthenic measure, but a contemporary of Aristotle, Androtion, believed it was passed in 487, rather than a useful political weapon left in cold storage for 20 years. Early each spring the people were asked if they wished to expel any citizens for a period of ten years; if more than 6,000 so desired they wrote the names of their candidates on potsherds (*ostraka*) and the "winner" was required to leave Attica. The measure was said to have been aimed originally at the old tyrant's party, who may have acted treacherously at Marathon, though it was soon turned against others and used as a not entirely foolproof device for getting rid of political opponents. Themistocles is thought to have been behind the ostracisms of the later 480s, though there was a well-organized attempt to banish him in one of these years – a dump of 191 ostraka with his name was found on the north slope of the Acropolis, but they had been prepared for distribution by only 14 hands. Themistocles did eventually succumb, but not till 471.

Beyond these checks of 487, all archons and other officials became accountable to the people for their actions at the end of their term of office, and although judgment at law was still given by the presiding officer of the court (juries came in in 461), there was right of appeal to the people. These more democratic measures may both have been Solonian reforms.

Xerxes' invasion. A further characteristic of a democratic government is the publication of measures passed by its sovereign body, and it is soon after Cleisthenes' reforms that we find the first decrees inscribed on stone at Athens – the first of a very long line of invaluable petrified documents. Related to these is an inscription published in 1960 and found at Troizen on the opposite coast of the Saronic Gulf, a 3rd-century copy of a decree allegedly proposed by Themistocles outlining action to be taken by the Athenian people in view of the impending invasion of Xerxes in 480. An orderly evacuation of Attica is planned, to Troizen in particular, and a system worked out for manning the fleet with the available crews; this was the fleet of 200 triremes largely built through Themistocles' insistence after 483.

Unfortunately the inscription does not tie in with Herodotus' account, which implies hastier action, and many scholars believe it a later fabrication. Such is the state

Right: one of the sadly fragmentary pair of inscriptions beautifully inscribed on marble metopes originally prepared for the temple of Athena erected by the Pisistratids. It sets out regulations for cult practices and correct observance on the Acropolis. Dated to 485–484.

Opposite page: ostraka cast against Megacles in 487. One is a fragment of the rim of a krater made by the Kleophrades painter, other sherds of which were used for votes against Themistocles. Over 4,000 ostraka were found in a well in the Kerameikos in 1968.

of our knowledge of the key year of Athenian history that agreement about the authenticity of a major document cannot be reached. The inscription implies that the Athenians were already planning evacuation after the decision was taken by the Hellenic council to abandon the forward position in the vale of Tempe, but before battle was joined at Thermopylae. In view of their experience of the Persians in 490 we may well believe that the Athenians, and the farsighted Themistocles in particular, took long-term precautions against the new offensive.

We have noted the successful outcome for the Greeks of the campaigns of 480 and 479, which were rounded off by the courageous attack at Plataea, where they eventually committed their 40,000 hoplites to battle on ground not entirely unsuited to the large cavalry forces of the enemy. Earlier, Spartan heroism had been the order of the day at Thermopylae, and the cajoling and threats of Themistocles

ensured that the combined Greek fleet stood at Salamis bay. The Athenian fleet also figured prominently in the follow-up campaign in 479, when Greek and Persian naval forces fought a battle on land at Cape Mycale in Ionia, traditionally on the same day as the battle of Plataea. The Ionians began to recover their freedom once more and exiles returned; a Rhodian poet, Nicocreon, complained that Themistocles took money not to restore him to his home. Greece was getting back to normal.

Warfare. The hoplite army and the trireme proved their worth in these battles after much practice in interstate warfare. The essence of war in Greece had been short campaigns, the only course open for states which had no standing army and soldiers who had farms to care for. Siege warfare was the way of easterners, and the siege mounds of Alyattes at Smyrna and of Darius' general

Artybius at Paphos are eloquent testimony to this. Greek campaigns often consisted of a single pitched battle, a set piece in which the winner was the army which won the field. The Spartan hoplite force was 10,000 strong at Plataea and was backed by the traditional parting words of the women "Come back with your shield or on it"; Athens contributed 8,000 hoplites, the Sicyonians and Megarians 3,000 each.

Boundary disputes and the ill-treatment of visitors were frequent causes of warfare, and although arbitration could be and was resorted to, it did not prevent an impressive array of campaigns, often mentioned only in passing in our sources.

The hoplite force of a city was its main strength – a compact line of men armed with breastplate, greaves, helmet, shield, spear and sword, regulated in depth by tactical considerations and available manpower. Tyrtaeus, writing at Sparta in the mid-7th century, gives a vivid picture of the confusion of a hoplite battle: "A man should come close, hand-to-hand, and take his foe, thrusting with spear or sword; foot against foot, shield pressed on shield, helmet by helmet, plumes touching, let him fight face-to-face, grasping the hilt of his sword or the long spear."

In practice there was a tendency for hoplite lines to move crabwise, as the exposed right wing tried to outflank the enemy. At Athens vase-paintings tell us that the richer hoplites rode to the front with their squires. As the Greeks knew of neither saddles nor stirrups the apparent superiority of cavalry over infantry was much reduced; in addition the lack of open ground in many parts of central and southern Greece further impaired their effectiveness, with the result that most states used cavalry only in small numbers for harassing the enemy. Phidippides ran from Marathon to Athens; he did not ride.

Tyrtaeus continued his advice: "You light-armed men should lurk here and there behind the shields and throw rocks and javelins at the enemy, standing beside the fully armed troops." On broken ground light-armed forces, drawn from the poorer classes, could be most effective and before the later 8th century they probably formed the bulk of an "army" in support of their better-equipped champions. Cretan archers gained some renown, using a bow akin to Bronze Age types, simpler than the famous weapon deployed by the Cimmerians and Scythians, whose accuracy at long range lends a sinister air to the enrollment of Scythians by Pisistratus as a kind of police force at Athens, along with a brigade of Thessalian cavalry for the army. Both sets of newcomers were soon introduced into the repertoire of the vase-painters.

Warfare at sea was scarcely less common than on land. Geometric vases depict many battles with ships, more

Two lines of hoplites converge – the earliest and one of the most effective representations of the basic tactic of Greek warfare, painted on a Corinthian jug of about 650 found at Veii near Rome. The painter, named after the MacMillan aryballos in the British Museum, is a major exponent of Corinthian polychrome decoration.

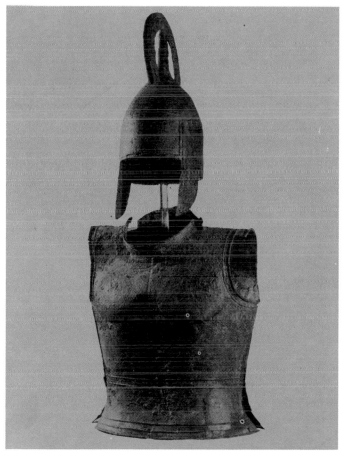

Above: Athenian cavalryman, dressed in a Thessalian cloak, portrayed on the inside of a red-figure cup painted by Euphronios in about 510 BC. Coral red is used on the surrounding surface.

Left: bronze helmet and cuirass from the aristocratic Warrior Grave at Argos, dated about 720, the earliest known armor from Iron Age Greece.

Below: part of the frieze of hoplites and chariots on the neck of the 6-foot high bronze krater found at Vix near Châtillon-sur-Seine in France. Laconian work of the mid-6th century.

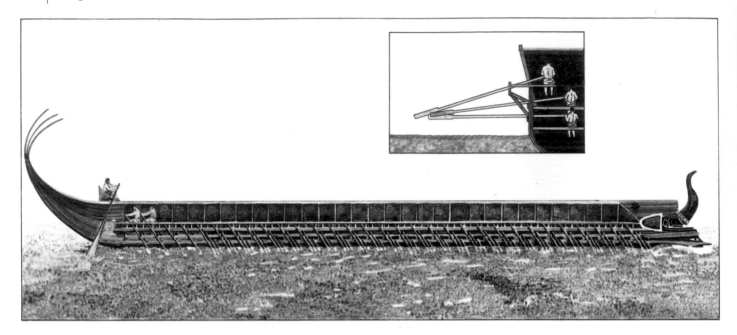

often raiding parties than fights at sea, first known to Thucydides in 663 and reported regularly in the following centuries. Not unnaturally the islanders figure prominently among the earlier exponents of naval warfare. Samians were responsible for the major innovation of the period – the introduction of the trireme (and subsequently its large-scale use under Polycrates). Some fleets still included 50-oared ships in 480, but the trireme had three banks of oars on either side, the upper ones on outriggers, and was designed to increase the speed at which the enemy could be rammed and, one hoped, sunk – the basic tactic of the period. From Geometric times the ram was a feature of all warships, which were lightly built, glorified racing shells. Yet they also carried marines who could board the enemy, though we do not hear of a great deal of hand-to-hand fighting at Salamis. Major drawbacks of the stream-lined Greek warship were its inability to ride out difficult conditions and its need to keep close to land; rarely could a coastal town be effectively blockaded when merchantmen even of modest proportions were far superior sailers. No Greek ship of the Archaic period has yet been fully excavated (an Etruscan merchantman off Antibes is of 6th-century date), but we may well hope for more information about them in the future.

As well as poor weather the trader had to contend with piracy, which was widely practiced. The Phocaeans living in exile at Alalia plagued Etruscan and Carthaginian shipping, as did the Cnidian settlers on Lipari. An agreement about piratical behavior between two neighboring states on the Corinthian Gulf is preserved for us on a bronze tablet and dates to the early 5th century; activity on the high seas is allowed, but "illegal seizure" was to be fined.

Commerce. Despite these difficulties trade flourished throughout the Mediterranean in the 7th and 6th cen-

Above: a Greek trireme with the upper bank of oars on outriggers, ram at the prow and steersman at the steering oar. Introduced in the 6th century, the trireme did not completely replace the simple 50-oar boats until after the Persian wars.

Opposite page: an example of the earlier 50-oar ships is seen attacking a merchantman on the high seas on a black-figure cup painted in Athens in about 520.

turies, though judging from the interest rates charged in later years on maritime loans it was probably a high-risk business. Individuals and cities grew rich on trade, notably the Corinthians with their important position on the Isthmus and large pottery industry, and the Ionian Greeks. In the later 7th century Miletus planted numerous colonies in the Black Sea area and was foremost among the Greeks setting up shop and shrines at Naucratis in Egypt. A Samian, Colaeus, was the most successful of all traders known to Herodotus; his ship was blown beyond Gibraltar in about 630 and he discovered the rich silver-mining area of Tartessus in southwest Spain (long known to the Phoenicians). The Phocaeans developed this route and founded Massilia and other trading posts in southern France. Chiot wine jars are found at an increasing number of sites. Parians persevered in their activities around Mount Pangaion in the northern Aegean, losing men in battle there in the later 6th century. The Aeginetans were lone mainlanders (to stretch a meaning) sharing the Hellenion sanctuary at Naucratis, and indeed the first mainlanders to issue coinage around 540. Ionians were responsible for carrying on the bulk of the massive 6th-century trade with Etruria, though their exact origins in Ionia yet elude us – Samians were certainly among them; common types of Ionian pottery and terracottas are widely imported and imitated. The Corinthians may have carried much of their own pottery west, down to the mid-6th century, but a good deal of the trade in Attic vases

was in the hands of the Ionian traders.

What were the commodities traded in return by the Greeks? Judging from archaeological evidence, or the lack of it, raw materials and perishable goods must have made up the bulk. Metals came from many areas including Spain and Etruria; Cyprus gives its name to copper. The main product of Cyrenaica was silphium, a species of asafetida used as a type of health food by the Greeks. In 480 Xerxes saw Aeginetan ships laden with grain passing down the Dardanelles from one of the Black Sea colonies, from where certainly in later years quantities of dried fish were imported.

In all these transactions we hear little of dues and taxes – indeed taxation of any kind is rarely mentioned in our period, which knew of coinage only in its later days. Periander grew rich on tolls charged for the haul across the Isthmus; lead tablets from Corcyra of about 500 record large sums lent out, perhaps as maritime loans. In Dorian states the individual had to contribute in kind to the common mess. The tithe system operated widely, and we often hear of personal contributions to building projects.

One import of significance must have been slaves, in particular from the Thracian region. Only in the Classical period does our information on slavery become full, but slave-owning was certainly widespread and taken for granted in earlier centuries. Hesiod recommends the use of slaves on the farm, Solon was concerned with the plight of Athenians sold into slavery, and a unique letter on a lead tablet found near Olbia on the north coast of the Black Sea records the complaints of a slave-owner about the activities of an associate in claiming his slaves and house. There were various kinds of serfdom – in some places, like Sparta, Thessaly and Syracuse, the indigenous peoples lived at a level not far removed from that of chattel slaves, while on Crete the Gortys legal code distinguishes between slave and serf. In a period when the rights of individuals varied so much from class to class and state to state, such a situation causes few surprises. By the Classical period we find that virtually all slaves are non-Greek – a situation which must have emerged during the Archaic period as a result of the expansion of trade.

Religion. Most of the artistic achievements of the Greeks at this period were prompted by religious considerations. The gods were housed lavishly, were thanked, appeased and persuaded by a vast range of offerings, and were represented by statues of increasing size and grandeur.

We now know that many of the deities of Classical Greece were worshiped in the Bronze Age, and some may have been at home in Greece before any Greek speakers arrived; but the successive strata of gods and cults are far more difficult to read than any archaeological section. New gods could be introduced who then assimilated any number of older cults, while particular states could develop aspects of a deity rarely found elsewhere. In the Archaic period we first discover the richness of these cults and realize the importance of religion in Greece.

The Greek gods were basically the overseers of all aspects of mortal life, and so the relationship between man and his anthropomorphic gods was one of cult offering, sacrifice and initiation, administered under strict rules of observance by priests and priestesses largely drawn from aristocratic families. It cannot be doubted that the gods could inspire awe and respect of their laws, and were the objects of individual prayer, but this was not their major role, and religion was part of everyday civic life. Few voices were raised against this system in the Archaic period; rather, divine sanction was fatalistically accepted. In about 500 two philosophers voiced doubts: Heraclitus of Miletus said that praying to a statue was as stupid as talking to a house, while Xenophanes of Colophon commented on the Ethiopians' claim that their gods were black and snub-nosed and the Thracians' claim that theirs were blue-eyed blonds; he believed in a single ruling force in the universe.

We may separate religious observances into three rough categories. First, there were state cults involving the Olympian deities as protectors of cities and their tribes – Athena at Athens, Apollo at Corinth, Zeus on Aegina and so on. Second, there were the more local cults, very often concerned with the fertility of crops and animals; these could be part of the state religion, but were often more personal, centered on demigods or nymphs residing in springs or caves. The character of their rites was usually more primitive and ritualistic than the first category, and often only the initiated could be admitted. The best-known example is the cult of Demeter and Persephone at Eleusis, which was promoted as a state cult by Pisistratus. Third, we should note hero cults and ancestor worship, first apparent in the 8th century when rediscovered Mycenaean tombs and structures attract offerings and the heroes of Troy are given shrines – Agamemnon at Sparta and Mycenae, perhaps Odysseus on Ithaca. Founder cults are common in cities of both recent and distant foundation.

We have surmised that at a few sites cult observance continued uninterrupted from the Mycenaean period, though the archaeological remains leave room for doubt. Temples also arise on the ruins of Mycenaean palaces (where they were perhaps dedicated exclusively to Athena) on the Acropolis, at Tiryns and at Mycenae; in this guise Athena would be Polias, the protectress of the citadel and inheritor of the mantle of the Mycenaean king. A number of sanctuaries of Hera have yielded Bronze Age material, probably not of a cult nature, for example on Samos, at Olympia and the Argive Heraion. Athena and Hera are deities known from the Linear B tablets; Poseidon is another, and his major title, "the earth-shaker," belongs in the seismic belt of the Aegean. Zeus, however, is the skygod of the Greek-speaking settlers; his original consort, Dione, retains her position only at Dodona in the northwest, for elsewhere she has to yield her throne to the popularity of Hera's cults.

In a brief survey one can only stress the varied makeup

Below left: a necklace of gold plaques stamped over a matrix depicting a winged goddess "potnia theron" – mistress of the animals. Mid-7th century.

Below right: a similar figure (we may think of her as Artemis) appears on the side of a handle on the Attic "François" vase, a krater painted by Cleitias in about 570 with a compendium of mythological scenes.

Opposite page: "Nikosthenes made me" – the signature separates the bloodied boxers with their paunches and heavy thighs, incongruous on a small and delicately modeled Attic vase. About 525.

of the other Olympians. Apollo and Aphrodite have stronger connections with the Near East, as Aphrodite's birth at Paphos suggests (although we may note that Homer ignores this). Artemis was the goddess of hunting man and retained a number of her aspects as such; she assimilates features of the eastern mother goddess and mistress of the animals, as do Athena and Hera occasionally. Dionysus has Aegean connections of an agrarian character in his role as the god of wine. At Aghia Irene on Kea there may have been unbroken observance at the Bronze Age temple shrine, and we know that by the 6th century at the latest Dionysus was its occupant.

Cult practices. The essence of Greek religious practice was the sacrifice of animals, usually burned, at an altar dedicated to the deity, and if possible within sight of the cult statue. We have noted the relationship between altar, statue and temple, and seen that in Crete, at Dreros in particular, hearth, statues and tables of offerings could all be found within the temple. It was not unusual for deities to share a sanctuary or even a temple, as Leto's family at Dreros; the two inner chambers of the temple of Apollo at Corinth and of Athena on the Acropolis are good examples, and Hermes and Aphrodite shared a large temple in the temenos of Hera on Samos.

A number of scenes of sacrificial processions are found in Archaic art. They follow a pattern: the priest, and sometimes the cult statue also, stands by the altar facing a young flute-player, attendants with the sacrificial animals, and girls carrying instruments of sacrifice in distinctive wicker baskets balanced on their heads. The periodic changing of the dress of the cult statue was often a solemn occasion – Homer recounts it at Troy, and such a scene may be depicted on one of the large pithoi from Tenos. It most certainly formed the heart of the major festival at Athens, the four-yearly Greater Panathenaea.

Divination was commonly practiced. For instance scenes of extispicy (examination of the entrails of sacrificial victims for propitious signs) are portrayed on vases. On more than one occasion adverse readings prevented a Spartan army crossing the frontier. Oracles were particularly favored; at such shrines the god revealed the future to his priests or priestesses in various ways, and they interpreted it to the petitioner. Delphi was the most famous of the oracles, and was much frequented by foreign potentates, especially the Lydian kings from the time of Gyges onward. The oracle here originally belonged to Ge, Mother Earth, but was taken over by Apollo, and the seat of his priestess was within the temple. Excavation has revealed nothing of the latter, not even the underground spring whose vapors inspired the priestess to utter the gibberish which the suspiciously venal priests then interpreted. Another famous oracle was that of Zeus at Dodona, though we know little of it in the Archaic period; like many sanctuaries of the sky-god, it was not given a temple till the Classical period. Apollo had two further oracles in Ionia, at Claros and at Didyma. Croesus made rich offerings at Didyma as well as Delphi, and the geographer Hecataeus vainly urged the Ionians in revolt to use them to finance trireme construction.

The competitive spirit. Other shrines owed much of their importance to the annual gatherings of ethnic groups, such as that of the Ionians at Delos, and of the Dorians at the as yet unlocated sanctuary of Apollo Triopius near Cnidos, and initially at Olympia. Contests in sport and music were an important part of these occasions; we should not underestimate the competitive character of the Greek world in the Archaic period, manifested not only in the numbers of such contests, but also in general attitudes to commerce and warfare.

The competitions in music, song and dancing were the forerunners of the major branches of Greek literature, and included the tragedy and satyr plays performed in honor of Dionysus, whose origins lay in extempore performances in Peloponnesian shrines. Prizes ranged from tripods through jars of wine to goats (the "tragos" of tragedy).

The major athletic festivals were held at Olympia, Isthmia, Delphi (the Pythian games) and Nemea. They were all established (in that order) before 550, and were held at intervals of two, three or four years. True to Archaic style the greatest rewards went to the winner of the four-horse chariot race, victory in which meant so much to the Sicilian tyrants of the early 5th century. Political advantages could also be gained by winning, as illustrated by the career of Miltiades' father, Cimon the Dim-wit. He won the race at Olympia three times in succession, but had enough gumption to present the title to Pisistratus on the second occasion; however, the third victory led to his discreet assassination by Hippias, who saw in him a dangerous rival for power.

By the later 6th century the emphasis in vase-paintings at least had turned to athletics. The program consisted of long and short track races, in which the athletes of Croton notched up an impressive series of victories in the mid-6th century, and the long jump, in which weights of up to nine pounds apiece were swung in the hands to gain momentum. Another Crotoniate, Phayllus, who fought at Salamis in his own ship, is claimed by an anonymous epigrammatist to have leapt 55 feet by this method, though tests have proved this to be impossible. The discus and the javelin were also thrown, the latter with the aid of a thong twisted round the shaft. Milo of Croton was one of the most successful wrestlers of the late 6th century, and to complete the strong men's program there was boxing and a marginally regulated all-in brawl, the pankration. The Burgon vase illustrates the mule-cart race, which the tyrant of Rhegion, Anaxilas, was proud to win at Olympia in 480. Practice in running in the part-armed race, the hoplitodromos, must have literally given impetus to the charge of the Athenian hoplites at Marathon.

Animals and Monsters

As in all ancient cultures, animals, pictured on artifacts of many kinds, play a large part in Greek art. Here we illustrate a minute proportion of the varieties of creatures found in good and bad work, on terracotta, ivory, metal and stone throughout the period 1000–480 BC. In the Dark Ages the range is mostly limited to domestic creatures, especially the horse and ox – with the singular exception of the Leukandi centaur (see page 43). The Orientalizing period introduced creatures of fact and fable from the Near East, adopted with alacrity and sometimes obvious bewilderment by Greek artists. The 7th century saw many curious experiments in hybridization, and battles between heroes and all kinds of hybrids and monsters are the order of the day. In Corinth and east Greece the animal frieze became a basic ingredient of many arts. As the 6th century progressed a more stereotyped range of creatures, employed in conventional ways, tended to evolve, although in skill and care of representation the artists outdid their predecessors.

Many cultures have their horrid masks intended to scare off evil spirits. In the Near East this was the lined visage of Humbaba; in Greece it was the Gorgon's head that turned all who looked at it to stone. The story of Medusa and her sisters is popular in Archaic art, while the isolated head, the Gorgoneion, modeled on a lion's mask, appears in many unlikely places – on coins, in the interior of cups, and on the knees of bronze greaves, as well as more suitably in temple pediments. Below we see Perseus pursued by Medusa's sisters on a mixing-bowl painted in Athens, under heavy Corinthian influence, in the early 6th century.

Left: wild boar roamed the mountains of Greece, but the fiercest one was the legendary monster that terrorized Calydon in Aetolia, and was eventually killed by Atalanta and Meleager, in company with a host of other heroes. On the François vase of about 570, shown here, Cleitias painted a full treatment of the scene, not sparing us the disemboweled hunting dog. In the lower frieze we see the galloping chariots of the funeral games of Patroclus at Troy, with the prizes depicted in among them.

Left: deer are a stock motif of east Greek art and appear in the late Geometric period at Athens. They also play a part in mythology. Here we see Herakles capturing the hind of Mount Keryneia in Arcadia, painted by the Antiphon painter on a cup of about 480 in the Louvre. Literary sources vary concerning the cause of the capture; the animal may have been sacred to Artemis, or was it causing a nuisance to the local inhabitants? It had golden horns, which may suggest some garbled knowledge of the reindeer, for only the buck of more southern species has horns. Herakles pursued it for a year around the Peloponnese, eventually springing on to its back.

Left: a black-figure Attic cup of about 520 has a charming scene of goats browsing in a vineyard. This is the regular background for Dionysiac scenes on Greek vases, and indeed we often see goats accompanying Dionysus. Occasionally he rides a goat, as does Aphrodite – a suggestive representation of beauty and the beast. On the other side of this cup, amid similar foliage, is a gathering of unique female sea serpents.

Left: birds also figure in Greek mythology, for example the eagle of Zeus sent to tear at the liver of the bound Prometheus, punishment for his taking fire to man. Here we see Herakles, on an Attic amphora of about 550–540, endeavoring to rid Lake Stymphalus in Arcadia from the overpopulation of bird life which threatened the livelihood of the inhabitants. This is another of the more local labors of Herakles and one that gained much in the telling.

Right: a team of horses, a common device, forms the handle of the lid of an Attic late Geometric box from the Agora in Athens.

Lower right: Nessos, the horse-man centaur, who molested Herakles' wife Deianeira when ferrying her across the river Euenos, is killed by the hero on the neck of an Attic burial amphora, about 620 BC.

Below: on the neck of a pithos of about 675, found on the island of Mykonos, we see the earliest representation of the wooden horse, disgorging its load of armed Greek warriors at Troy.

Left: Corinthian vase-painters led the way in the 7th century in developing the range and iconography of animals and hybrids in Greek art. They also copied, as did other Greeks from time to time, an eastern practice of giving vases animal or human heads. Here is the miniature masterpiece of the Macmillan painter, a lion-headed aryballos found in a grave at Thebes.

Below: the winged female-headed lion, the sphinx, first appeared in Greece in the late 8th century and became instantly popular. Here we see an illustration of the myth of Oedipus and the sphinx, painted at Athens by Douris at the end of the Archaic period. She has posed the riddle of the child, youth and elderly man, which Oedipus, in traveler's gear, is about to solve.

Left: most Greek lions of the 7th century imitate the slim maneless Syrian type. Here we see two of a row of such marble lions erected at the end of that century facing the sacred lake on the island of Delos. They border the way that led from the landing place to the temple of Leto and the precinct of her children, Artemis and Apollo.

Left: a hoplite is faced by a typically puzzling Protocorinthian hybrid on an aryballos of about 670, perhaps a variant of the story of Bellerophon and the Chimaera. A panther completes the symmetrical composition on the right

Far left: the Minotaur of Knossos is regularly portrayed as a bull-headed man. Here is the earliest known Iron Age creature of this type, one of a pair grasping the ring handle of a late Geometric bronze tripod.

Left: of the same period is this fibula engraved, probably in Thebes, with a duel involving a Siamese twin. Such twins are not rare in Geometric vase scenes. Here he may represent Geryon, later always triple-bodied, attacked by Herakles.

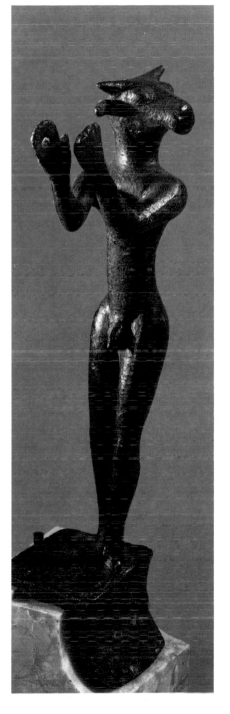

The griffon, a winged, eagle-headed lion, was well known to the Minoan and Mycenaean world, and Minoan gems with a griffon device were known and recut in the Cyclades in the 7th century. Another source for renewal of contact with the creature were the griffon heads used to decorate the rims of bronze cauldrons imported from Syria. The Greeks imitated them widely and here we see a later example with stylized topknot and ears.

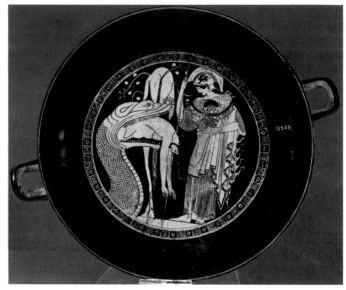

Above: a unique representation on a cup by Douris of about 480. The monstrous serpent guarding the golden fleece disgorges Jason, while Athena, holding her owl and wearing the aegis with the Gorgoneion and a helmet decorated with a sphinx, stands by to assist the hero.

Above left: frequently found on these eastern cauldrons was the human-headed bird, often male. The Greeks preferred to copy the female variety, the siren. On the "Harpy" tomb from Xanthos in Lycia, about 480, we see sirens carrying off the manikin souls of the dead.

Left: Typhon, son of Ge, was an elemental god of wind and storm. Here we see him painted on a hydria, made perhaps in Rhegion in about 540, battling with Zeus after the slaughter of his brothers, the Titans, by the young father of the gods.

5. Architecture and Art

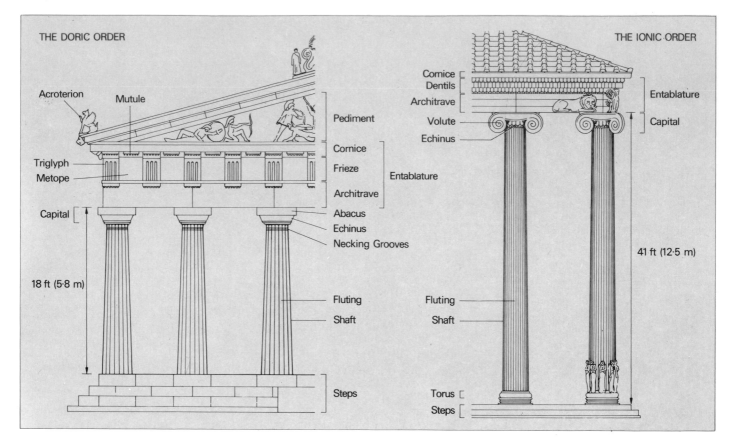

Temples. The awesome words "Doric and Ionic orders" have so far featured little in our considerations of architecture. The reason for this is simple: in earlier buildings virtually all those parts which could tell us most about their external appearance were made of perishable materials, notably wood and mudbrick, and so we can only guess, sometimes with a modicum of evidence, at details of the upper parts. When we do reach temples in which any number of these parts are in terracotta or stone, we see two distinct styles. Most of those on the Greek mainland are being built within a strict system of interdependent structural members, which many people have taken to be the invention of a single (perhaps Corinthian) architect, while in the east a great variety of more decorative treatments were tried. The first was the Doric order, the second could be better termed the "Ionic disorder."

Both types of temple are based on the concept of a long, narrow, central room, normally surrounded by a colonnade, with an entrance at one short end and the whole covered by a pitched, tiled roof. Where sufficient evidence exists it is clear that the ceilings and roof were supported by the prop-and-lintel system, imposing a dead weight on the walls below. This necessitated strong foundations, often sought in the rocky ground only a little way below the surface. However, some important cult sites were in valleys and marshy coastal plains, and here it was found that the simple one-step foundations of the early structures could not prevent subsidence and flood. The 6th-century

Above: the temples of Aphaea on Aegina and Apollo at Didyma serve as examples of the Archaic Doric and Ionic orders. The original colors, mainly red and blue, are omitted.

Previous page: columns of the Archaic temple of Apollo at Corinth.

Artemision at Ephesus is said to have been supported on a raft of charcoal and fleeces. To protect the lower ends of wooden columns from rotting on these low-lying sites they were often placed on separate stone bases, thus originating one of the lasting differences between Ionic and Doric temples. Other striking differences between the two styles lie in the column capitals and the frieze above them, though we have but slight knowledge of the upper parts of all the large Ionic temples of the period. The needs of the cult as well as the choice of building materials could also affect the final plan and appearance – a particularly important consideration in this period when the transition was made from the use of wood to stone, and in turn marble.

The Doric column is topped by a capital consisting of a square abacus above a rounded echinus, which slopes down on its underside to join the narrowing top of the column. On Archaic temples we find a number of decorative treatments at this join, notably the pendent leaf pattern on the temple of Artemis on Corfu, a pattern which imitates that of the beaten bronze cladding known from examples at Olympia to have protected wooden capitals at this point. The capital is a simplification of a Mycenaean type, and has echoes in the moldings used on

Painted terracotta revetments on the pediment of the mid-6th-century treasury, built by the Sicilian city of Gela on the terrace above the stadium at Olympia. The treasury is the earliest of more than a dozen such structures.

the elaborate bronze dress pins of the late Geometric period. The slim stems and flat capitals of our earliest stone columns, at the Argive Heraion and Delphi, indicate that they supported wooden upper parts, but by about 560 a thickset forest of stout columns is used to support the stone frieze of one of the earliest monumental temples in Sicily, that of Apollo at Syracuse.

Above the architrave ran the Doric frieze, consisting of alternating carved triglyphs and blank, non-load-bearing metopes. Alternate triglyphs are centered over a column, and the pegs for fixing the members have become petrified in the stone. Above this were overhanging eaves, protected on most early buildings by boldly painted terracotta revetments. These were originally intended to protect the ends of the wooden ceiling beams and rafters, but in many cases were retained as a purely decorative feature when stone blocks were set in this position. Many other features of the Doric order suggest forms in wood, notably the triglyphs and the thickened ends of the walls flanking the porch, which were originally mudbrick encased in boards. Yet there was no simple changeover from wood to stone; this is shown by the fact that beams could never have been the size of the triglyph, and in any case the ceiling beams of a stone temple are regularly set at a higher level than the triglyphs.

For complex reasons concerned with the gradual thickening of the architrave blocks it became impossible for the architect to place triglyphs at the corner of the building so as to be both at the end of the frieze and central over the corner column. In order to retain metopes of equal size to the rest at this point he was forced to bring the corner column closer to its companions. Such "corner contraction" became regular in Doric temples, with the result that the central columns were wider spaced than those at the sides; but the system demanded considerable architectural skill. In Ionic temples there was no such triglyph problem and the space between columns could be altered freely. We normally find a closer spacing at the sides and lesser end than at the main entrance, which allowed, or encouraged, a greater emphasis on the porch in Ionic temples, where columns multiply in profusion in the 6th century. The Sicilians copied this style in their Doric structures, a trend largely ignored on the mainland. Here strictly symmetrical groundplans evolved during the same period, a simple porch with two columns between the wing *antae* being mirrored by a dummy porch at the rear, used often as a storeroom for dedications.

The Ionic capital owed much to eastern models, though its exact origins are obscure. It emerges at about the same time as the Aeolic capital, named after its main area of use, Lesbos and the mainland nearby. Both types are essentially two-sided capitals in which the top of the column branches out into a supporting surface, whose faces are decorated with carved volutes. In the Aeolic form these spring from the shaft itself, whereas in the Ionic they spring from an echinus-like "cushion." A simpler capital, which may have also been used as a base, consisted of a leaf-clad drum, more obviously related to Syrian types and in use before the Ionic and Aeolic capitals in Asia Minor.

To our limited knowledge treatment of the upper works of Ionic temples varied in the Archaic period. The little treasury of the Siphnians at Delphi had a plain architrave surmounted by a continuous sculpted frieze, framed between richly carved moldings. At Didyma we find the more typical architrave imitative of triple overlapped boarding, but with an animal frieze carved on it. Dentils (closely set "ceiling beam" ends) are found at Didyma, but are rare elsewhere – they have been attempted by the Ionian stonemasons cutting the blocks for the tomb of Cyrus at Pasargadae in Iran.

Ionic columns were very tall compared with Doric, thus making the rather flimsy upper parts less integral to the whole architectural concept than in the carefully composed and balanced Doric elevation. The bases of Ionic columns also received decorative rather than architectural treatment, and usually took the form of two horizontally grooved or modeled drums. On the 6th-century temples at Ephesus and Didyma the effect was increased by placing sculptural decoration (a sacrificial procession in stone) on the lower parts of the columns. The Dorian architect was more concerned with the harmony of the whole, and experimented with his columns with this end in view. Not only do they taper upward, they also bulge outward as they taper – an effect most clearly seen in the two juxtaposed temples of Hera at Paestum. Doric columns also tend to lean inward slightly, and already in the Archaic period were placed on a foundation which was not flat but raised a little at the center, curving modestly away to the corners.

Both architectural and decorative approaches called for careful masonry work. At first softer stone was used; the column bases at Samos were turned on a lathe, and everywhere the marks of the pick and chisel can be seen. Visible surfaces were smoothed, while for adjoining surfaces a new technique was rapidly evolved in which only the outer parts were smoothed and the central area cut further back. A tighter fit was thus ensured by allowing only a limited part of the two surfaces to come into contact – a technique termed anathyrosis. The pegs on the stone Doric frieze and cornice suggest the main method used for fixing members in wooden structures and such wooden dowels continued to be used to secure stone blocks in the earliest temples, just for column drums till much later. Metal dowels can be found sporadically on all temples. Much more general was the use of metal clamps to tie in blocks horizontally with their neighbors; in the 6th century these are extravagantly large butterfly-shaped clamps of bronze or iron secured with molten lead.

Other holes we may find cut on stone blocks were used in moving and lifting the pieces. Until about 525 large and heavy blocks, for instance monolithic columns, were often used in temples, but later individual blocks are cut down to a much smaller size, rarely more than 15 tons. This implies a change in the method used to raise blocks, from ramp and rollers to winched cranes.

Among the last jobs to be done were the detailed carving of moldings and the fluting of the columns. The ceiling beams and rafters were laid in notches cut in the back of the cornice blocks, the tiles were often laid directly over the rafters, and the terracotta cladding of the cornice was nailed into position, together with any gargoyle-like embellishments of the guttering.

Few Doric temples of the Archaic period survive in any fair condition. The second temple of Apollo at Corinth was built in about 540, and seven monolithic columns still stand at the west end. Cuttings in the rock for the rest of the foundations show that, like the Parthenon and all its predecessors on the Athenian Acropolis, it had a *cella* divided into at least two rooms. We have noted the remains of the temple of Hera at Olympia, built in about 600 with a repertoire of later replacement columns in stone. It had a foundation of two steps instead of the later three, and walls of mudbrick above the tall socle of stone, their debris preserving for us the Hermes of Praxiteles which stood in the interior. At Delphi the temple of Apollo is of the 4th century, but follows the plan of its late 6th-century predecessor, while in the precinct of Athena Pronoia a very early temple was also replaced in about 500. Better preserved and delightfully situated is the temple of Aphaea on Aegina, built around 510. There is a double line of columns in the cella, structurally unnecessary in such a small building, but a regular feature of Doric temples, with a second range of columns superimposed to gain the height needed to reach ceiling level.

The use of marble for buildings was promoted in Ionia, but hardly before the mid-6th century. Earlier the attack of Alyattes on Smyrna in about 610 had brought to a halt work on an impressive temple of Athena – a large building, yet dwarfed by the monsters erected by Samos and Ephesus in the next century in obvious, and probably not wholly friendly, rivalry. The once conspicuous Hecatompedon on Samos was replaced by a structure four times as large, soon burned down and restored in a similar shape by the tyrant Polycrates, though little remains to be seen today. At Ephesus the temple of Artemis again replaced a smaller shrine and was slightly larger than the Samos giant. Marble was used for the first time here for structural members in a large building, though a little earlier the men of Cnidos had erected a marble treasury at Delphi. Its use was earlier confined to sculpture, notably on the islands of Naxos, Delos and Samos where marble

The columns (foreground) of the first temple of Hera at Paestum (Posidonia) show the exaggerated bulge and taper of Archaic Doric columns. The second temple, dating from perhaps 100 years later, has far more subdued forms.

was at hand as well as a supply of emery (of which Naxos is still a leading producer) to aid the working of the hard stone. The variety and care in the carving of the capitals of the Ephesus temple and the sculptured columns show the concern and expense lavished on its building. The cella was probably left open to the sky, as at nearby Didyma, and both these temples were rebuilt in the 4th century, though not finished until the Roman period.

The best-preserved Archaic temples are in the west – the "Basilica" and "Temple of Ceres" at Paestum. The former retains the older plan with a central row of columns in the cella, as well as including a number of refinements of more Ionic taste, especially the molded courses of red sandstone in the entablature, sandwiched between limestone courses. The "Ceres" temple is the first known to us to employ a mixture of Doric and Ionic columns, the latter in the porch where their slimness and height lent a more airy atmosphere to the entrance. Some temples in Sicily went further in imitating the large porches and bigger co-lonnades of Ionia, though not employing the double colonnade of Samos and Ephesus. An early example is the temple of Artemis on Corfu, whose broad front concealed doubly wide colonnades and a narrow cella in the old tradition. The crowning glory was the sculpture of the pediments – to our knowledge the first large-scale pediments to be decorated, even if in the shallowest relief, replacing the hipped roofs of earlier temples built in the Corinthian sphere of influence.

Towns. All these costly and extensive programs of development or, to a large degree, redevelopment in the sanctuaries of 6th-century Greece had precious few counterparts in the field of civil architecture. It is a period when civic centers begin to take shape, but it cannot boast the marbled halls and meeting places of later years. At Athens the Agora seems to have been reserved for public use from the early 6th century – earlier it was used for housing and burials. A complex structure in its southwest corner may have been used by state officials, but most public business even in a democratic state could be conducted in the open air, inside a sanctuary or even inside the headman's house. We can see such a system at work perhaps in the village of Emporio on Chios: on the acropolis was a small temple and a large building with a central hearth but no apparent sacral character, interpreted as the chieftain's house. On the hillside were scattered the rest of the houses, which were of very modest

Construction techniques illustrating the use of levers and clamps in Greek ashlar masonry walls. The levers are used to assist the close fitting of the blocks.

standards, regularly equipped with sleeping-benches in their single rooms but little else. The roofs were flat and constructed of branches and mud with simple chimney-pipes.

Housing was generally of a similar mean standard, though our evidence is far from extensive. Among the types found are freestanding houses of single rooms, some with porches, as well as rows of such buildings, and units consisting of more than one room in a variety of plans. None of them have any refinements such as decorated floors or walls – the rule was beaten mud or pebbles for the floor, and mudbrick on a stone foundation for the walls. The two main house forms of ensuing centuries, and their grouping in regular blocks, had their origin in the Archaic period. The first type, "prostas," was based on a porched main room; the other, "pastas," had a series of rooms leading off a central corridor running across the block. It is not unusual for traces of industry, in particular metal working, to be found in buildings no different from the ordinary house.

The pediment of the Archaic temple of Artemis at Garitsa, Corfu, restored from the fragmentary remains. Blanks in each corner indicate where slabs are missing.

After the reforms of Cleisthenes at Athens, public buildings begin to multiply in the Agora among the minor shrines. About this time the simple stoa of the archon basileus was built, where that official conducted much of his business in very open court, and also the first council house to accommodate the Boule of 500 – a plain, square building provided with tiered wooden seats. All these buildings were carefully aligned down the western side of the Agora, parallel to another useful amenity – a large, stone-lined drain.

Provision and disposal of water was a basic necessity not overlooked by the architect. Wells were frequently dug, filled up and dug elsewhere, but water could also be led through pipes to a fountain-house, and these are among the most ambitious of Archaic buildings outside sanctuaries. We have already noted the hydraulic achievements of the tyrants of Athens, Megara and Samos, but it is worth noting a few details of the aqueduct which Polycrates had hacked out of the rock above his city. It was 1,040 meters long, with a main bore about 1.80 meters high. The two parts, cut from each end, met at a right angle with an error of less than 2 meters in height; to one side was a channel of varying depth in which the waterpipe was laid. Masons' marks show that the work was split between gangs, and on one stretch where the walls had to be lined with cut blocks a large painted notice on one block, which reads "EXEMPLAR," tells us how the foreman ensured a supply of correctly measured stones. More important, we may assume that a similar procedure was followed in the building of more visible structures.

No coherent pattern emerges from consideration of the remaining public buildings of the period. A theater was built at Thorikos in about 500, but it was not until about 450 that stone seats were provided in the auditorium, whose irregular shape follow the contours of the hillside. At Athens and Corinth there is evidence that musical, theatrical and equestrian contests were held in the Agora without any specialized buildings or tracks.

Attention was often paid to fortifications. Many city walls were built in the 7th and 6th centuries, though few are well preserved and none have the grandeur of the Mycenaean or sophistication of the Hellenistic periods. A common method of construction was to sandwich a rubble core between two built faces, stone below and mudbrick above, with occasional towers. As siege warfare was hardly practiced by Greeks, there was no inducement to improve defensive systems. Types of stone walling varied, but typical of the Archaic period was the use of irregularly shaped stones with a single smoothed surface, carefully arranged to fit tightly. The best example of such "polygonal" walling is the retaining wall of the temple terrace at Delphi. Many Archaic city walls comprise an area far greater than the inhabited quarters, and infinitely larger than a single stronghold of the ruler. At Corinth, Athens and Samos the Archaic walls embrace the lower-lying ground as well as higher vantage points.

Above: a view of the temple of Aphaea at Aegina showing the columns rising in two registers to support the ceiling, with an architrave between. Late 6th century.

Below: plan of the Athenian Agora soon after the reforms of Cleisthenes about 500 BC. The public buildings, including the solidly built drain, are confined to the west side of the square.

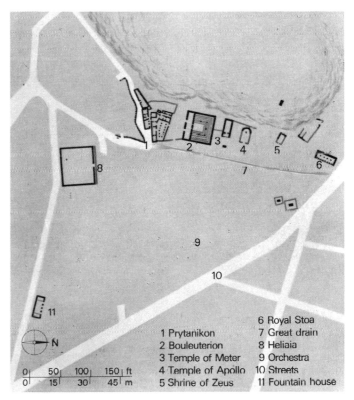

1 Prytanikon	6 Royal Stoa
2 Bouleuterion	7 Great drain
3 Temple of Meter	8 Heliaia
4 Temple of Apollo	9 Orchestra
5 Shrine of Zeus	10 Streets
	11 Fountain house

Extreme left: marble statue of Artemis, found in the sanctuary of the goddess on Delos in 1878. Nikandre ("preeminent among all the women of Naxos") had her dedicatory inscription cut into the right flank.

Left: the earliest of the kore statues dedicated in the Heraion on Samos, the "Hera" of Cheramyes (inscribed down the front of the plain drapery). She holds her offering to Hera, perhaps a bird, in the left hand. About 570.

Opposite page: korai statues dedicated to Athena on the Acropolis between 525 and 480. The first shown here, the superb Peplos kore, retains the heavier dress of earlier pieces such as the Merenda statue, while later pieces have extravagantly pleated chitons and diagonally draped mantles – virtuoso coloring and carving. By 480 this virtuosity and the smiling features give way to a greater severity, seen in the torso of the kore dedicated by Euthydikos, shown on the extreme right.

Sculpture. Religion stimulated advances in the plastic arts as it did in architecture. No building outside a sanctuary is known to have carried sculpted decoration before the 5th century, and virtually all freestanding statues or reliefs of the Archaic period were set up as dedications in sanctuaries or as memorial markers over tombs. Although one grave of about 700 on Paros boasted a crudely carved marble slab, depicting a seated figure, as its marker, the position of the most important Geometric graves was indicated by plain stones or at best a large, painted vase. One hundred and fifty years later the tombstones of Athenian aristocrats were among the most ostentatious of sculptural tours de force, against which the new democracy reacted strongly, since no decorated headstones are found in Attica between 510 and 430.

It is a little more difficult to envisage the appearance of an Archaic sanctuary, containing not only the altar, temple and other subsidiary buildings, but also lines and clusters of dedicated offerings, ranging from the smallest pot of honey to extravagant statues raised high on columns. There is a marked decrease in the amount of expensive material buried with the dead at the end of the Geometric period, and a greater concentration on the display of piety and wealth in the sanctuaries, where rich and poor citizens offered the traditional tenth of their gains to their divine protectors. The increase in the prosperity of at least the ruling classes gave scope for experimentation and specialization to the artists commissioned to provide suitable objects in which the gods would take delight. However, it is clear that there remained a number of craftsmen who could turn their hands to more than one particular job – marble-work, architecture, gem-carving and the like.

We saw the large bronze tripods dedicated in the 8th century; by 600 a vogue for large marble statues had developed. How did this happen? The urge to monumentality was already there, perhaps, but marble statues were unknown in the 8th century. The oldest stone carving we have dates from the years 675–650 and is almost wholly restricted to Cretan work in soft local limestone, using the tools and the paint of the carpenter. A life-size cult statue from west of Heraklion, architectural decoration from Gortys and later Prinias, and hammered sheet-bronze statues from Dreros all combine features derived from Minoan tradition with strong Near Eastern influence, especially in the placing and iconography of the architectural reliefs.

The legendary inventor with Cretan connections lends his name to the "Daedalic" style which evolves throughout the Greek world in the 7th century in vase-painting as well

as the plastic arts – terracottas, bronzes and large-scale sculpture. We see a strong frontal emphasis, deliberately ordered proportions and especially large facial features framed by wig-like hair, the whole a Greek schematization of the current styles of Syrian ivory and metalwork. Such features can be discerned on the worn surface of our earliest marble statue, an Artemis dedicated by Nikandre of Naxos in about 640. A minimum amount of marble has been cut away from the thin slab of hard stone so that the statue has a board-like appearance. Throughout the rest of the Archaic period sculpture did not break free from the constraint imposed by the shape of the original blocks.

By about 500 the bronze-founders of Greece had acquired enough technical expertise in casting large figures to allow them to experiment with a range of new postures – a trend which also began to have an effect on stone sculpture. "Nikandre" was a forerunner of a long series of standing female statues or *korai*, paralleled by a nude male type (*kouros*), both dedicated in numbers at sanctuaries in Greece and Ionia. Within the framework of the basic types we can see the sculptors gradually coming to terms with the human body and its clothing, and eventually we see them beginning to move beyond that framework.

These kouroi and korai are perhaps the best-known monuments of Archaic Greece. They owe something of their origin to Egyptian models, some certainly being cut with the help of gridded guide lines painted on the front of the block in the Egyptian manner, but from the start we see considerable individuality and a keen interest in bodily form. Monumentality was a major consideration in the early days of the 6th century, when many pieces were larger than life size, and an unfinished Dionysus lying in a quarry on Naxos would have measured 34 feet if the block had not broken. Muscles and bones are rendered by ridges and grooves on the surface, in imitation of repoussé-work breastplates, while ears and hair are delightfully rendered patterns. Few korai are as early; the bodies of early Ionian examples are treated like fluted columns with added arms, a description which belies their undoubted grace.

Various deities were the recipients of these statues, a fact which proves that they were intended to represent, for the most part, the idealized votary – not necessarily the actual dedicator, since men could dedicate korai. Noteworthy is a group from the Heraion on Samos – three korai, a kouros, a seated and a reclining figure. Their names, carved on the base, include Phileia, Ornithe and Philippe. They may have been members of the priestess's clan or related to the dedicator, Geneleos.

Some figures closely modeled on the Syrian Astarte

type, and nearly all of the 7th century, were nude, but otherwise these females are always clothed, and the sculptors took delight in the ornamental treatment of the drapery and its painted embroidery. Though the fashion of wearing a light tunic or "chiton" with sleeves under a cloak draped diagonally across the shoulders prevailed, two of the finest pieces wear a heavier dress or "peplos" over the chiton – the "Peplos Kore" found on the Acropolis in 1886 and the recently discovered grave statue of Phrasikleia from Merenda in the Mesogeia plain of Attica. The smiles on the lips of these figures cannot simply be explained away as the result of inexpert carving, but must surely be a reflection of the sculptors' joie de vivre. This characteristic disappeared by the time of the latest korai dedicated on the Acropolis before 480. In Euthydikos' kore, interest in decorative drapery is minimal and the face is built around the stark axes of the straight-set eyes and nose.

In the male figures we see a reaction from monumental beginnings into smooth slimness in the middle of the 6th century, but by 480 aggressive athleticism dominates. These later pieces show a considerable departure from the inherited strict symmetry – heads turn, shoulders slope and the weight begins to fall clearly on one foot in contrast to the uncertain traditional pose. As for developments in the sculpting of the face, a comparison between a head of about 600 from the cemetery by the Dipylon gate and the famous Blond Boy from the Acropolis tells all.

The adornment of temples as well as the temenos gave scope to the artist, who was no doubt usually working under the patronage of the leading families of the state. The fragments of architectural sculpture from Crete have little to do with developments elsewhere, but our record for the 7th century on the mainland is sketchy. We have noted the painted panels at Isthmia. Painted metopes from the temples at Thermon and Calydon form the next considerable body of material from the later 7th century. They consist of square slabs of terracotta decorated in a style closely related to that of Corinthian vase-painting. The range of scenes portrayed is remarkable – Thermon has the tragic death of Itys, killed by his mother Procne; Orion returning from the hunt, his prey slung over his shoulder; Perseus, seated deities and a copulating couple. The head of Medusa, the Gorgoneion, is also found, and recurs frequently as an apotropaic symbol on temples elsewhere, especially in Sicily. The pediments of the temple of Artemis on Corfu showed Medusa with her offspring Pegasus and Chrysaor as their central figure, flanked by leopards, tame to Artemis but not man, with the wings filled with mythological scenes; such a disunited whole deliberately avoids the problems of scale which tested composers of later unitary pediments.

Relief sculpture includes figures in active poses, but not till the end of the Archaic period do we begin to find active bodies portrayed in a truly convincing manner, tensed and contorted in lifelike rhythms. The successive sets of

Opposite page: bronze statuette found at Prizren in Albania. It was one of three or four running female figures attached to the rim of the lid of a large bronze vase similar to the Vix krater. About 520.

The earliest kouros head from Attic soil and the last carved before the Persian sack. *Left*: the "Dipylon" head of about 600 belonged to a grave statue. *Below*: the "Blond Boy" (thus named after the traces of yellow paint in his hair) is more natural in treatment and far from symmetrical.

sculpture at Delphi demonstrate these changes. At Athens a large temple of Athena of about 560 had painted limestone sculptures in its pediments; in one corner Herakles grapples with a seamonster, while a three-bodied, snake-tailed creature fills the other corner – a figure whose identity has tested scholarship. The temple was refurbished by the Pisistratids and given marble pediments in which Athena plays the central part in a battle between gods and giants. She also appears centrally in the west pediment of the temple of Apollo at Eretria (rebuilt not too long before its destruction by the Persians in 490), illustrating a theme which had great appeal in the following years, especially at Athens – Theseus is shown carrying off Antiope from among the Amazons. Athena again dominates both pediments of Aphaea's late Archaic temple on Aegina (we must assume that Athena had annexed the cult of Aphaea, presumably before this period, when Athens and Aegina were almost constant enemies). In all these later pediments the figures are sculpted in the round and then doweled to the wall and floor of the pediment.

The provincial nature of western art becomes clear when we turn to the metopes of the early temples at Selinus, where unconvincing frontal heads look out at us and the broken-backed bull on which Europa rides can scarcely be excused by considerations of available head-room. A rich series of scenes is depicted in the metopes from the mid-6th-century Hera temple at the mouth of the Sele river near Paestum. Heracles, the leitmotif of Archaic heroism and violence, performs many of his feats, including rescuing Hera from an attack by satyrs. We also find Trojan scenes, the death of Agamemnon, the damned in Tartarus and an unexplained tortoise-riding gentleman. The unfinished work on a number of the metopes shows the manner in which Greeks carved reliefs by cutting back the contours silhouette-style and then adding details.

Literary sources tell us that large-scale bronze-casting was first practiced by Rhoecus (the architect of the Hera temple on Samos) and Theodorus in the mid-6th century in Ionia. We have no assured pieces of this date, but a number of bases to which bronze, not marble, statues were attached are known from the later 6th century, and in the Agora at Athens were found substantial remains of the mold in which the bronze cult statue of Apollo Patrous was hollow-cast in about 540.

Minor arts. Smaller bronzes are among the most pleasing achievements of Archaic art, whether individual pieces or parts of larger ensembles. Examples of the latter are the figures applied as friezes to the necks of the huge bronze kraters made at Corinth and Sparta, of which the Vix krater is the outstanding example. Earlier we may note the quality and variety of decorative bronzework in 7th-century Crete, especially the chased helmets and breast-plates, while at Argos and on Samos mythological scenes are stamped and beaten onto bronze shield-bands and

plaques. Indeed few artifacts have come down to us from this period without some decorative features on them. Careful attention was paid to the moldings on pins and the butt ends of spears.

Influence from the east is particularly strong in those skills in which the east excelled, especially ivory-carving, which never took full root in Greece. Understandably the Ionians practiced it more widely, and carved ivory lyre-frames of around 600 from Samos and Ionia are exquisitely cut, as are some of the statuettes of priests and priestesses found by Hogarth at Ephesus. Standards were lower at Sparta, where bone was a common substitute for very ordinary figures of Artemis Orthia; even less significant and more common are the small, stamped-out lead figurines dedicated in their thousands at Sparta and elsewhere in the Peloponnese.

At such sites ivory and bone seals of the 7th century also occur. No Bronze Age Greek of any standing went without his sealstone, but the habit did not recover after the Dark Ages. As well as these Peloponnesian pieces, stone seals were made in fair numbers in the Cyclades; the range of motifs is wide, a number recalling Minoan types – indeed we even find some Minoan gems recut in the Archaic period.

Currency and coins. Metal was also used as currency. From early texts and inscriptions we learn of forms of currency in Greece before the 6th century. The relative values of gold and silver used as bullion are mentioned by Homer, and on a more mundane level we hear of animals (especially oxen) and bronze and iron objects being used as

---

1: a coin selected from the deposit of primitive electrum coins found beneath the temple of Artemis at Ephesus, about 600.

2: shortly afterwards the earliest inscribed Greek coins were privately issued, by Phanes perhaps at Ephesus or Halicarnassus. Despite the fine detail, doubts raised about the authenticity of the piece reflect the skills of the present-day forger.

3: large silver coins were exported from the metal-rich area of Mount Pangaion, Macedonia. This piece carries the name of one of the tribes in the area – the Derrones. About 500. Weight over 40g.

4: the earliest silver coins from a Greek homeland state were minted on Aegina in the mid-6th century. Her type was the sea-turtle or tortoise.

5: Corinth soon followed with Pegasus, the offspring of Medusa, bridled by Bellerophon at the fountain of Peirene in the town. ϙ is the initial letter of Corinth in the Archaic script.

6: on the early coins of Sybaris and other Italian colonies the reverse has the same design as the obverse, but in intaglio (incuse).

7: Himera uses a punning type – the cock announcing the dawn (*hemera*). She was the first city in Sicily to issue coined metal.

8: a coin of Sicilian Zancle shows its harbor in the shape of a sickle (*dankle*). The shell on the reverse celebrates a major Zanclean product. About 500.

currency. In Crete fines were paid in tripods and cauldrons, terminology later transferred to actual coins, while on the mainland as well there is a strong literary tradition that iron spits were used as a medium of exchange. Sets of such large roasting spits (drachmae of six obols, the names given in literary and inscriptional sources) have been found at a number of sites, not least in the Argos Warrior Grave, while a good-time girl from Naucratis, Rhodopis, dedicated a set at Delphi in about 550 which Herodotus saw and commented on.

Weighed metal bars had been in use as currency in the Near East in the 2nd millennium, but in the Iron Age our first evidence for such a practice further west comes from Hogarth's delvings into the foundation deposit of the temple of Artemis at Ephesus, where over 50 pieces of electrum (a mixture of gold and silver) and four silver lumps were found. Some of the electrum pieces are plain, others have a roughly striated surface, while many have a true stamped type (mostly crudely cut animals) and four bear a Lydian inscription. For a long time these finds were dated to the early 7th century, but a more thorough analysis of the objects from the foundation deposit suggests that none of the electrum pieces are likely to have been manufactured before 625, which is then the date of the earliest coinage known to us.

These coins were issued by Lydians and Ionian Greeks – from which city we cannot say. The metal must have come mainly from the alluvial deposits of the river Pactolus, flowing past Sardis. All the coins, plain or stamped, are of a fixed weight or fractions of that weight – a basic essential of a coinage system. It was hoped to inspire confidence in the user by producing coins with types and to a set weight, but it should be remembered that either the mixture of gold and silver in the alloy could not be regulated by the issuer, so that the pieces were in fact of varying worth, or the issuer could himself manipulate the mixture. Refining installations found at Sardis do not go back further than about 570, but it was earlier than this that Alcaeus and his friends were given 2,000 staters by the Lydians, probably to finance a military operation. Another important point is that even the smallest pieces (and they are very small, one ninety-sixth of the unit) were no small change but could purchase a considerable amount.

The Ionian Greeks took up this idea and many electrum issues of the years 600–540 are known, several on the same Lydian weight standard, others employing different standards without apparent difficulties of exchange. The types punched on the face of most coins are animals, taken from the repertoire of vase painter and gem engraver, while the reverse consists of squares and oblongs, the ends of the punches struck by the mallet of the mint-master. Three bear a Greek inscription which reads "I am the symbol of Phanes" – he probably lived in Ephesus, though we cannot tell whether he was a private citizen or a state official.

By the late 6th century one electrum coinage had emerged from the rest as a medium of international exchange – that of Cyzicus in the Sea of Marmara. Her coins are found widely in the Black Sea area and the Balkans to the exclusion of most other mints, including that of Miletus, founder of so many colonies in the area. Byzantium, focal point of the trade routes, managed without coinage till the late 5th century.

On the mainland only silver was used for the early coinages, first that of Aegina in about 540, followed by Corinth, Athens and some of the Cycladic islands. The tribes of Macedonia and the Greeks of Thasos coined the silver extracted from mines around Mount Pangaion, the tribes minting large, childishly decorated pieces which were mostly exported to Egypt and the Near East as bullion. Many of the pieces found in those areas have been clipped to prove the full silver content, but the practice is rare in Greece, showing that coinage was accepted at face value.

The use of iron spit currency was perpetuated in Argos and Arcadia by the issuing of iron coins. Bronze, however, was not minted until the mid-5th century or later.

In the west, Sybaris had been issuing coins for some time before her destruction in 510, but she was probably the earliest coiner, in about 540. All the cities in southern Italian states who coined in the 6th century, together with Zancle across the straits in Sicily, adopted a most curious minting technique which is best regarded as imitative of repoussé metalwork. The obverse was struck as usual in relief on a very thin blank, while a mirror image in intaglio was stamped into the reverse; the process necessitated the careful alignment of the two dies to avoid splitting the blank. The Achaean colonies and Taranto used a standard derived from that of Corinth, reflecting close trading contacts with Corinth earlier in the century; the Euboean colonies brought their own standard, which was the same as that of Athens but used subdivisions of thirds, not quarters. In Sicily the westernmost colonies Himera and Selinus coined first, an indication that their silver came from yet further west (Spain) via Carthage; a number of silver ingots were among a hoard of coins found at Taranto in 1911 and one of them was marked with a Selinuntine stamp. Syracuse did not start coining till about 500, and regular issues do not appear until after Gelon captured the city in 485.

Few coins apart from those of silver-exporting states strayed far from home; only five south Italian coins have been found outside that area. It was clearly in the interests of most cities not to allow their stocks of bullion to leave the country, and therefore coins were stamped to show that the state guaranteed their exchange value.

The value of the smallest coins was still far from trivial, and there were few of them, the main denominations weighing from 8 to 17 grams. This was not small change for everyday use, but for larger internal or state transactions such as payment of taxes and fines and of wage bills for officials and mercenaries, and for the buying of large amounts of produce. So possession of coinage was not an everyday matter in 500, and on this point we must beware of many modern (and ancient) interpretations.

Artistically coins have much in common with gems, for gem-engraving and the cutting of coin dies are essentially the same process. The range of types is largely animal and vegetable, with human or divine figures appearing as full types only late in the century, the earliest including the Athena of Athens, Apollo of Caulonia and Dionysus of Sicilian Naxos. Other types advertise the local way of life and produce – horses in Thessaly, ox-carts in Macedonia, an ear of corn at Metapontum and cattle at Eretria and Sybaris. Mythology appears rarely, being hampered by the restricted size of the coin, though the Pegasus of Corinth is indeed based on myth. The cutting is at times bold and far deeper than we are used to in modern coinage.

Some mints produced heads of considerable charm and accomplishment in the later years of the period, notably Syracuse, Athens and Corinth. In the first two places these were years of intense coining in which very much poorer work also appeared. At Athens heavy minting followed the discovery of the richest vein of ore at Laurion in 483, in order to finance the crash program of trireme-building, while at Syracuse the massive indemnity paid by the Carthaginians after their defeat at Himera in 480 was turned into coin.

The versatility of clay. Most civilizations produced terracotta works of accomplishment and interest, but it is arguable that the Greeks were among the greatest exponents of the modeling, and especially decoration, of clay artifacts, and in the later Archaic period they produced some of their finest works. Terracotta figurines were made in many areas, mostly for dedication at local shrines. They were the ordinary man's dedication, and though usually attractively painted they do not shine forth as works of art. We have noted the use of terracotta in architectural construction and decoration; in Corinth and the western colonies small, portable clay altars were decorated with a variety of lively scenes, including the deeds of Herakles and the battle between the pygmies and cranes.

The production of vases kept many men and slaves at work. In the 7th century there was a great diversity of local styles, though Corinthian ware prevailed in the export trade. Local production gradually fell off during the 6th century (save for undecorated containers and kitchen ware), and Attic vases took over the major role from Corinthian, until by the early 5th century Athens had no serious competitors at all.

Few changes occurred in the pattern of usage of clay vases which had been established in the Dark Ages and indeed went back to the Bronze Age. Metal and wood were also used for vessels of various types, and we have seen that the bronze ware of the period was impressive work, but the clay vase, decorated or not, was the basic container, from the huge storage jars of Crete and the islands to the smallest miniature toy or dedicatory bowl.

The frieze and panel forms for figure decoration, already established in the Geometric period, also persisted. Rarely do we find such decoration bereft of a groundline and floating free on the surface of the pot. The use of the frieze encouraged the drawing of well-populated narrative scenes, while the increase in the use of the panel probably owed more to outside influences, such as the painted metopes on temples.

In the 7th century the eastern Greeks and the areas whose art they influenced were slow to discard the chains of the Geometric style, but at Athens and Corinth and other less productive areas, such as Argos, Naxos (Cycladic and Sicilian) and Megara Hyblaea, vase-painters admitted a whole host of new ideas and influences. These came especially from artifacts imported from the east, which included no vases, but metalwork, ivories and probably textiles. From this material the painters became acquainted with the animal file which was to dominate Corinthian pottery, a whole range of floral motifs unknown to the Geometric artist, and a style of drawing of the human body, in particular the head, which we have already encountered as the Daedalic style. In vase-painting two contrasting innovations in technique accompanied these changes, the first substituting a contour-based system for the Geometric silhouette, the other enlivening that silhouette by incising lines on it to bring out detail – a technique borrowed from the bronzesmith and one which we term black-figure. Despite its artificiality, black-figure dominated the outline style in the Archaic period, although outline did flourish in some places in the 7th century, especially at Corinth around 650 in the hands of

The masterpiece of the Kleophrades painter – a wine amphora decorated with the god of wine (left) and his cavorting followers – the aggressive maenads and lustful satyrs. About 490.

the painter of the Chigi vase (page 80). Here and on its replica recently excavated at Erythrae in Ionia, the outline style is combined with a number of accessory colors to give a near-polychrome effect. Tucked away by the handle is an explicitly labeled mythological interlude, the Judgment of Paris – its first certain appearance in Greek art.

A number of earlier Corinthian vases seem to portray mythological scenes, but these are not labeled and we have difficulty in recognizing the characters, who do not appear with the regular attributes and in the rather stereotyped episodes of the later Archaic period. Some identifications, however, cannot be denied, for example the Wooden Horse of Troy on the neck of a pithos decorated in relief found on the island of Mykonos (page 89). The panels on the body are replete with the brutalities of the sack of a city, bringing home to us the stark realities of life in those years. Attic artists had a lengthy flirtation with the outline style and some of their products are forceful, even if they were only learning to cope with the large field for decoration they allowed themselves.

After 650 the black-figured animal frieze style became the staple of Corinthian production and was exported to all corners of the Greek world. Attic artists took up the cue and towards the end of the 7th century began to imitate this style. Up till this point no Attic vase, save oil amphoras, had traveled further than the island of Aegina since the mid-8th century. However, Athens' trade built up slowly through the 6th century, until by 525 considerable numbers of vases were being shipped from Phaleron Bay – most of the more pretentious pieces to Etruria, and lesser ware to even more places than Corinth had supplied.

It was during the early 6th century that an improvement in technique was achieved at Athens which, aided by careful brushwork, resulted in a full contrast between dark, lustrous "glaze" and a rich, deep orange ground. The Corinthian artist could not match this contrast with his pale clay and friable glaze, although he did resort to a red-orange wash in an attempt to rival Attic work during the last two decades of large-scale production at Corinth around 560. In other areas a whiter ground was used to cover somber, uneven or porous clay surfaces; it is usual in a number of eastern workshops – centers where an independent animal style, mainly deer and goats, flourished in the 7th and 6th centuries. Perhaps the most attractive of these products are those of Chios, whose plain amphoras full of wine were often exported in the company of distinctively shaped, deep drinking cups. The best of these cups featured mythological scenes in outline and color.

Artisans in Laconia also produced finely made and painted vases, especially elegant stemmed shallow cups, a shape which had an instant appeal and was widely imitated. The Laconians (whose identity and place of work we do not know) also used a creamy white slip on which to place their heavy, framed figures. One of the most interesting is a very rare contemporary document, a tondo scene showing King Arcesilas of Cyrene seated beneath a canopy supervising the weighing and package of some product among a rich African fauna acutely observed (page 75). On the whole, however, the school is labored in its work, and is far more repetitive than any other which regularly attempted human representations.

Artistically the black-figure painters could make few advances, being hampered by the restraints of the silhouette technique and the unnatural additional colors available to them. Until the end of black-figure production the pattern of profile head and legs combined with frontal torso remains perceptible. On the other hand, the range of shapes and scenes developed constantly; there was much hack work in all schools, but also considerable variety and experimentation among the broad range of iconography used, from Zeus in Olympus to revelers in the street. The deeds of Heracles were great favorites; at Athens his struggle with the lion of Nemea outnumbers by far any other episode, and later in the century Dionysus with his attendant maenad women and horse-men satyrs appears increasingly frequently.

The most accomplished Athenian users of the black-figure technique were thoughtful in the arrangement of their figures on the surface, and cut the incised lines fine and true. Many of them may not have been Athenian citizens, for example a man who signs his work "the Lydian," and another, Amasis, who signs as maker rather than painter of vases – this was a common Egyptian name and that of the contemporary pharaoh. These two were very able artists, but were overshadowed by the greatest exponent of the technique. Exekias, the nobility of whose figures brings a premature glimpse of full Classical art of a hundred years later. His boldness was in daring to isolate his figures in the field, while lesser artists could not leave space unfilled. He is at his best on larger vases – the "Noah" cup in Munich is the largest known up to its date of manufacture (page 119). It is remarkable not only for its tondo scene, which shows Dionysus transforming Etruscan pirates who have captured him into dolphins, but also for two of the many technical innovations which Exekias introduced. These were first the use of a coral red ground for the tondo (a pleasant but seemingly technically difficult alternative), and second the fact that it is the first known vase of this particular shape – a shape which develops in the next two generations into the most elegant cups ever produced by Greek potters.

From about 530 onward Attic artists were also painting in red-figure, filling in a dark background around figures left the color of the clay ground. At first they drew the details of these figures with a brush, and used the traditional extra colors, but there soon prevailed the use of a thicker, wiry line. Red-figure virtually displaced black by 480, and was the technique preferred by most artists of more than average ability from as early as 520. The first to use it was a pupil of Exekias, the Andocides painter, given

his name from a tag he paints on one of his vases, which reads "Andocides is handsome"; these "kalos" names were in praise of the aristocratic youths who were courted by the men-about-town, as explicit vase scenes demonstrate. Some of the youths were later to have careers known to us from the historians, and besides offering us a glimpse of their upbringing the tags afford useful dating criteria for the vases in question.

Among the everyday pots, tiles, drainage pipes and terracotta figures, the Athenian potters' quarters produced red-figure vases of superlative quality in the period 520–480. Artists soon threw off the shackles of the silhouette and began depicting the human anatomy in a whole range of poses in a spirit of enthusiastic competition, illustrated by the remarks they paint on some vases – "Here's one for you, Euthymides," or "Euphronios never did anything like this." Athletes were the favored subjects for these experiments, as well as the muscle-bound Herakles, but the new technique also allowed details of dress, furnishings and the like to be portrayed far more convincingly than did black-figure; the richness of the pleated drapery vies with that of the marble korai statues being carved along the street.

The leading artists of the early 5th century are a little more restrained, but the less expansive gestures of their figures often lend them greater inner strength. Two men concentrated on larger vases – the Kleophrades painter and the Berlin painter. The latter specialized in stately figures isolated on the dark surface of the pot, though late in his career they became wooden and repetitive, while the fires of the Kleophrades painter still burned bright in the 470s.

During these years the stemmed cup reaches its finest form and finds its most skillful decorators, among whom we may single out the Brygos painter, working for the potter Brygos, a name which can be associated with the Macedonian tribe of Bryges. His bright-eyed revelers, satyrs and maenads in their carefully arranged swirling drapery, are unmistakable. He uses a wash of diluted glaze to shade in large areas, and some of his best work is done on a white ground, a technique introduced to Attic vases in about 525, probably through the medium of wall painting. He was also far ahead of his time in using light stippling to denote shadow on areas of the human body.

Painting. The individuality and resource of the better vase-painters suffice to rule out any thought of direct dependence on free-painting, despite glimpses of borrowings here and there. Until recently we had pitifully little by way of "free" painting of any kind with which to test such ideas, but recent discoveries and publication have brought some precision. Painted wooden plaques found before World War II in a cave at Pitsa above Corinth date to about 550, the best preserved showing a sacrificial procession. Apart from a greater use of color, the style is closely linked with that of contemporary vases – with contour drawing the basic ingredient. The same applies to the painted decoration on the walls of two stone burial chambers of the end of the century, uncovered in 1969 and 1970 in the high inland plain of Elmalı in Lycia in southern Turkey. Painstaking conservation work has resulted in the rescue of large areas of the original paintings, which had been applied directly onto the stone.

Less care went into the decoration of the Diver tomb at Paestum (page 125). The haste was due to the fact that true fresco technique was used on the still damp plaster lining of the sarcophagus. As on many Attic vases a rough sketch was first made with a pointed tool, then the paint was applied, large areas of red and blue predominating; but these areas and some slight departures from the obligatory contour style are not enough to suggest that free painting in Greece was in any way a higher art than that of the vase-painter in the Archaic period.

Syracuse

For much of its ancient history Syracuse was the leading Greek colony in Sicily. It owed its importance to its strategic position on a low promontory commanding two harbors, a small one to the north and the Grand Harbor, the largest in Sicily, to the south, while the heights of Epipolae dominated its rear (see map *opposite page*). The spring of Arethousa on the Ortygia peninsula provided fresh water. Not surprisingly, the Corinthians who settled here in 733 had to win the site from the local Sicel inhabitants. Not surprisingly, too, Syracuse still flourishes today, which makes excavation difficult. The few remains of the ancient city huddle amidst modern buildings, as shown below. The history of the ancient city was a stormy one. From 550 onward struggles for supremacy with other Sicilian cities were punctuated by major clashes with the Carthaginians while at home military dictators dominated the scene. Periods of constitutional government were fleeting and all too often terminated by bloody civil war. Interfering in local quarrels, the Athenians were disastrously defeated in 413, as memorialized by the historian Thucydides. Finally – and despite the ingenious defensive devices of the great mathematician and inventor, Archimedes – the city fell to the Romans in 212 BC.

The center of the ancient city was on the isthmus connecting Ortygia with the mainland, where a temple dedicated to Apollo and Artemis was built in about 560 BC. Its remains, cleared of the overlying medieval buildings some years ago, can still be seen today (*opposite page*) next door to the modern meat and vegetable markets. The Archaic market, on the other hand, along with later public buildings, seems to have been sited on the mainland, with the city cemeteries – which have provided the sole indication of the wealth of the city before the mid-6th century – spread out on the lower slopes behind. At this time the city was dominated by a ruling class of landowners, the Gamoroi, who were replaced by a short-lived democracy in 493. In 485 Gelon, tyrant of Gela, took the city, made it his capital and five years later soundly defeated the invading Carthaginians at Himera. It was the practice in those years for the rich tyrants of Sicily to make ostentatious dedications at Delphi and Olympia, and the famous bronze Charioteer of Delphi (*left*) was part of a team and car set up at Delphi in 474 by Polyzelos, brother of Gelon.

However in 465 the family tyranny collapsed, to give place again to a democracy. The destruction of the Athenian expeditionary force in 413 was followed by another and more serious invasion by Carthage, whose troops reached the city gates in 405. The hero who led the Syracusans to a precarious victory over the Carthaginians was the famous Dionysios, who set himself up as tyrant and in time brought much of the east coast of Sicily and parts of south Italy under his control. In the meantime, with a massive army equipped with the latest stone-throwing artillery, he besieged and captured Motya, the main Carthaginian post in the west, in 398.

And so it went – periods of democracy giving way to more frequent tyrannies, recurrent wars with Carthage, and under Hiero II a long alliance with Rome whose power was in the ascendant. Unwisely joining with Hannibal against Rome in 214, Syracuse was besieged by Marcellus and two years later fell. Archimedes, who almost saved the city, died in the debacle at the hands of a Roman soldier.

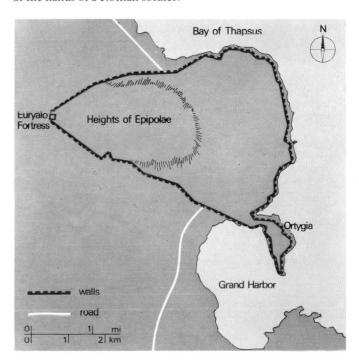

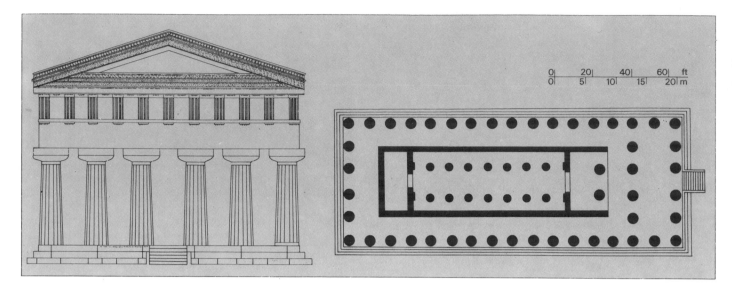

The Apollo temple (*above and p. 110*) is the earliest known stone temple in the western colonies, built in the second quarter of the 6th century. Modest remains still stand and testify to the early date with columns thicker-set than in any other temple, supporting a remarkably heavy entablature, originally decorated with painted terracotta revetments. Uniquely, there is a mason's signature cut on the upper step at the east end including some specific reference to the columns. In the plan we see already the influence of Ionic fashion, with emphasis placed on the porch.

Below: on the highest point of Ortygia was placed a temenos of Athena, graced with a wood and mudbrick temple first, but replaced with a stone temple around 500 BC. The fabric, complete with architrave and Doric frieze, has been built into the medieval cathedral, contrasting nicely with the baroque pilasters of the mid-18th-century facade. Orsi's excavation alongside the cathedral brought to light many objects dedicated to Athena – pottery, bronzes, faience and ivory – while below he uncovered the huts of the Sicels burned down by the Corinthian settlers.

The finest coin struck by the mint of Syracuse in the period 500–450 is a 10-drachma piece, known from less than 20 specimens – the so-called Demareteion. Once thought to have been struck from a gift of bullion given to Gelon's wife Demarete by the Carthaginians after their defeat in 480, as part of their indemnity, it is now recognized to have been struck about ten years later on some unknown occasion. The traditional chariot gains a Nike figure crowning its driver and a lion below. On the other side is the culmination of a series of fine heads of Arethousa, surrounded by four dolphins representing the sea lapping around Ortygia and her fountain. Some have seen the same hand in the die-carving for a single known specimen of a tetradrachm of Hiero's refounded Aetna (previously Katane) – another delicate masterpiece.

The aisle of the cathedral (*above*), the one flourishing example of pagan temple turned into Christian church. Many temples in Sicily, and indeed the Parthenon too, were converted to Christian use, but have since fallen into disuse. Close alongside the cathedral the Syracusans, in about 530, began to build the only known Sicilian temple in the Ionic order, but it was never completed and the scant remains lie in the cellar of the palace across the road. Had it been completed the Christian architects would have been faced with an embarrassing choice for their cathedral.

Found built into a Byzantine structure beside the cathedral was an exquisite marble torso of a Nike (winged victory) some 2 feet high (*right*). Nike figures were dedicated at many Greek sanctuaries from the late Archaic period onward, both for military and competitive victories. The first one was said to have been carved by a Chiot, Archermos, and it may well be a piece found in the excavations of Delos. This Syracusan example follows the Ionian pattern, with its soft modeling and cloak worn diagonally across the shoulders. The carving of the drapery folds suggests a date late in the 6th century.

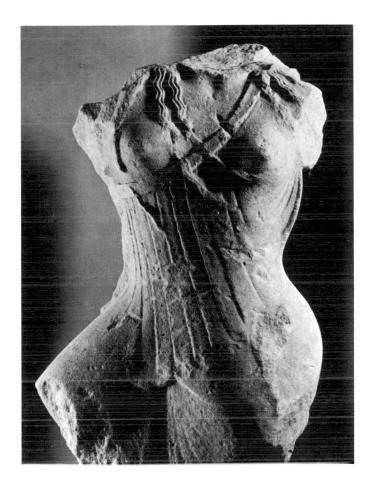

Above: during the 5th century the Syracuse mint continued to produce heads of charm and variety. Here we see three different hair-styles in vogue, together with a head in three-quarter view signed by the artist, Kimon, in about 410; he also adds the goddess's name, Arethousa.

As a thank-offering for his victory over the Etruscan fleet off Cumae in 474, Hiero sent captured spoils to Olympia and Delphi. The ship going to Delphi sank en route, but some of the Olympian armor has come to light. On the helmet (*below*) is a terse explanatory dedication: "Hiero, the son of Deinomenes, and the Syracusans, to Zeus, from (the spoils of) the Etruscans, from Cumae." The type of helmet is typically Etruscan, though another helmet with a similar dedication, found recently at Olympia, is of the standard Greek "Corinthian" type with nose and cheek guards. We may wonder which of Hiero's opponents wore it. During this period the tyrants took a keen interest in affairs north of Sicily, but later Syracusans were taken up by events closer to home, especially the warfare of the 420s and the Athenian invasion of Sicily in 415. The Athenian generals attempted to blockade the city by land and sea, and nearly succeeded in throwing a wall across Epipolae. Eventually, however, the marshy climate of the Great Harbor took its toll, a naval battle within the harbor was lost and the Athenian remnant fled up country. Nearly all were either killed, or captured and imprisoned in the quarries on the slopes above the city. The quarries were then no doubt of less extent than now, and did not enclose a botanical garden to afford some shade from the beating sun. Here we see, in the quarries (*below*), the so-called "Ear of Dionysios" – whose projects demanded much building stone.

Above: possession of the heights of Epipolae was of crucial importance for any attacker. Dionysios threw a wall around the whole perimeter and built a gate at the vulnerable west end. Succeeding generations continually sought to improve the works at this point (Euryalo), and in its final version – engineered, we are told, by the mathematician Archimedes – the gate itself is overshadowed by the huge artillery battery on the crag above with its complex of forward ditches and bastions, designed to keep the most modern machines out of range of the battery.

A postern gate (*below, left*) in the circuit wall of Epipolae below the strongpoint of Euryalo. The heart of these defenses was the main battery, which housed lesser pieces as well as five mammoth machines capable of throwing a 100lb stone to good effect 200 yards away. In front of the battery is a rock-cut ditch reached by a number of underground passages from inside the walls. These lead into a gallery (*below, right*) running along the inner side of the ditch, where lurking defenders could take infiltrating opponents nastily by surprise.

1

2

3

4

5

6

7

8

9

10

11

12

1. A silver decadrachm from dies cut by Kimon to celebrate the victory of 413. The set of armor below the chariot is often labeled "prizes" – perhaps for victors in contests instituted after the victory.

2. Gold coins as well as decadrachms were minted by Dionysios to pay his mercenaries. Euainetos was the artist who designed this piece, equivalent to two silver decadrachms and showing Herakles wrestling with the lion of Nemea.

3. A rare half-drachma issued jointly by Leontini and Katane in their last struggle with Dionysios. The bull of Katane joins a fine Apollo head of Leontini.

4. The Carthaginian posts attacked by Dionysios were issuing their own coins, closely modeled on Greek types. Motya used the crab and eagle of Akragas.

5. On this coin of Panormos the types copy Syracusan originals; the chariot (complete with Scylla in the exergue) was struck at Syracuse in 413, before the Arethousa head that accompanies it here.

6–7. With Timoleon's arrival in Syracuse (345 BC) coins very similar to those of Corinth were issued. On one of these pieces the archaic "koppa" (page 105) is even retained by the Syracusan mint.

8. Agathokles issued electrum coins to pay his mercenaries in the late 4th century. On this issue we see two heads of deities, Apollo and Artemis, on the same piece.

9. In imitation of Alexander and his successors Agathokles took the title "King," and on his gold staters he also borrows Alexander's types, the thunderbolt of Zeus and head of Athena.

10. Agathokles resumed minting silver tetradrachms. A fine head of Demeter is on the obverse of this piece, showing a Nike decorating a trophy of captured arms.

11. The coinage of Hiero II (275–215) is very extensive. A frequent tetradrachm type bears the old chariot design on the reverse with the head of Hiero's wife, Philistis, on the face, as shown here.

12. The head of Hiero himself appears far more rarely. We see it on some bronze issues, and here on an isolated tetradrachm from early in his reign – a piece of coronation propaganda.

The wheatfields of Sicily supplied Rome, as they had supplied Greece in earlier centuries. Mainland Greece was particularly dependent on imported wheat in the later 4th century – at Athens a man from Akragas was praised for his diligence in this respect. It is no surprise then to find the cult of Demeter so firmly rooted and the humble wheat-ear elevated to the heights seen in this magnificent 3rd-century gold spray – found in 1900 in a tomb near Syracuse, perhaps of a priestess of Demeter. It underlines the prosperity of Hiero's reign. He seized control of Syracuse in 269 BC.

The remains of Greek Syracuse lie embedded in the modern town. Arabic inscriptions are cut on the walls of the Apollo temple, the cathedral retains its religious importance, the fountain of Arethousa, now tainted with salt water, is a pastiche of architectural fragments of different ages, and the excavated theater is once more used for public entertainment.

The coins of Syracuse, too, were rediscovered. One of Euainetos' decadrachms of the early 4th century was set in a gold band, perhaps in northern Italy in the years around 1200 AD, and graced with a fine inscription, "quia pretium sanguinis est," a quotation from Matthew (ch. 29) relating the betrayal of Jesus by Judas for 30 pieces of silver. The pious owner of the piece took the head of Arethousa, with her wreath of wheat-ears, for the thorn-crowned head of Jesus. It is the earliest known example of this particular interpretation of rediscovered ancient coins, but one that was soon fostered by the crusaders passing through Rhodes, with her coins bearing the head of Helios surrounded by the sun's rays.

6. The Greek West

In ships such as this the early Greeks sailed west to found their colonies in Italy and Sicily. The cup, signed by Exekias, the leading Athenian painter of around 540, was found in an Etruscan tomb. It shows Dionysus with the Etruscan pirates whom he had transformed into dolphins.

Our knowledge of the political history of the western colonies in the Archaic period is extremely sparse. Herodotus and Thucydides allude to events in the area from time to time, but one of our main sources is Diodorus of Agyrion in Sicily, below Etna, who patched together a universal history in the 1st century BC. He drew his material from a number of earlier writers but abbreviated their accounts drastically and put accurate chronology second to a nicely ordered flow of pedestrian narrative.

Sicily before the battle of Himera.

Early in the 6th century the last major colonies were planted, about 150 years after the first Greek settlement on Sicily. Syracuse secured her control in the southeast by founding Camarina in 598, and Gela expanded westward along the coast to Acragas in 580. One of the various wars mentioned in our sources is the destruction of Camarina by Syracuse in 552, apparently for not following her line of suppressing the Sicels; excavation, however, tells us that Camarina still existed after this date.

In the west of the island we have noted the attempts of the Cnidians under Pentathlus and the followers of Dorieus of Sparta to settle at Eryx in about 580 and 510 respectively. They were repulsed by the local Elymians together with the Phoenicians from Motya. The Cnidians settled on the island of Lipari, adopting a communist society, albeit with the few native islanders as slaves. Dorieus had previously attempted to found a colony in another area of Phoenician influence at Cinyps in Libya; he was killed at Eryx, but his few surviving would-be colonists remained to cause trouble for the Greeks at Selinus and Minoa. The latter was a coastal outpost of Selinus, later taken by Theron, tyrant of Acragas.

We also saw the rise of the tyranny at Gela, where Cleander was succeeded by his brother Hippocrates in 497. A series of hard campaigns won him the whole of the east of the island by 491 save for Syracuse, which was forced to hand over Camarina as a result of mediation by Corinth and Corcyra, and Zancle, where Hippocrates was bought off by a body of aristocratic exiles from Samos, fleeing after the collapse of the Ionian revolt; on treacherously taking the city from the control of Anaxilas, tyrant of Rhegion across the water, they appeased Hippocrates with half the property and slaves and most of the free inhabitants as well. Anaxilas eventually regained the town in 487 and installed Messenians in flight from the Peloponnese after a revolt against Sparta.

Hippocrates' successor was Gelon, one of his commanders. It was he who eventually took Syracuse and transferred his seat of power there in 485. He also transferred the inhabitants of Megara Hyblaea and Camarina – the latter only recently "recolonized" by Hippocrates. This began a long sequence of population shifts in Sicily and Italy carried out merely to suit the political and strategic convenience of military rulers. When Theron of Acragas took Minoa he may even have moved

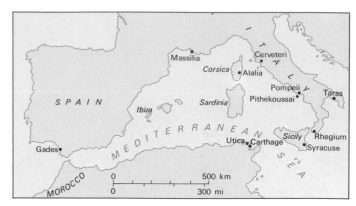

The principal colonial settlements of the western Mediterranean.

its site a few miles nearer Acragas, but his main aim was to take Himera, which he did in 483, thus giving himself control over both coasts of the island. We saw how the ousted tyrant of Himera, Terillus, turned to Carthage for assistance, and the subsequent victory of Gelon and Theron before Himera in 480. It is worth stressing the number of Greeks who opposed the Acragas/Syracuse coalition – not only Terillus, but also Rhegion and Selinus, while Hamilcar, the Carthaginian commander, had a Syracusan wife.

The tyrants of Acragas and Syracuse gained not only prestige from their victory, but also a huge indemnity and many captives, who were set to work at Himera, Syracuse and Acragas on the temples built to commemorate their defeat. The largest Doric temple ever attempted was built just inside the city walls at Acragas, with unique Atlas figures supporting the architrave on their shoulders.

Phoenicians in the west.

This was probably the second large-scale Carthaginian intervention in Sicilian affairs. The early history of this colony of Tyre is as obscure as that of the rest of the western world, depending on much the same source material, very little of which is known to stem from Carthage itself.

Carthage was one of a number of settlements dispatched westward from Phoenicia in the Early Iron Age. As in the case of the Greek colonies, we find Phoenician settlements mainly beside the sea on promontories or sometimes offshore islands, as Tyre and Arados in the homeland. At Kition on Cyprus in the 10th century the Mycenaean temple provided the foundations for a shrine of Astarte, and further Cypriot settlements followed. Further west, literary sources give a number of foundation dates for the colonies, which are most difficult to reconcile with available archaeological evidence. Pliny and other writers place Utica, on the north coast of Tunisia, and Gades (Cadiz) in Spain around 1100 BC, with Carthage 287 years later in 814. No material persuasively earlier than about 740 has been found at Carthage or Utica, while Cadiz has been little explored owing to the difficulties of excavating in the modern city.

Above: the acropolis ridge at Velia south of Paestum. Beneath the lighthouse are the remains of a Doric temple and around it the walls of the original 6th-century colony.

Below: a model in cork of the gigantic temple of Zeus at Agrigento. It was built after 480 as a memorial of the defeat of the Carthaginians that year. The Atlas figures hint at the subjection of the African people.

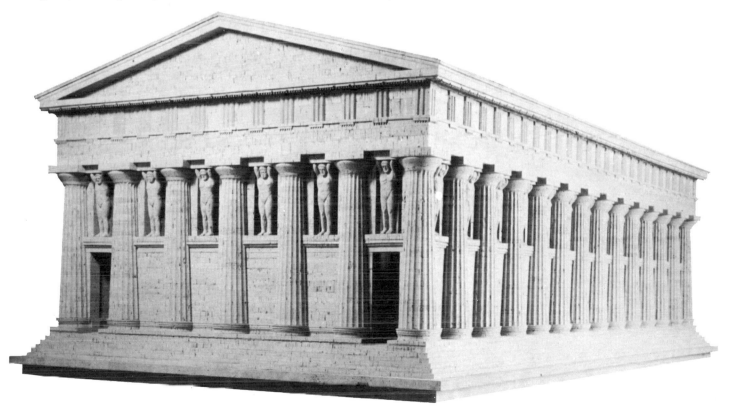

Excavation has yielded further evidence for Phoenician expansion in the 8th century. Thucydides speaks of Phoenicians trading in western Sicily before the Greeks arrived, though the only sign of this noted so far is some possible eastern influence on local Sicel pottery and metalwork; more tangible is a Phoenician embossed bronze bowl which was discovered in an 8th-century grave at Francavilla near Sybaris. In the west of Sicily the earliest material from Motya is contemporary with that of Carthage, while to the north a very few finds on Sardinia suggest a slightly earlier date for the first Phoenician arrivals. They were no doubt in search of the island's mineral wealth, and may have arrived at the same time as Euboeans came to Pithekoussai.

Yet further west, recent excavations have established a Phoenician presence in southern Spain in the late 8th and 7th centuries. There can be no doubt that the main attraction was once again the mineral riches of gold, silver, copper, iron (the use of which the Phoenicians probably introduced) and tin, the last mentioned brought from northwest Spain as well as Brittany and Cornwall. The valley of the Guadalquivir river (the region which went under the name of Tartessus in Greek) was the focal point for a thriving native industry in gold and bronze work, which was considerably boosted by the arrival of Phoenician merchants and ideas. A Greek fable expressed the wealth of the area by telling how the amount of silver obtained by one Phoenician captain for his cargo was so great that he had to resort to replacing his lead anchors with ones of silver.

Phoenician expansion continued through the 7th century with settlements along the Atlantic coast of Morocco and also in Algeria, Tunisia, Sicily and Sardinia. Carthage is said to have sent colonists to Ibiza in the middle of the century, though Majorca remained untouched. The increasing pace of colonization must have been connected with increasing pressure at home, where Assyria was a constant threat during these years, inflicting apparently severe defeats on some of the Phoenician cities by 671. The colonies were dependent on the homeland in many respects, but display differences among themselves in aspects of culture, as indeed do the Greek foundations. In southern Spain a school of ivory-carving emerges, while at Carthage and elsewhere we often find grotesque terracotta masks in graves. However, artistic achievement was largely on a low level and Egyptian-inspired, and the colonists did not spend their acquired wealth on temples and dedications in the way the Greeks did. At Toscanos in southwest Spain the only considerable architectural remains of the period have been found, consisting of a large building with an eastern ground plan and part of a fortification wall of large, well-squared blocks, strangely similar to a contemporary wall at Leontini.

Our knowledge of early Carthage is at present slight and poorly published. It comes mainly from a few cemeteries and a Topheth, the gruesome depository for the ritual child sacrifices or "molk," carried out in the colonies long after their apparent abandonment in Phoenicia. These deposits were often marked by headstones which by the 6th century carry a variety of carved or painted decoration, stylistically impoverished and eventually owing much to Greek influence, though solidly based on Phoenician iconography.

Greek artifacts are found fairly frequently in the colonies – about 100 sherds have been excavated at Toscanos, and modest Corinthian vases are common enough at Motya and Carthage, while Cypriot pottery of the 7th and 6th centuries has been found at Toscanos and Mogador. Early 6th-century graves at Carthage contain good numbers of vases in the unmistakable soapy dark gray ware of Etruria, known as bucchero (found on Greek sites as well – Camarina, Metapontum, Corinth, Samos), and during the same period and even earlier the Etruscans were carrying on a brisk trade with settlements in southern France.

Rivalries in the west. The relationship between Greeks, Etruscans and Carthaginians in the western Mediterranean poses challenging problems, rarely elucidated by any clear correlation between the archaeological material and what meager literary evidence we have. Some modern historians have posited a system of trading cartels and protectionism which rests on insufficient evidence and much anachronistic economic theory, yet it would be going against the grain of human nature to deny any attempts by individuals or states to protect their own interests and markets as best they could, if they believed competition would not be in those interests. A perusal of the extent of interaction between the peoples concerned will reveal the complexity of the actual situation.

In the far west some Phoenician posts additional to Lixus and Mogador were established in Morocco in the 6th century and become more recognizably Carthaginian. In Spain the south is still dominated by Phoenician and Carthaginian influence and imports; the one Greek colony said to have been planted in the area, Mainake, has not been located and was probably short-lived. Herodotus relates how Colaeus of Samos "discovered" Tartessus in about 630 and the men of Phocaea developed the trade with Spain, but the founding of Himera and then Selinus, soon after Carthage colonized Ibiza, suggests that Sicilians too were interested in profiting from trade with the Phoenician colonies. In later years Selinus more often sided with Carthage than neighboring Greeks.

The Phoenician element on Malta seems to have kept closer links with the east than other colonies did, and certainly mixed peacefully with the native inhabitants, probably taking wives from among them. We are told this was the case at Carthage in its early years, and it is also suggested by the amount of native handmade pottery found at Motya. Peaceful coexistence seems to have prevailed in Spain, but in Sardinia there are clear signs of a

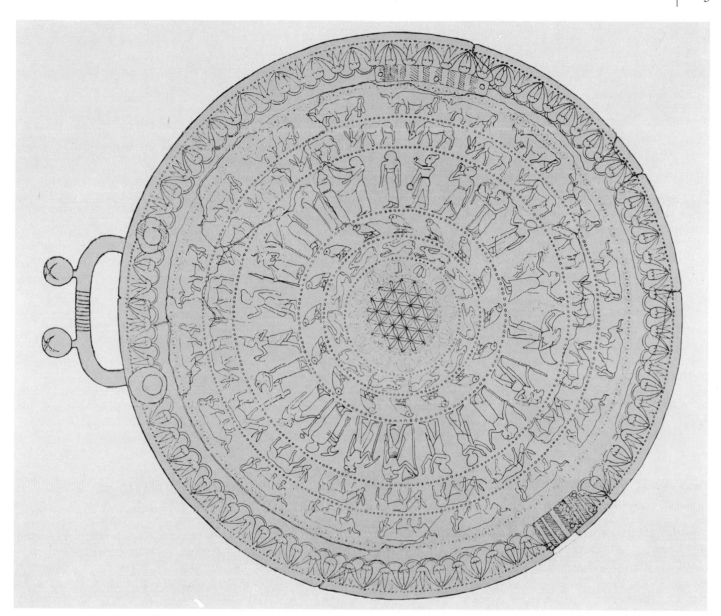

Phoenician or Phoenician-inspired embossed bronze bowl from an 8th-century tomb at Francavilla, a native settlement on the hillside above Sybaris in Italy.

more aggressive policy, with Phoenician outposts guarding the river valleys while the Sardinians strengthen their walls elsewhere.

In Sicily Motya clearly flourished in the 7th and 6th centuries, probably outgrowing the bounds of the original island site, which was fortified in about 600. The very site of Archaic Solous is disputed, though it was probably by the sea close to the Hellenistic Greek town of the same name. Although at Palermo the medieval and modern city hampers the excavation of Panormus, it becomes increasingly clear that here there were Greeks living cheek by jowl with Phoenicians from some time in the 6th century onward. We can judge that the west was still open to Greek traders from the large amounts of presumably Spanish silver used for Sicilian coinage in the later 6th

century and from the high proportion of tin regularly found in Archaic Greek bronzes.

Yet the picture of general goodwill does become clouded. Greeks rapidly occupied areas of the Mediterranean where Phoenicians had not settled; in Libya Cyrene and her colonies were founded after the setbacks suffered by Tyre and Sidon, and were able to exercise some control over one of the main routes westward. After Rhodian pioneers had opened up contacts, Phocaeans founded Massilia in about 600 and soon developed trade along the French coast as far as Ampurias, as well as up the Rhône valley, to the detriment of the previous Etruscan commerce. A major aim here may have been to tap the tin routes from Brittany via the Rhône and from Spain through the Mediterranean coast, both independent of routes through the straits of Gibraltar. Soon after, Pentathlus troubled areas of Phoenician influence in the west of Sicily, and an inscription set up in the sanctuary of Hera on Samos in about 575 tells of some Samian adventurers taking part in a victory won by Himera over the local Sicans – a Samian interest in the area which had not previously been suspected.

Not long after this comes the Carthaginian Malcho's campaign in unspecified areas of Sicily and then in Sardinia. A relic of the hostilities of this period is the tombstone of a Selinuntine who fell in battle beneath the walls of Motya; yet at the same time Greeks and Phoenicians were living together in harmony at Panormus. Another contemporary event was the settling of Phocaeans at Alalia on Corsica; from there they harassed Etruscan, Carthaginian and more than likely Greek shipping. The Cnidians on Lipari set up two extravagant dedications at Delphi as thank-offerings for victories over Etruscan fleets – and indeed Etruscans also made dedications at both Delphi and Olympia. Yet all this time Etruria was importing huge quantities of Greek artifacts.

From such an uneven pattern of evidence it would be foolish to extract sweeping conclusions about national or ethnic enmities or friendships. Only in one area does a consistent pattern seem to emerge – the strongly Phocaean domination of the south of France throughout the 6th century. Even here the Ionian wine amphoras and cups which replace the Etruscan trade give way in turn to local Massiliote products, and we should not forget the Vix krater. This is of Peloponnesian manufacture, and is one of a series of 6th-century bronze masterpieces sent from Greece to the Balkans and further north, though none is so magnificently preserved.

Two precious documents of the years around 500 shed further light on the question of western interrelationships. We have noted the gold plaques found at the port of Cerveteri, Pyrgi, with their inscribed texts in Punic and Etruscan. Although they refer only to the regulation of affairs in the two temples sited in the port, they prove a long-suspected Carthaginian influence at Pyrgi. The second document is a treaty quoted by the two historians of early Rome, the Greek Polybius and Italian Livy, which defines areas in which the respective parties, Carthage and Rome, could ply their trade in the western Mediterranean. The two authors unfortunately assign different dates to the agreement, but there are good reasons for accepting Polybius' 509, the year in which Rome gained independence from the Tarquinii. We may conclude that Carthage already had such agreements with the Etruscans, and possibly some Greek states as well. In particular the Romans were required not to sail past a certain cape north of Carthage, presumably westward towards Gibraltar, or if carried there by contrary winds not to carry on any trading activities. Amasis of Egypt laid down similar rules for the Greeks using Naucratis 50 years before.

When we are discussing the 6th century the use of the adjectives "Phoenician," "Carthaginian" and "Punic" (the latter implying "belonging to the wider field of Carthaginian influence") is not a simple choice. It depends much on subjective impressions about when links with the homeland become so weak and the growing influence of Carthage among all the colonies so strong that a shift of emphasis is necessary. The start of this process can be seen in events in Phoenicia in 671 and the founding of Ibiza by Carthage, and it has clearly been largely completed with the expedition of Malcho. Certainly, Phoenician fleets are confined to service with the Persian kings from about 525 until the spectacular capture of Tyre by Alexander in 331. For the western colonies we are desperately ill-informed about events of the 5th and 4th centuries; only where Greeks become involved, as in 480, do we have any reasonable narrative. This means that for most areas, especially Spain, our knowledge is almost purely archaeological, and while Greek civilization aspires to its highest level in these centuries, Carthage and the other Punic settlements go through a period of relative stagnation.

Carthage experienced political changes at this time. The family of Mago, of whom Hamilcar was a member, had been heads of state since Malcho's failure in Sardinia, but after three generations were replaced by a system of selected suffetes, "Judges," though an oligarchic council of 100 seems to have existed throughout. However, a further contributory factor to Carthaginian inactivity was the defeat inflicted on her Etruscan allies by Hiero's Syracusan fleet at Cumae in 474. The dedication of helmets, among other spoils, to Zeus at Olympia by Hiero says much for the character of naval engagements at the time.

The early history of the Italian colonies. Cumae had taken over the role of Pithekoussai as the most northerly of the Greek colonies on the mainland, and carried on a brisk trade with the inland towns of Capua and Nola. A combined attack by Etruscans and Daunians was beaten off in 524, and troops were reluctantly sent to the aid of the Romans and their allies in revolt against the Etruscans in 506. Their leader, Aristodemus, after winning a victory at Aricia in Latium, set himself up as tyrant and demagogue; his name is painted as black as that of Phalaris in the tradition that has come down to us.

Other Greek settlements arose around the Bay of Naples. Dicaearchia was founded by Samian refugees from Polycrates' tyranny in 531, on the site of later Pozzuoli. Naples itself is of doubtful vintage; traditionally a Rhodian foundation of before the first Olympiad, some material of the early 7th century has been recovered. We can be more certain of the expansion of the colony in 470 under Cumaean leadership, when its name was changed from Parthenope to Neapolis. Another famous Roman site, Pompeii, housed Greeks in the Archaic period, but was a mixed settlement, as is shown by the peculiarities of its early 6th-century Doric temple.

All these colonies came under pressure from inland tribes in the 5th century, especially after the weakening of Etruscan control in the area after the battle of Cumae.

Right: the temple of Athena at Paestum, constructed in about 520, viewed from the west. The inner walls of all the Paestum temples have almost completely disappeared.

Below: the second temple of Hera at Paestum, c. 430. The steps in the foreground lead up to the cella, whose ceiling is supported by columns.

Left: a unique painted sarcophagus from Paestum, dating from about 480. The inside of the lid depicts a young diver plunging from an elaborate platform. It may be a memorial to an athlete or may have a symbolic significance.

These tribes were of Indo-European origin – Samnites and Lucanians who spoke the Oscan language. Cumae fell to them in 420, Dicaearchia probably soon after, although Neapolis stood against them, as did Velia further south. The capture of Posidonia towards the end of the century resulted in the change of name to Paestum, clearly demonstrated in the coin series.

Further south the Greek colonies also had to deal with hostile neighbors, but these seem to have been fellow Greeks as often as indigenous peoples. We know virtually nothing of their political history before the later 6th century; in about 530 the Ionian foundation of Siris was destroyed by the combined forces of her Achaean neighbors, and probably soon after they turned their attention to little Locri, whose subsequent victory was soon to become a legend.

Archaeological evidence, especially from Taranto and

Sybarite sway in the later 6th century, and archaeological evidence suggests that Greeks lived in a number of them. At Francavilla, just above Sybaris itself, Greek-style sanctuaries were constructed and dedications were made there by successful Greeks. Croton was in more restricted territory, and after being thwarted in her southward expansion by Locri seems to have turned jealous eyes northward. Pythagoras the mathematician, exiled from Samos, settled in Croton in about 530, where his mystical religious views combined with forceful oligarchic leanings to have a powerful influence on affairs. His political "societies" were no doubt among those who urged an attack against the demagogic tyrant of Sybaris, Telys, who had had murdered 30 Crotoniate envoys sent to explain their city's refusal to hand over oligarchic refugees from Telys' rule. Sybaris may not have been unprepared for conflict; a copy on bronze of an alliance between the city

Locri and increasingly from Sybaris, reveals the same prosperity as elsewhere in the west. The quantities of imported Ionian cups found at Sybaris, as well as many other sites, nicely demonstrate reports of special ties between Sybaris and Miletus. From about 550 onwards such vases and also Greek bronzes, armor and architectural ideas permeate up the river valleys from Metapontum and Sybaris. A number of the colonies plant secondary settlements on the west coast – Croton at Terina, Locri at Hipponion (later Vibo) and Sybaris at Laos and Pyxous – strongly suggesting that they were using portage routes (at least in emergencies) across the toe of Italy, avoiding the Straits of Messina, where the Chalcidian colonists were perhaps not always ready to allow passage.

Sybaris had by this time become a byword for luxurious living, and her situation was certainly excellent regarding both local farming and trade with many parts of the mountainous hinterland. The Ionian geographer Hecataeus compiled a list of 25 native towns under

and her allies with an unknown people called the Serdaioi has been found at Olympia, and must date to the years before 510 when Croton attacked and destroyed Sybaris. The victory was followed by an ostentatious issue of coins from Croton in alliance with a number of towns in the area, including the remnants of the Sybarites themselves.

Croton probably held a position of supremacy in south Italy for much of the early 5th century. Taras and perhaps Metapontum too were under greater pressure from native populations than was the Achaean colony. Certainly Taras, in alliance with Anaxilas of Rhegion, suffered an extremely severe defeat at the hands of the Messapians and Peucetians in 473, although dedications of bronze sculpture at Delphi by the Tarentines for victories over each of these tribes indicate that they were able at least to hold their own. Anaxilas sought Tarentine friendship because of increasing pressure exerted by Syracuse; Rhegine dedications at Olympia come from a battle against Locri and the Syracusans in 477. In the next year we hear of the

Sybarite remnants calling in Syracusan aid against Croton.

The refoundation of Sybaris brought Athens to the west. More than one attempt was made in the 450s before it emerged under Athenian sponsorship as a Panhellenic colony named Thurii, but in spite of the adoption of Athena's head on the coinage, the colony never became a really trustworthy ally of Athens. The new colonists soon had to contend with Tarentine aggression over possession of the lands which once belonged to Siris to the north. Eventually they settled their differences long enough to found a joint colony in 432 near or possibly on the old site of Siris, giving it the full-blooded Doric name of Heraclea. Not long after, all the colonies were faced with the takeover of the hinterland by the Lucanians, a branch of the tribe who captured Posidonia around 400, and the 4th century saw them squeezed between Italians and new tyrants of Syracuse.

interior, now well Hellenized. After some initial successes he was forced to seek sanctuary in Syracuse, from where he was exiled to Corinth. Many of the Greek sites of the interior that have been excavated have thick, burned levels, proving the destruction wrought upon them by the victorious Sicels. Ducetius was allowed to return to Sicily and founded a colony at Kale Acte on the north coast; the Acragantines were sufficiently upset by Syracuse allowing this for a war to break out between them.

So despite the return of constitutional government, and democracy at least at Syracuse, there seems to have been no end to inter-city hostilities. Selinus and Segesta remained at enmity; elsewhere ill-feeling tended to polarize Dorian and Ionian colonies, especially Syracuse and her Ionian neighbors, Leontini in particular. There was much campaigning in the 420s, in which the Athenians intervened to slight effect on behalf of the Ionians.

A handsome Attic cup painted by "the Lydian" and found in a tomb at Taranto. It shows (left) a duel being halted by a man in the presence of the warriors' white-haired fathers. The other side portrays Herakles in a winged chariot guided by Hermes, being conveyed to his eternal home in Olympus, where his mentor Athena will introduce him to Zeus and his enemy Hera.

Below: the major Greek, Carthaginian and Sicel sites in Sicily. Many of the Sicel sites were taken over by Greeks or were thoroughly Hellenized by the 5th century.

Sicily between the Carthaginian invasions. Despite their military and Olympic successes the tyrannies of Acragas and Syracuse did not last long after 480. Theron was deposed in 472 and Acragas lost control of Himera at the same time. To the east Hiero continued his predecessors' practice of population removals by installing Naxians and Catanians near at hand in Leontini, replacing them with various new settlers and changing the name of Catane to Aetna. Discontent grew as a result of such autocratic treatment; Gela seems to have fallen away first, and at Syracuse Hiero's son Thrasybulus was removed from power after only a few months in 465. The exiles returned to their homes, Camarina was refounded a second time and the tyrants' mercenaries were left to roam the island fending for themselves.

The Sicels, led by Ducetius, helped the Syracusans attack Hiero's colonists in Aetna/Catane. Soon afterwards he struck out on his own to set up a strong Sicel empire, launching his attacks from a number of Sicel towns of the

A metope from temple C at Selinus in Sicily shows Europa brought across the sea on a bull by Zeus. A striking feature of all the sculptures of this period (around 550) is the way in which the heads are turned to face the visitor to the shrine.

Despite a peace settlement in 424 quarrels broke out once more, together with a further round of bickering between Selinus and Segesta, which caused the dispatch of a very large force from Athens in 415. After a desultory and difficult siege of Syracuse, the Athenians lost a naval battle within the confines of the Grand Harbor and were cut to pieces on the retreat up the river Anopos in 413. Thanks to the full narrative of Thucydides, this is the best-known and most clearly documented episode in Sicilian history.

Athenian ignorance of Sicilian conditions was a large factor in their defeat, but so was the help sent to Syracuse from Corinth and Sparta. In return Syracuse and Selinus sent triremes to assist Sparta in the war against Athens in the Aegean, under Hermocrates, a capable general who had won his spurs during the siege. A democratic backlash at Syracuse in 410 led to his recall and replacement; he decided to obtain Persian gold and try to force his way back into Syracuse, but by the time he returned to Sicily a new phase in the island's history had begun to unfold.

Carthage returns to the offensive. An appeal by Segesta against Selinuntine aggression had once more brought Carthaginian forces to the island, this time in the shape of a very sizable army led by Hannibal, who soon made it clear that Carthage was looking for revenge for the events of 480. In 409 Himera and Selinus were

destroyed; the Carthaginians did not return till 406, by which time Hermocrates had established himself in the ruins of Selinus and had gathered adherents for an attempt on Syracuse. This was delivered unsuccessfully in 407, but one of his followers (and son-in-law), Dionysius, managed to get elected to the board of generals the following year and was soon given absolute powers against the renewed Carthaginian assault. In 406 Acragas submitted to a siege, and in the next year Gela was abandoned and Syracuse invested. An outbreak of disease in the Carthaginian camp came to the latter's rescue, and Dionysius was able to conclude a treaty recognizing Carthaginian control of the western part of the island and the independence of Greek cities on the east coast.

Dionysius did not remain inactive. He ignored the treaty by taking Catane and Naxos and selling the inhabitants into slavery, and then attempted to take over Rhegion and Messana. Failing with the former, he contracted a marriage with the daughter of a leading Locrian (taking a Syracusan wife at the same time). Diodorus describes at length the preparations which he made for renewed war against the Carthaginians, stressing the number and quality of the armorers he brought to Syracuse, the enrollment of mercenaries and the experiments with catapults. In 398 Dionysius set out west and took Motya after a difficult siege. The town never recovered its position, though excavation has proved that it was inhabited subsequently. A new settlement arose nearby at Lilybaeum where deeper water was available for shipping than in the shallow lagoon at Motya. After the fall of Motya the Carthaginians soon retaliated and reached the walls of Syracuse; but again we are told that plague struck and Dionysius was able to defeat the depleted forces and regain control of "Greek" Sicily.

Italians, Sicels and Greeks. The relations between the Greeks and natives over the years varied considerably. The founding of some colonies saw the decline or abandonment of nearby settlements, though elsewhere, especially in the areas occupied by the Chalcidians, coexistence can be demonstrated. In the toe of Italy at Torre Galli and near Locri Greek potters seem to have been at work in native settlements of the 8th and 7th centuries. Further north the villages near Sybaris had early contacts with the Greeks, though standards seem to have been depressed for most of the 7th and early 6th century when the Greeks were consolidating their hold on the plains of the coastal strip. During the 6th century both in Sicily and Italy Greek influence and imports increase – vases and metalwork are imported and imitated, Greek architectural styles copied and by 500 some places were striking Greek-inspired coinage. The process seems to have been more thorough in the enclosed environment of Sicily than up the river valleys of southern Italy. Hostilities seem to have resulted mainly from Greek expansion, especially on the part of the tyrants of Acragas and Syracuse, which destroyed the

The late 5th-century
Doric temple at Segesta
still stands unfinished,
with its columns unfluted
and the interior never
begun. Though the city
was peopled by non-
Greek Elymians, Athens
made an alliance with her
which led to the Athenian
disaster at Syracuse in 413
and presumably the
collapse of the Segestan
treasury.

established system of landholdings. We have seen the struggles of Taras against the local populations, and may note that Taras and Thurii enrolled the support of opposing sets of tribes in the wars of the 440s. Athens sought non-Greek aid during the Sicilian expedition, winning assistance from Caere in Etruria and from the Campanians, whose mercenary service for Carthaginians and Syracuse was a prominent feature of later Sicilian and Italian warfare.

The 4th century. In our visual story we followed the succession of events at Syracuse down to its capture by Roman forces in 212. With the exception of Taras, no other city is able to make any lasting impression on the history of the 4th and 3rd centuries. Although our sources have no doubt preserved for us the major episodes of the period, we should note that they are concerned mainly with the personalities who emerged and the battles that were fought and not with other aspects of life. Indeed they are virtually silent about many of the colonies. We should also note that much of the material preserved for us goes back to two contemporary writers with something of an ax to grind – Philistus, a trusted general of Dionysius, and Timaeus of Tauromenion, whose father assisted in the overthrow of Dionysius' son in 344 and who himself was exiled from Sicily by Agathocles.

The wars of the late 5th century had brought chaos to Sicily, and the first half of the 4th saw further depletions of resources, with many towns deserted or leading a token existence. Dionysius continued with the population game, settling Campanian mercenaries at Entella and Catane in 404–403, other mercenaries at Leontini in 396, and planting a mixed settlement in captured Messana in 389. What he did not capture or control was in Carthaginian hands, as finds of Punic cults and material in 4th-century Selinus testify. Only Syracuse and the Carthaginians were able to continue coining in gold and silver, and this merely to supply pay to mercenaries, despite the high artistic quality of the products. Elsewhere 5th-century coin met 4th-century needs.

In Italy many of the Greek states apart from Syracuse's ally Locri had formed a league led by Croton to oppose the Lucanians. When Dionysius attacked Rhegion in 393 to counter the Carthaginian capture of Messana, the League came to her support and did so again in 390. Dionysius disowned a peace treaty between the League and the Lucanians negotiated by his brother-in-law and admiral Leptines, by returning to the attack in 389, taking Caulonia and defeating the League forces, which were led by a Syracusan exile. Rhegion fell after a ten-month siege in 386, and the lesser colonies were captured more or less en route. Rhegion and Locri were the favorite haunts of the younger Dionysius after his father's death in 367, until he returned to hold precarious power at Syracuse for a few years after 346.

By this time Taras had emerged as champion of the Italian Greek cities under Archytas, a military leader whose exact dates "in power" are unknown, but were certainly in the 360s and 350s. Archytas had a strong interest in Pythagoreanism and the moral instruction of the Tarentines. Plato is said to have conversed with him on his journeys to the west in his fruitless attempts to convert the soft-living younger Dionysius into his ideal Philosopher King. From the evidence we have, consisting mainly of sculpture, pottery and jewelry, it would seem that Taras flourished during these years, when she extended her control over many of the neighboring tribes and planted colonies among them. Syracuse was an ally, a fact which accounts, in part at least, for the elder Dionysius' passing interest in the affairs of the Adriatic around 385, when he established a post at Lissus on the Dalmatian coast and allied himself with Alcetas, king of the Molossi in Epirus.

To maintain her position against the Messapian and Lucanian tribes Taras subsequently had recourse to various external sources of aid. First to help was a Spartan king, Archidamus, who died in Italy, then another Molossian king, a namesake of Alexander the Great (in fact both his uncle and brother-in-law). The latter crossed to Italy in 333 in hopes of emulating his Macedonian relative, and indeed campaigned with some success until his death in 331, though in the meantime he had broken with the Tarentines.

Between Rome and Epirus. By this time the power of Rome was already more than just a speck on the horizon. From 327 the Romans were campaigning bitterly against the Samnites of Campania and the interior, and in that year Naples came to terms with Rome. In this series of campaigns the Lucanians were for much of the time allies of Rome and still hostile to Taras. A peace treaty between all three parties was concluded in 302. In 325 the Athenians sent a colony to Spina under the leadership of a descendant of the great Miltiades – a move clearly designed to secure supplies of corn from the Po valley, as the preserved foundation charter specifies.

Taras capitulated to Rome in 272, and her allies were in no position to do otherwise, but much had happened in the decade 282–272. The old hostility between Taras and Thurii led to the latter appealing for aid from Rome when faced with yet further waves of pressure from the Lucanians in the years 284–282. In contravention of the treaty of 302, a Roman garrison arrived in 282 and other Greek cities, Croton and Locri included, accepted Roman troops. For the last time Taras looked abroad for help and found it with another Molossian king, Pyrrhus, who cut his losses in the mighty squabbles of the successors of Alexander and crossed to Italy in 280. For five years he campaigned at the head of a mixed army of Illyrians, Greeks and Italians, winning notable victories over

A view along the scarp and southern wall of Agrigento, from the porch of the "temple of Juno" to the finely preserved "temple of Concord," both 5th-century Doric shrines.

Roman armies and at one stage gaining control of all Sicily save Lilybaeum. But his victories were expensive – "Pyrrhic" – and his aims too high; his ambitions in Greece too contributed to his decision to return home in 274, after a defeat at Beneventum, when his elephants were captured and the beast made its first appearance at Rome. Taras' resistance soon crumbled, and in 272 she became an independent ally of Rome.

Sicily and the rulers of Syracuse. In Syracuse the return from exile of the younger Dionysius did not put an end to internal power struggles. An appeal made by one of the parties to the mother city Corinth resulted in the dispatch of a 70-year-old general named Timoleon with a small and motley force to restore order in the island. Although he was only active in Sicily for six or seven years, his success in restoring stability and constitutional government, as well as in throwing back the Carthaginians, was somewhat more lasting. In the archaeological record we find time after time the destruction levels of the late 5th century being followed by a renewed building activity in the "Timoleontic" period, lasting far longer than those few active years.

The next figure to feature prominently in our sources is Agathocles, although much of what they have to say about him concerns his mean birth and debased nature and is probably largely fiction. He rose to power through a military career both in Syracusan service and as a condottiere in Italy and Sicily, securing a position as generalissimo in Syracuse in 317, largely through the support of his mercenary troops. He did not find it easy to root his tyranny; Syracusan exiles stirred up the other Greek cities against him and consecutively called in a banished, and as it turned out ineffective, Spartan prince, Acrotatus, and the Carthaginians to assist them in removing the tyrant. The renewed spirit of independence among the cities stemmed from the Timoleontic revival (which included the influx of many new colonists from Greece), and archaeology and written sources show that Acragas and Gela were among the leading contenders. In 311–310 the Carthaginians with their Greek allies were pressing hard on Syracuse itself, when Agathocles took a gamble such as few leaders have dared. He set sail with a large force to attack the Carthaginians at home, and in unsuspecting Libya he met with considerable success, campaigning there till 307, though unable to take Carthage itself. It was during this period he adopted the title "king" in imitation of the successors of Alexander. His return to Sicily was caused partly by a lack of resources to pay his mercenaries, and partly by a worsening state of affairs at home, where his generals had relieved the siege of Syracuse and held the city for him, but where he still had many enemies, both within the city and in the rest of the island. So he made peace with Carthage in 306, on much the same terms as Dionysius 99 years before, and a relatively quiet period ensued in which Agathocles was able to extend his control over much of Sicily and perhaps south Italy also. It ended with his murder in 289.

His successor Hicetas is a shadowy figure, but not so King Pyrrhus of Epirus, who crossed into Sicily in 278 during his Italian campaigns; he had been for a few years Agathocles' son-in-law and was initially welcomed at Syracuse. He proceeded to take control of the whole island save Lilybaeum, and Messana where Agathocles' Campanian mercenaries, the Mamertines, had taken control in 288. But his demands on the Greeks were excessive and his schemes too ambitious; so he withdrew in 276, leaving the way open for a new Carthaginian invasion and a new ruler of Syracuse. In fact it was with the aid of troops he was leading against the Carthaginians that Hiero, perhaps from the family of the old Deinomenid tyrants, seized control of the city in 275. His subsequent reign (he took the title of king in 269, no doubt in imitation of Agathocles and Pyrrhus) lasted to within three years of the Roman capture of Syracuse, and from 262 until his death he was an ally of Rome.

At first, however, they came into hostile contact on the Straits. Hiero was intent on dislodging the Mamertines from Messana, though his first campaign was frustrated by Carthaginian intervention on their behalf in 269. In 264 he marched again and this time the Mamertines appealed to both Carthage and Rome; both sent help, and came to blows as a result. At first Hiero chose to oppose Rome, though he was a distrustful ally of Carthage; yet he was forced to come to terms with the Roman consuls, Otacilius and Valerius, after being blockaded in Syracuse by their legions. This agreement ensured that Syracuse was little affected by the havoc wrought on the rest of the island during the wars between Carthage and Rome, when Acragas, a major port used by the Carthaginians, was twice sacked, in 262 and 210. Only when Hiero's grandson and advisers, perhaps overawed by Hannibal's successes, deserted Rome in 214, did enemy forces return to the walls of Syracuse. A two-year siege by Marcellus ended with the capture of the whole city and the end of the independent existence of the western Greeks.

Architecture. So the Greek colonies slid into a succession of wars and autocratic military dictatorships – a sorry termination to the promise of the 6th and 5th centuries. We have already noted some of the social and artistic achievements of the western Greeks during that period, especially the tangible remains of the large number of temples, better preserved than most mainland ones.

The gods of the motherland traveled with the colonists and remained one of the strongest links with Greece. In addition, the agricultural wealth of the new lands led to an increase in the cults of the appropriate deities, notably Demeter and Persephone at Gela, Acragas and Locri, and Hera, whose aspect as guardian of cattle combined with her Achaean ancestry in flourishing sanctuaries at Posidonia and near Croton.

A marble relief, perhaps from a sacred pit in a temple at Locri,
found in the gardens of the politician and writer Sallust at Rome.
Aphrodite is seen rising from the waves, to be clothed by her
attendants. On the sides a modest wife burns incense, while a more
liberated follower of the goddess provides music. 470 BC.

Many of the surviving temples have been given fanciful names, masking our ignorance of their true occupants. This is especially the case at Acragas, whose 5th-century prosperity rings out loud from the row of temples along the south wall of the city, and at neighboring Selinus with imposing sanctuaries inside and outside the walls. In both places the surviving temples are Doric with massive upper members, conceding nothing to the lighter entablatures used in Greece from the Parthenon onward. Ionic temples are known from the meager fragments left at Syracuse (unfinished), Metapontum, Massilia and Locri, though this is not to deny the existence of ruined Doric temples too – for example three in the Agora of Metapontum and that of Athena at the east end of the Acropolis of Gela.

All these temples were built of local stone. Marble was employed only very occasionally, such as for the un-clothed parts of female figures depicted in the metopes of temple F at Selinus, which dates from about 460, and the two finely carved screens of the same period probably used to surround a sacred pit in the temple of Persephone at Locri. The lack of local marble meant that a far greater use was made of terracotta as a decorative material, especially for the brightly painted temple revetments, cornices and eaves tiles, but also for sculptural decoration of temples, now preserved mostly in wretched fragments.

The production of terracotta statuettes was an important industry in many colonies throughout their history. Enormous quantities have been found for example in temple dumps at Acragas, along with some of the molds used for their manufacture, and in graves at Taras, especially those dating from the 4th and 3rd centuries.

They performed the same role of minor dedications and grave goods as vases at Athens or small bronzes at Olympia or Delphi, and demonstrate the profoundly religious outlook of the western Greeks.

As was the case in the homeland, we are poorly informed about architecture outside the sanctuary. It has been demonstrated that many colonies were laid out on an axial system, but few non-sacral structures have been fully excavated. At Megara Hyblaea the central square, left free of buildings from the earliest days of the colony, was flanked in the 6th century by two small temples and two simple stoas, together with other buildings of less certain purpose (one perhaps a prytaneion where civic entertainments were held and some cults housed). At Himera the houses so far excavated lie within regularly spaced streets, but do not themselves have any basic or distinctive ground plans. At Naxos a grid system of the 6th century was replaced by a slightly different alignment in Hiero's colony; there were similar changes of axis at Locri and Metapontum, where the once impressive range of temples in the center of the Agora follow now the earlier, now the later alignment. We have noted the uniform-sized allotments of land around Metapontum, each with its farmstead; as at other colonies the plains were protected from attack by outposts on nearby hills.

The walls of some of the cities are their most impressive features. We noted the well-squared 7th-century stone

A postern gate in the fortification wall of Gela at Capo Soprano, Sicily, blocked by mud bricks which also cap the lower stone courses. The wall was built during the years between the refounding of the city after 340 and its destruction in 282.

A skyphos (deep cup) made at Taras in the mid-4th century. It shows Actaeon in the process of turning into a deer and being torn to pieces by his own hunting dogs. This was his punishment for offending Artemis, goddess of the hunt.

wall of Leontini; there were also attractive polygonal terracing and fortification walls at Velia and Naxos. Of particular interest are the works of the 4th and 3rd centuries, especially at the Euryalo fortress at Syracuse, the similar constructions at Selinus and the excellently preserved sections of the wall of Gela at Capo Soprano, dating from the period of Timoleon's ascendancy. The walls of Paestum and Pompeii too include defensive features of this period, though largely of Roman date.

Burials. Gela was one of the principal sites ravaged by tomb-robbers of the past (and probably the present too). Large numbers of cemeteries have been excavated in the western colonies, making a considerable contribution to our knowledge of their cultural and artistic history. Burial customs are related to those in Greece, both cremation and inhumation being practiced, and various forms of grave are found. Grave goods are often richer and more numerous than in mainland cemeteries, and we find a number of more impressive graves. At Taras chamber tombs were frequently cut – crypts in which several members of a family were buried. In one such Tarantine tomb was found the athlete's burial already noted, in a monumental stone sarcophagus, imitating a temple in its carving. Such large individual sarcophagi are rare in the Archaic and Classical periods – there is one from Gela, and we can add the Diver's tomb at Paestum.

At Taras too the 5th century sees the beginning of a long series of stone grave markers of various types, the more grandiose resembling shrines, which are also frequently depicted on the actual vases deposited in the tombs. Elsewhere visible grave markers are either not used at all or are plain, for example the rough-hewn headstones of Selinus with their crudely cut inscriptions. Standing rather apart, therefore, is a kouros statue set up over the grave of Somratidas at Megara Hyblaea. According to the inscription cut on the thigh he was a doctor – probably an Ionian following Ionian burial custom.

Pottery. Much of the pottery found in western tombs is imported – from Corinth, Ionian cities, Rhodes and increasingly from Athens in the 7th and 6th centuries, and almost exclusively from Athens in the 5th, when the Italian corn trade may have meant much to her. Local production was sporadic in the earlier period; Cumaeans imitated Corinthian work, tolerable black-figure was made in Metapontum and kilns of the 7th and 6th centuries have been excavated at Naxos and Megara. In the 5th century, however, home production of red-figure vases closely modeled on Attic work began on a large scale at the new colonies of Thurii and Heraclea, though one painter was working at Metapontum in around 400 as the recent discovery of kilns and their debris has amply demonstrated. In the 4th century production was stepped up, based at Taras and sites among the Lucanians of the hinterland, while in the later 5th century experimenters in red-figure in Sicily migrated to Campania, to Paestum, Cumae and Capua, where a second set of schools flourished and declined in the following century. Characteristic of much of their work is a free use of lavish floral scrolls and gilding, and a predilection for scenes involving Dionysus. Aphrodite and Eros. Massive Tarantine vases destined for immediate interment show graveside vigils and mythological tableaux, some based on stage versions used by the great Athenian tragedians and brought to the colonial theater in the 4th century. Less elevated stage shows are represented on many "Phlyax" vases, where exaggeratedly padded and masked buffoons parody the life of men, heroes and gods alike.

Coinage. Perhaps the greatest artistic achievement of the western colonies was their coinage, though admittedly some of the leading engravers may not have been native to the west. Metalwork in other forms also deserves mention, for example the bronze mirrors produced in Locri in the 5th century with their elaborate figured handles and stands, a superb bronze and silver "parade" helmet from a tomb at Metapontum and fine golden jewelry from Taras. The only bronze sculptor of note seems to have been Pythagoras of Rhegion, who probably received his training in Samos in the years around 500.

From the outset the engravers of coin dies in the colonies were ambitious, producing some of the earliest Greek coins with full human (or rather divine) figures as their types well before the end of the 6th century. Around 470 the Syracuse mint capped a long series of exquisite heads of Arethusa with the ten-drachma "Demareteion," which had a lasting effect not only on Syracusan coinage but on that of other western mints as well. Among coins of equal artistic standard we may single out the latest of only three known types minted at Hieron's foundation of Aetna on the site of Catane, and from a little later the first of only three issues of tetradrachms of Naxos in the years 461–405. During this period Selinus and Himera issued similar types showing a scene in the sanctuary of a river god, and it is remarkable how widespread the appearance of such deities is on coins in the west. The older type showing the god as a bull with a man's face is eventually supplanted by a youthful figure distinguished merely by small horns on the forehead. An exception is the Minotaur-like figure on a few mid-century issues from Metapontum, which bear the legend "games of Acheloos" – a clear indication that these pieces at least were issued more as commemorative medals than as currency.

We also see "games" inscribed beside a set of armor in the exergue on the reverse of some of the decadrachms of Syracuse signed by Cimon. Such signatures begin to appear only after 450 and are particularly common in Sicily in the later 5th century. Cimon's decadrachms are among the most attractive of all coins, but can be closely matched by other contemporary issues at Syracuse. One Syracusan engraver escaped the troubles and went to Lycia in Asia Minor where he resumed his art, while the only hoard of western coins found in the mainland, near Corinth, demonstrates that at least one family from Leontini found refuge in Greece.

Sicilians were also the first to begin using other metals for their coins. Bronze was struck or cast at Himera and Acragas from about 450, often in large pieces which attempt to reflect the silver-bronze ratio – an attempt soon abandoned for a purely fiduciary bronze coinage. During the Carthaginian invasions gold from the temple treasuries was coined in emergency at a number of cities, though Messana and perhaps Syracuse had struck gold earlier.

Few of the Italian colonies can match the production of Sicily, though there are individual masterpieces of careful engraving, especially at little Terina. Here Phrygillus, one of the Syracusan die-cutters, was active in the later 5th century; he sometimes "signs" with a finch (phrygilos). At Thurii and Heraclea, and a number of imitative mints, the Athena heads wear helmets bristling with monsters. Croton, Rhegion and Taras have series depicting the mythological founders of the colonies and during the years of the Italian league the head of Hera Lacinia appears on the coins of several of its members. In the 4th and 3rd centuries Taras mints the most heavily: her horseman staters are interspersed occasionally with issues clearly reflecting contemporary events – the appeal to Sparta for aid, the passage of Alexander the Molossian and the campaigns of Pyrrhus.

On some coins of lesser value from Sicilian mints (and also on most Etruscan coins from the 4th century onward) we see small globules indicating numbers of onkiai of the litra (or ounces of the libra as it becomes in Rome). Such an indication of value is very rare, and we also see in Sicily a local system of weights being used concurrently with the Greek drachma – more proof of the close relationship between Greeks and Sicilians in the Classical period.

Further Reading

GENERAL HISTORY

Bury, J. B. and **Meiggs, R.**, *A History of Greece to the Death of Alexander the Great* (4th edn, London, 1975).

Ehrenberg, V., *From Solon to Socrates* (2nd edn, London, 1973).

PARTICULAR PERIODS AND AREAS

Andrewes, A., *Greek Tyrants* (London, 1956).

Burn, A. R., *Lyric Age of Greece* (London, 1960).

Burn, A. R., *Persia and the Greeks* (London, 1962).

Desborough, V. R. d'A., *The Greek Dark Ages* (London, 1972)

Dunbabin, T. J., *The Western Greeks* (Oxford, 1948).

Forrest, W. G., *A History of Sparta, 950 BC–192 BC* (London, 1968).

Hignett, C., *Xerxes' Invasion of Greece* (Oxford, 1963).

Huxley, G. L., *The Early Ionians* (London, 1966).

Moscati, S., *The World of the Phoenicians* (London, 1968).

Woodhead, A. G., *The Greeks in the West* (London, 1962).

SOCIAL AND ECONOMIC HISTORY

Boardman, J., *The Greeks Overseas* (2nd edn, Harmondsworth, 1973).

French, A., *The Growth of the Athenian Economy* (London, 1964).

Graham, A. J., *Colony and Mother City in Ancient Greece* (Manchester, 1964).

Harris, H. A., *Greek Athletes and Athletics* (London, 1964).

Nilsson, M. P., *A History of Greek Religion* (2nd edn, Oxford, 1949).

Snodgrass, A. M., *Arms and Armour of the Greeks* (London, 1967).

Willetts, R. F., *Aristocratic Society in Ancient Crete* (London, 1955).

ART, GENERAL

Boardman, J., *Preclassical* (Harmondsworth, 1967).

Boardman, Dörig, Füchs and **Hirmer**, *The Art and Architecture of Ancient Greece* (London, 1967).

Charbonneaux, Martin and **Villard**, *Archaic Greek Art* (London and New York, 1971).

ART, REGIONAL AND PERIODS

Homann-Wedeking, E., *Archaic Greece* (London, 1968).

Langlotz, E. and **Hirmer, M.**, *The Art of Magna Graecia* (London, 1965).

Schweitzer, B., *Greek Geometric Art* (London and New York, 1971).

SCULPTURE

Blümel, C., *Greek Sculptors at Work* (2nd edn, London, 1969).

Lawrence, A. W., *Greek and Roman Sculpture* (3rd edn, London, 1972).

Payne, H. and **Mackworth-Young, G.**, *Archaic Marble Sculpture from the Acropolis* (London, 1936 and 1950).

Richter, G. M. A., *Korai: Archaic Greek Maidens* (London, 1968).

Richter, G. M. A., *Kouroi: Archaic Greek Youths* (3rd edn, London, 1970).

POTTERY

Boardman, J., *Athenian Black Figure Vases* (London, 1974).

Boardman, J., *Athenian Red Figure Vases of the Archaic Period* (London, 1975).

Coldstream, J. N., *Greek Geometric Pottery* (London, 1968).

Cook, R. M., *Greek Painted Pottery* (2nd edn, London, 1972).

Payne, H., *Necrocorinthia* (Oxford, 1931).

Shefton, Arias and **Hirmer, M.**, *A History of Greek Vase Painting* (London, 1962).

COINS

Jenkins, G. K., *Ancient Greek Coins* (London, 1972).

Kraay, C. M. and **Hirmer, M.**, *Greek Coins* (London, 1966).

Price, M. J. and **Waggoner, N.**, *Archaic Greek Coinage* (London, 1976).

ARCHITECTURE

Dinsmoor, W. B., *The Architecture of Ancient Greece* (3rd edn, London and New York, 1950).

Lawrence, A. W., *Greek Architecture* (3rd edn, Harmondsworth, 1973).

Winter, F. E., *Greek Fortifications* (London, 1971).

Acknowledgments

Unless otherwise stated, all the illustrations on a given page are credited to the same source.

Acropolis Museum, Athens; photo D. A. Harissiadis 101 left.
Agora Museum, Athens; photo Ekdotike Athenon, S.A., Athens 89 center.
Badisches Landesmuseum, Karlsruhe 135.
Dick Barnard, London 51, 52, 56 bottom, 68 bottom left, 82, 98 top, 112 bottom, 115 top.
C. Bérard, Lausanne, Switzerland 45 top.
Bibliothèque Nationale, Paris 75.
John Boardman, Oxford 35 lower left.
British Museum, London 10 top, 28, 48 bottom, 85, 90 top left.
British Museum, London; photo John R. Freeman 11 bottom, 83.
British Museum, London; photo Michael Holford 21 bottom, 50, 53, 84 left, 89 top left, 103.
British Museum, London; photo Angelo Hornak 18, 92 top left.
British School at Athens; photo Vincent Desborough by permission of the Managing Committee 42.
British School at Athens; photo M. R. Popham and L. H. Sackett by permission of the Managing Committee 43 center left, 44 left and center right.
British School at Athens; photo L. H. Sackett by permission of the Managing Committee 44 top right.
Dr Oscar Broneer, Old Corinth 56 top.
Dr Giorgio Buchner, Ischia 47.
M. D. C. Cuss, Oxford 11 top.
Cyprus Museum, Nicosia; photo Ekdotike Athenon, S.A., Athens 60.
Deutsches Archäologisches Institut, Athens 15, 29 top, 35 right and top left, 46 bottom, 59 top left, 78, 79, 95, 102 bottom.
Deutsches Archäologisches Institut, Rome 121 bottom.
École Française d'Archéologie, Athens 31, 66 bottom, 67 top center and right.
Elsevier, Amsterdam 67 top left, 68 right, 69 left, 73, 125 bottom.
Professor P. R. Franke, Saarbrücken, West Germany 105 (2).
Ray Gardner, London 21 top, 48 top, 69 center and bottom right, 105 (1), 105 (3), 105 (4), 105 (5), 105 (6), 105 (7), 105 (8), 113 top center and right, 114 top, 116.
Roger Gorringe, London 38, 54, 55 bottom, 62, 66 top, 77, 91 top, 98 bottom, 99 bottom, 111 bottom, 123.
D. A. Harissiadis, Athens 70 top.
Drs A. A. M. van der Heyden, Amsterdam frontispiece, 9, 23, 29 bottom, 69 top right, 70 bottom, 74, 111 top.
Michael Holford Library, London 27 top, 33, 93, 97, 99 top, 114 bottom left, 131.
Lovell Johns, Oxford 12, 13, 43 bottom right, 57, 120, 127 bottom.
Dr Alan Johnston, London 45 bottom, 110, 112 top, 115 bottom right, 121 top, 125 top left, 134.
Victor Kennett, London 114 bottom right, 115 bottom left.

N. Kondos, Athens 25.
Howard Loxton, London 68 top left.
The Mansell Collection, London 27 bottom, 34, 100, 102 top, 113 top left, 128, 133.
Leonard von Matt, Buochs, Switzerland 39 bottom, 43 top, 113 bottom.
The Metropolitan Museum of Art, New York 76.
Musée de Châtillon-sur-Seine, France; photo R. V. Schoder, S.J. 81 bottom.
Musée du Louvre, Paris; photo Maurice Chuzeville 87.
Musée du Louvre, Paris; photo Giraudon 88 center, 91 bottom left.
Museo Archeologico, Florence; photo Mauro Pucciarelli 84 right, 88 top.
Museo Arqueologico Nacional, Madrid 40.
Museo Nazionale Etrusco di Villa Giuila, Rome; photo Mauro Pucciarelli 80.
Museum of Fine Arts, Boston, U.S.A.; photo R. V. Schoder, S.J. 17, 37.
Museum of Mykonos; photo Ekdotike Athenon, S.A., Athens 89 bottom left.
National Archaeological Museum, Athens; photo Ekdotike Athenon, S.A., Athens 22, 49, 55 top, 58, 59 right and bottom left, 89 bottom right, 91 center, 109.
Norbert Schimmel Collection, New York 71, 117.
Olympia Museum, Greece; photo Ekdotike Athenon, S.A., Athens 91 bottom right.
Oxford Illustrators, Oxford 94.
Oxford Illustrators, Oxford after M. R. Popham 44 bottom right.
Pieterse-Davison International Limited, Dublin by courtesy of John Hunt 118.
Radio Times Hulton Picture Library, London 36, 39 top.
Robert Harding Associates, London 90 bottom, 125 top right.
David Ridgway, Edinburgh 43 center right.
R. V. Schoder, S.J., Chicago, U.S.A. 10 bottom, 46 top, 63, 67 bottom.
Professor A. M. Snodgrass, Edinburgh 81 top left.
Soprintendenza alle Antichità della Basilicata, Potenza 41, 127 top.
Soprintendenza alle Antichità della Puglia, Taranto 126.
Spectrum Colour Library, London 20, 65, 70 center, 129.
Staatliche Antikensammlungen, Munich; photo Caecilia H. Moessner 81 top right, 88 bottom, 92 bottom, 119.
Staatliche Antikensammlungen, Munich; photo R. V. Schoder, S.J. 107.
Vatican Museum, Rome; photo Mauro Pucciarelli 90 top right, 92 top right.

The Publishers have attempted to observe the legal requirements with respect to the rights of the suppliers of photographic materials. Nevertheless, persons who have claims are invited to apply to the Publishers.

Glossary

Acropolis "The high city." A term used to describe the isolated defensible hilltops, usually of modest height, on which the kernel of so many Greek cities was placed. Used in particular of the Athenian Acropolis, which was originally the administrative and defensive heart of Athens.

Acroterion The decoration set above the peak of a pediment,* and also at its corners on either side. Outstanding examples of the Archaic period are the eight-foot diameter terracotta painted disk of the Temple of Hera at Olympia and the elaborate marble floral flanked by korai figures of the Temple of Aphaea on Aegina.

Acroterion

Alcaeus Aristocratic poet and contemporary of Sappho in Mytilene on the island of Lesbos. Prominent in political upheavals in the years around 600, but later in exile, traveling widely. His lyric poetry, preserved only in fragments, covers a wide field of themes, including attacks on his political opponents.

Alcman Composed poems at Sparta in the later 7th century, though of Lydian origin. The little of his work that survives consists mainly of choral hymns in honor of several deities, and throws a gentler light on the military aspects of Spartan life which dominate our historical sources.

Amphictiony An association of "dwellers around," meeting together at a common sanctuary. An amphictiony could acquire political importance, as exemplified on several occasions by the Amphictions who organized the affairs of Apollo at Delphi after extending their control over it from their original seat at Thermopylae, probably in the 7th century.

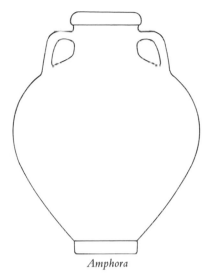

Amphora

Amphora Originally "amphiphora" ("held on both sides"). The standard, all-purpose portable container of the Greek world, normally made of clay. They display a considerable variety of size and shape, from huge burial jars, via standard oil or wine containers to miniature replicas or souvenirs of the prize amphoras of the Panathenaic games.

Anax *or* **wanax** The title of king found in Mycenaean and Homeric Greek. It does not appear in official use in the Iron Age* and presumably went out of use after the collapse of the strong monarchies of the Bronze Age.*

Anta The projecting wing of a porch or, more strictly, its terminating part. Originally the part of a mudbrick wall exposed to the elements and given a timber sheathing, hence the increased width of the anta in a Doric stone temple.

Apotropaic Deterring, turning away, especially of objects intended to ward off evil, eg the Gorgoneion on temple pediments,* and perhaps the eyes painted on the prows of warships and on many 6th-century vases.

Apsidal With an apse, ie a curving, not straight wall, usually at the short end of a

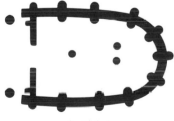

Apsidal plan

rectangular building. More suited to wattle-and-daub type construction than the rectangular plan, and often found in Dark Age* settlements, though rare later.

Archilochus A 7th-century poet of Paros, whose father may have led the Parian colonists to Thasos, where later Archilochus lived and felt homesick. Noted for his vitriolic attacks in verse on Lycambes, who had refused him the hand of his daughter Cleoboule (the original "barbed iambs").

Architrave The course of stone or wood in a building lying immediately above the columns.

Archon "Ruler" or "leader." The most commonly used Greek term denoting an official holding any kind of administrative power sanctioned by his fellow citizens. At Athens it refers to the chief magistrate, by whose name the year was identified – the *archon eponymos*.

Archon basileus The magistrate at Athens who performed the religious duties of the king after his replacement by a board of non-hereditary officials. In a sense the religious head of the polis* of Athens.

Areopagus The senior council in Archaic Athens, named after the Hill of Ares, opposite the Acropolis,* where the council met. After the reforms of Cleisthenes, their function was largely limited to trying cases of murder, but earlier they probably had wide-ranging powers, especially for initiating legislation. Composed of ex-archons*.

Apotropaic device

Beazley, Sir John (1885–1970) Although not a practicing archaeologist, Beazley has had a profound influence on Classical archaeology through his work in museums and at the Ashmolean library in Oxford, England, on Attic figured pottery. Particularly noteworthy is his achievement in isolating many hundreds of individual painters and workshops of both black-* and red-figure* vases. An outstanding classical scholar with a remarkable visual memory.

Black-figure A technique of vase decoration in which figures in dark "glaze"★ are set off against the natural ground of the clay. The figures are tricked out with red and white, and lines incised with a sharp point are used to show detail within the silhouette. The technique first appears just before 700, but has its heyday in the 6th century.

Boule A deliberative council, one of several terms used to describe such a selected or elected body in Greece. At Athens the name was originally applied to the Areopagus★, but was later transferred to the broader-based elected Boule introduced by Cleisthenes (or possibly earlier by Solon).

Bronze Age The period of history in any culture or civilization in which bronze is the dominant metal used for implements and weapons, prior to the adoption of iron. In Greece this period stretches from about 3000 to 1050 BC, encompassing the Minoan and Mycenaean civilizations.

Burgon, Thomas (1787–1858) A merchant resident in Smyrna till 1814. He excavated in Athens and Melos, bringing to light the first (and still perhaps the earliest) Panathenaic prize amphora recognized as such in 1813. Later employed in the Coin Department of the British Museum after the failure of his business concerns.

Capital The crowning part of a pillar or column, designed to ease the burden of the overlying members on the top surface of a vertically grained wooden column. In the early period the capitals themselves were of wood, later of stone and of three main varieties, Doric, Ionic and Aeolic. Corinthian capitals were an invention of the later 5th century.

Carbon 14 A radioactive isotope of carbon present in minute quantities in wood and other carboniferous substances. The amount decreases at a steady progression after the object ceases to be a living organism. Thus the approximate calendar date of manufacture of any object, or of ashes, etc., made from such a substance can be calculated from the amount of C 14 remaining in it.

Cella *or* **naos** The main room of a temple, excluding any porch or false porch at the rear.

Chalcidice "The Chalcidian land," applied to the three-pronged peninsula of northern Greece, east of Salonica, colonized largely by Euboeans from Chalcis and Eretria in the late 8th and 7th centuries. The most significant colonies were Acanthus, Torone, Mende, Stagira and Potidaea (founded by Corinth).

Chiton A garment of light material and full length (the shorter variety is normally termed

chitoniskos). Generously cut with a full skirt and breadth of shoulder, but generally fashioned from plain strips of cloth. Pinned with fibulas★ or buttoned on shoulder and arms.

Chiton

Cist A plain pit grave, lined and covered with stone slabs. A common form of individual burial in the Greek world, especially in the Dark Ages.

Cornice *or* **geison** The crowning course of the entablature of a temple, against which the tiles abutted on the long sides. On the short sides it ran up to the peak of the pediment★ (the raking cornice), but a horizontal cornice was also provided, giving the "floor" line of the pediment.

Crater A bowl used for mixing wine and water (probably with a wider usage in the early period). Geometric craters usually have tall feet, while in the 6th century three distinct varieties emerge: the column or "Corinthian" crater, with column-like handles; the volute or "Laconian" crater, named after its high-curving volute handles and best exemplified

by the François vase and the bronze Vix crater; and the calyx-crater, with its broad, cup-shaped body specifically designed to hold a "psykter" or cooling jar, filled with snow or spring water, which floated on the wine.

Cult statue The statue of the deity worshiped in any given temple. In fact the raison d'être of the temple was the protection of the statue. Many cult statues were venerable antiques by the Classical period, a large proportion being wooden, some of them aniconic and of alleged miraculous origin.

Cyclopean masonry Massively built walls of huge rough masonry, believed by later Greeks to have been constructed by the one-eyed giants, the Cyclopes. Best known from Bronze Age★ monuments, eg the walls of Tiryns, but also (though rarely) found in the Iron Age★, for example the retaining wall of the terrace of the temple of Argive Hera across the plain from Tiryns.

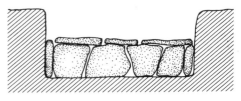

Cist grave

Dark Ages The name applied to the centuries (c. 1100–800) following the decline of the Mycenaean civilization. Living standards sank to a very low level, and no form of historical records was kept. This contrasts with the considerable information we have for the previous and subsequent periods.

Dedication *See* **Votive offering.**

Deme Derived from "demos," the people, but in a narrower sense "a township," particularly used of the villages with their own local administration in Attica upon which Cleisthenes built his tribal reforms in 507. He had to set up seemingly artificial demes within

Column-crater

Calyx-crater

the city of Athens to provide a balance of city and country demes in each tribe.

Democratia "Rule by the people," a word not known earlier than the mid-5th century, although a number of states had already developed forms of government in which the citizen body ("demos") of adult free males had extensive powers under the constitution. The word used to describe such a situation before the adoption of *democratia* was "isonomia" – equality in the recognition of rights.

Dentils "Little teeth," Latin. The course above the frieze★, sometimes the architrave★, in an Ionic temple, representing the ends of ceiling beams with only narrow spaces between. A far less monumental rendering than the Doric frieze of a similar origin.

Diodorus From Agyrion in Sicily. He compiled a *Universal History* in the 1st century BC, covering the timespan from the Creation of the Universe to his own day. For many periods he is our sole surviving source of historical information, and his highly compressed narrative (sometimes only preserved in summary form) causes many difficulties of interpretation in crucial events and developments.

Dörpfeld, Wilhelm (1853–1940) Best known as Schliemann's assistant in his excavations at Troy, Dörpfeld took part in or directed numerous excavations, particularly in the last decades of the 19th century, notably those at Olympia and on the Athenian Acropolis★.

Drachma In origin thought to mean "handful," a set of iron spits used as currency in the days before coinage, and thence transferred to a basic denomination of coinage, similarly composed of six obols "spits." Often found in compounds such as didrachm, decadrachm, etc.

Dress pin Large-scale use of simple bronze pins, often with elaborately molded heads, began in Iron Age★ Greece. Used principally to fasten heavy garments at the shoulder, they can attain impressive lengths.

Dromos Greek for race or racecourse, but applied in particular by archaeologists to the long passageways leading (usually downwards) to burial chambers. Particularly common in more elaborate Mycenaean burials, but also found in the Iron Age★, though normally in a less monumental form. The dromos was filled in after each burial within the chamber.

Ecclesia "A calling-forth," the name given to the general assembly of the people in Athens. Transferred at a much later date to the congregation and the building of the Christian church.

Elgin, Thomas Bruce (1766–1841) The seventh Earl of Elgin. Best known to the modern world as the procurer of the Parthenon marbles via his Italian agent in Athens, Lusieri, while he was British Ambassador to the Porte in Istanbul, 1799–1803. However he sent many other antiquities to Britain, especially from the Geometric and Archaic periods. Some were obtained by the British Museum and some retained till recently in the family seat at Broomhall, Fifeshire in Scotland.

Elymian Descriptive of the Elymoi, a people who lived in the west of Sicily, notably at Segesta and at Eryx, who were seemingly independent of other non-Greek Sicilian culture and, in unreliable Greek tradition, brought as fugitives from Troy.

Enceinte A circuit of defensive walls.

Ephor "Overseer." In particular the name of a magistrate at Sparta – one of an annually elected college of five concerned with administrative affairs. Their origin and constitutional position vis-à-vis the kings are not clear from our limited evidence.

Euxine "Hospitable," the name rather euphemistically given by the Greeks to the Black Sea, as it was frequently the opposite. Compare "Cape of Good Hope."

Extispicy The inspection of entrails, especially the liver, for signs of good or bad omen. A regular part of animal sacrifices made to appease the gods with regard to some projected undertaking by the individual or state.

Fibula Akin to the modern safety-pin in design and purpose, with pin, bow and catch-plate. It was in use from the late Bronze Age in many areas of the Mediterranean world. The fibula was used more widely than the plain pin, judging from finds *in situ* in graves. Usually of bronze, though gold fibulas are also found.

Filigree A manner of decorating objects of gold with strips of wire fashioned into the desired shape. Often precious stones and the like were encased in such mountings of filigree. The technique is similar to granulation★, save of course for the preparation of the wire, which was by hammering out bars or fusing together globules of gold.

Frieze A long horizontal band in architecture (above the architrave★) or in the minor arts, decorated in a variety of ways, normally either with a continuous flow of figures, as on Ionic temples and most Corinthian vases, or split into individual panels separated by narrow vertical strips, as in the frieze on Doric temples.

Frieze

Furtwängler, Adolf (1853–1907) Eminent German archaeologist who produced work of first importance on many topics, from Mycenaean pottery to Classical sculpture. From 1894 he was director of the Munich Glyptotek, and it was in search of further evidence for the history of the temple of Aphaea on Aegina, whose sculptures were in his care, that he met his death from gastric fever in 1907.

Genos "Family," used in a literal and extended sense, the latter akin to the Scots "clan." The noble *gene* in Attica and other states controlled and quarreled over leading positions in civil and religious administration in the Archaic period, though later they only retained their religious functions.

Gerhard, Edouard (1795–1867) Founder and energetic leading light of the Institute of Archaeological Correspondence at Rome in 1828, almost coincidental with the discovery of the rich Etruscan cemetery of Vulci. He pioneered thorough studies of various aspects of art and archaeology in Italy, notably Etruscan mirrors and Greek vases.

Gerousia The assembly of elders at Sparta and other states. In Sparta they were 28 in number and were joined by the two kings to form the main council of the state.

Glaze A term rather misleadingly applied to the glossy dark surface of Greek vases. It is in fact a form of sintered lamina, not a true vitrified glaze (obtained by firing at higher temperatures). The various clays used in Greece result in differing degrees of sheen and intensity of color.

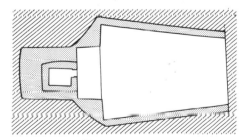

Dromos to a tomb

Graffito An inscription scratched onto any surface in an informal manner. Most of the earliest Greek inscriptions are of this type, and graffiti in general afford much evidence for dialect, language and other topics.

Granulation A technique of jewelry decoration in gold where surfaces or figures are covered with very small globules of metal, applied with a glue and then fused onto the surface in a variety of ways according to the size of the granules. A technique probably lost to the Greeks in the Dark Ages★, and later much used by Etruscan goldsmiths.

Greater Panathenaea The Athenians celebrated a festival of Athena each year in July or August, but every fourth year it was a more splendid occasion, centered around the bringing of a new robe to the old seated wooden statue of the goddess on the Acropolis★. Athletic and other contests were held. The festival was given the form in which we know it in the year 566.

Hecatompedon "Hundred-footer," used by the Greeks to describe temples whose length approximated to 100 local feet (all such were close to our foot). The size was particularly in vogue during the 7th and 6th centuries, eg the older temples of Hera on Samos and the first temple of Athena on the Acropolis★.

Helot The name applied to a serf – one of the class working the land of the Spartiates★ in Laconia and Messenia. It is uncertain whether they were of similar Dorian stock or of an earlier Bronze Age★ people indigenous to the area – perhaps both. Their name may be connected with that of the town of Helos ("Marsh") in southern Laconia.

Herodotus "The father of history," born c. 485 at Halicarnassus and later exiled and resident at Athens and Thurii. The nine books of his *Histories* narrate the relations between Greeks and Persians down to the end of the Persian wars, and include a wealth of incidental material on many far-ranging topics.

Hoplito-dromos

Hesiod Perhaps a younger contemporary of Homer★, but living on the Greek mainland, at Ascra in Boeotia. He composed several epic poems, including *The Birth of the Gods*, as well as a seasonal farming manual in the same verse meter – *The Works and Days*.

Himation A cloak or wrap consisting of a single square of material draped in a variety of ways. Often the sole garment worn by men; females could wear it symmetrically draped over the shoulders, but an Ionic fashion, seen on many korai★ statues, was to pass it diagonally under one arm.

Hogarth, D. G. (1862–1927) Excavated with Evans at Knossos and also at Naucratis. He was later keeper of the Ashmolean Museum in Oxford, England, and military diplomat in Mesopotamia during World War I. He directed the excavations at Ephesus in 1904–05, revealing the rich deposits of votive★ material belonging to the earliest phase of the history of the "Temple of Diana of the Ephesians."

Hollow-casting A method of casting bronze statues (or statuettes) in which the space inside the mold is largely taken up by a core roughly shaped as the finished object. The statue, when cast, will therefore have walls of only slight thickness, instead of being a solid, expensive mass of metal.

Homer The famous blind poet, probably from Smyrna or Chios, composer of the *Iliad* and *Odyssey* and traditionally the founder of the Greek line of epic poets. His precise role in giving the two works their final form towards the end of the 8th century is hotly debated.

Hoplite The armed warrior peculiar to the Greek state, fighting in close order with spear and sword as weapons. The hoplite shield was "worn" on the arm, with a central armhole and a handgrip near the rim.

Hoplitodromos A race in armor (originally helmet, greaves and shield) introduced at the Olympic festival in 520 BC and seen depicted on Attic vases of the 6th and 5th centuries.

Hydria A jar for carrying water, exemplified on p. 9 of this book. The essential difference between amphora and hydria was the addition of a vertical handle at the back of the latter for dipping and pouring. Regularly found at the bottom of wells in excavations.

Iliad The epic poem in 24 books composed by Homer★ on the theme of Achilles' quarrel with Agamemnon in the Greek camp at Troy. It was very likely based on an actual Greek war against Troy in the years around 1200 BC.

Iron Age Subsequent to a Bronze Age★, most cultures adopted the use of iron for principal

Himation

implements. In Greece and many adjacent areas this change began around 1050 BC.

Isonomia *See* **Democratia.**

Kalos "Fine," "handsome," the basic Greek adjective of approval, in particular used of youths, and more rarely girls (*kale*) to denote an admirer's attraction. Such *kalos* tags are painted on vases with some frequency in the period 550–430.

Kerameikos The potters' quarter. Applicable to any town but used in particular of Athens, where the area (and later deme★) covered territory within and outside the walls, including the Agora, the Sacred and Dipylon gates and a major burial ground flanking the roads leading from the gates, in use throughout the Iron Age★ from the Submycenaean period onward.

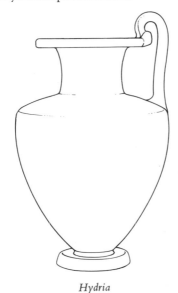

Hydria

Knight "Hippeus," a member of the second class of Athenian citizens under Solon's incomes assessment, producing between 300 and 500 measures per annum, with extensive rights. Although they all nominally owned a horse (*hippos*), they served as foot soldiers or hoplites★ in battle.

Komos A revel with alcoholic and musical accompaniment (attended by *komasts*). Often pictured on vases, most noticeably on Archaic red-figure★ cups, which were used on such occasions.

Komos

Kore "Maiden," used in two important specific senses, to describe the female standing figure typical of Archaic sculpture (a modern application) and, as a proper name, to refer to the daughter of Demeter, known also as Persephatta (or Persephone, a name of non-Greek origin).

Kouros "Youth," used more specifically by modern art-historians to describe the nude male standing figure of Archaic sculpture and other arts, previously dubbed "Apollos."

Kurgan Russian word for barrow, used to describe the large burial mounds of Scythian aristocrats, found in many areas of southern Russia. Usually fully and richly furnished, most belong to the 5th and later centuries.

Kylix A drinking cup. A term used widely in antiquity, but limited in archaeological usage to the tall-stemmed "champagne glass" varieties of cup which evolved in many Greek states in the 6th century.

Kylix

Lekythos A small vase used for perfume or oil. Today the word usually refers to oil containers, of which the most characteristic type is the cylindrical, painted Athenian lekythos, used especially in funeral rites and found in large quantities in Greek graves.

Lekythos

Lerici Foundation An institute for archaeological surveying founded in Rome by C. Lerici in 1970. Using protonmagnetometers★ and similar instruments, members of the Institute have plotted the hidden remains of a number of cities and cemeteries in Etruria and southern Italy.

Linear B The script on clay tablets found accidentally baked in the Bronze Age★ palaces of Knossos, Thebes and Pylos. Derived from the Cretan syllabic script (Linear A), but used to write down an early form of Greek. This was a discovery of the 1950s which revolutionized the study of Bronze Age and early Iron Age Greece.

Maenad "Inspired, maddened woman," a female follower of Dionysus in his quasi-mythical entourage. Maenads are depicted wearing *chiton*★ and deerskin and carrying the *thyrsus* – a fennel stem topped by a cluster of pinecones. They are also apt to carry snakes and suffer the personal attention of satyrs★.

Magna Graecia "Great Greece," the name applied first perhaps by Pythagoras or his followers to the south of Italy and Sicily, an area colonized by the Greeks in the 8th to 6th centuries and the source of many influences on the developing culture of Rome in the 3rd and 2nd centuries BC.

Megaron A term used by Homer and now applied to a particular form of rectangular structure, freestanding or embedded in a more complex building, where a main hall is fronted by a porch, or a porch and anteroom. Typical of Mycenaean palaces and Iron Age★ temples.

Metic An alien resident in a Greek state. In Athens their status emerged more clearly after the reforms of Cleisthenes in 507 had in the first place made clearer the legal definition of citizenship. Metics were obliged to pay taxes and could not own land in Attica.

Metope "Space between," the roughly square panels between the triglyphs★ in the Doric frieze★, also used to describe panel decoration in the other arts. In origin the blank areas between the ends of ceiling beams.

Moloch The ritual child sacrifice practiced in Phoenician cities according to literary sources including the Bible, and known from excavation in a number of Phoenician colonies (*see* **Tophet**). The children were cremated and buried in plain urns, sometimes with a stone with carved decoration set up above.

Naucrary An old division of Attica, predating the deme★-based administrative reforms of Cleisthenes; seemingly named after a basic naval function (*naus* = warship). The leaders of the naucraries are said to have had considerable powers.

Nomos "Law," with a widespread use in the sense of "custom," in which the recognition of one's proper position led to the preservation of law and order. It gradually takes over the meaning of "legal enactment" from various other words used in the Archaic period.

Odyssey Homer's epic poem in 24 books telling of the return of Odysseus (Ulysses) from Troy to his home on Ithaca, and of his wife and son, Penelope and Telemachus, who had waited for him.

Oecist The founder of a colony, always a citizen of the mother city or (in the case of a second-generation colony) of the original mother city.

Oenochoe A small jug of metal or clay used mainly for pouring wine into cups. Many have a pinched, trefoil lip for ease of pouring. In the Archaic period a considerable number were produced with neck and mouth fashioned into animal heads.

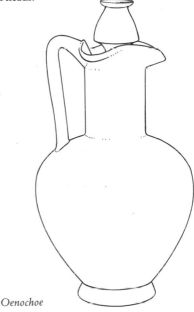

Oenochoe

Olympic games A four-yearly festival held in the sanctuary of Zeus and Hera at Olympia, first celebrated with athletic contests in 776, according to tradition. Victors' lists reported in various sources, which are probably reliable, demonstrate the gradual increase in popularity of the games, which grew from a local Peloponnesian occasion to a Panhellenic gathering. During the period of the games the Olympic truce was in force throughout Greece.

Oracle A place of divination where prophecies were made by priests and priestesses either by reading various natural phenomena or casting lots, or inspired directly by the god (as at Delphi in the Temple of Apollo). Other important oracles were at Claros and Didyma in Ionia, Lebadeia in northern Boeotia and Dodona in Epirus.

Orientalizing The name applied to the period (c. 720–600) in which Greek life came under and absorbed extensive influence from the Near East. Applied in particular to pottery styles in which eastern flora and fauna are introduced, but also detectable in literary forms, cult and myth.

Orsi, Paolo (1859–1935) Pioneer of archaeological research in southern Italy, though of northern birth. Worked in Crete before assuming office at Syracuse, and after 1907 in Calabria. He excavated at very many sites, not only Greek colonies, such as Gela, Megara Hyblaea and Camarina, but also a number of important native settlements.

Ostracism A constitutional device at Athens, first used in 487 and abandoned in 415, whereby a vote was taken by the citizens on whether to send into a ten-year exile any of their number who displeased them. It is uncertain whether the necessary minimum of 6,000 votes constituted a quorum for an election or the minimum for a candidate to be "successful." Named after the sherds or "ostraka" on which the candidate's name, his father's name and his deme★ were scratched.

Pankration

Pankration "All-in wrestling," a contest with very few rules (eg no gouging of eyes) which formed part of most athletic festivals. Introduced at Olympia in 648 and

supplemented by a boy's contest in 200 BC. It was not unknown for competitors to be killed in the pankration.

Panoply From the same root as "hoplite★." A full set of armor and weapons, consisting of breastplate, greaves, helmet, shield, spear and sword, perhaps thigh- and stomach-guard as well. Panoplies were regularly dedicated at shrines (especially Olympia) by victorious cities.

Panoply

Panther The name given by art-historians to the feline with facing head frequently found among the fauna of 7th- and 6th-century art. Probably modeled on the leopard, though rarely given a mottled coat – a striking exception is the pair on the pediment★ of the Temple of Artemis on Corfu.

Papyrus *Cyperus papyrus*, a marsh plant found predominantly in the Nile Delta, split down the middle and arranged in horizontal and vertical layers to form sheets of "paper" when pressed and dried out. Known to have been used for writing in Greece in the Archaic period, though no examples with Greek writing on them have been preserved in the dry sands of Egypt earlier than Alexander's takeover of the country in the later 4th century. In 5th-century Athens a sheet of papyrus cost twice as much as a whitened wooden board.

Pastas A type of house found in very many areas of the Greek world in the Classical period. The rooms open up on either side of a central corridor, and a courtyard is also frequently included. The concept is seen in several buildings of the Geometric period, eg the "sacred houses" at Eleusis and in the Academy at Athens.

Pausanias A native of Asia Minor who composed a ten-book guide to the antiquities and cults of Greece during the reigns of Hadrian and Antoninus in the 2nd century

AD. A thorough work displaying deep knowledge of Greece and its literature.

Payne, Humfry (1902–36) Oxford classical scholar and archaeologist, who excavated the sanctuary of Hera at Perachora near Corinth while Director of the British School at Athens, 1929–33. He had already written the basic work on Archaic Corinthian pottery, *Necrocorinthia*.

Pediment

Pediment The low triangular area above the columns and below the eaves at the short ends of a temple, often decorated with sculpture of stone or terracotta. In Greek architecture the emphasis laid on the ground line of the triangle gives the pediment its special importance.

Peloponnesian League A modern phrase used to describe the system of alliances made by Sparta with other, mainly Peloponnesian, states. It was primarily a military organization, with each party obliged to render mutual assistance in defense and offense. Originating in the years before 550, the League reached the peak of its influence later in the century.

Panther

Pentekonter "A 50-oared ship," the standard Greek warship in the Archaic period, still in use in several smaller states during the Persian wars. The oars were manned by 25 men on each side of the ship.

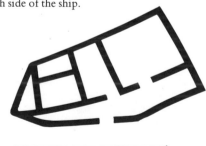

Pastas house

Pentekosiamedimnoi Under the class system introduced by Solon, the first division of Athenian citizens, whose land yielded over 500 measures of corn (or an equivalent) per annum. Only they were eligible for certain offices, possibly the archonship originally, while even in the Classical period the major financial positions, such as stewardship of the sanctuary and treasures of Athena, was reserved for them.

Peplos A full-length garment made of thicker material than the *chiton** and generally sleeveless. It was pinned up at the shoulders and normally worn with a belt. Simply wrapped round the body, it could be left open down one flank or sewn up, when it would be stepped into.

Peplos

Perioikoi "Dwellers around," the second class of the Spartan state, ranked below the true Spartiates*. They were freeborn, but little is known of their exact status, nor of their townships in Laconia. In the Classical period they supplied the daily needs of the Spartans, ever more preoccupied with military and athletic training, if not actual warfare.

Petrie, Flinders (1853–1942) Over 40 years Professor of Egyptology in London, he is best known to classical scholars as a pioneer of scientific methods in excavation, and for his discovery of the Greek trading post of Naucratis on the Nile Delta in 1884–85.

Phratry From the same root as the Latin *frater* ("brother"), the phratry was a "brotherhood," with little or no blood relationship involved, originally perhaps including the followers of a given noble *genos**. Enrollment in a phratry was a prerequisite of becoming a full Athenian citizen.

Pithos A storage jar with broad body and mouth, usually covered by a lid. Often of vast size, they were regularly sunk into the floor of houses or storerooms to afford ease of access to the contents. Of particular interest in the Archaic period were pithoi close to amphoras* in shape, which carried scenes in added clay showing molded figures. They were produced at Sparta and on Crete, Tenos and other islands.

Plutarch A prolific writer of the 1st century AD and native of Orchomenos in Boeotia. Among his more important works are the *Lives* – moralizing biographies of notable Greeks and Romans from the earliest period to his own day. They preserve for us much useful material from earlier sources which are now lost.

Polemarch "Leader in war." The title of the commander-in-chief of the army in most Greek states, including Athens, although in the Classical period he had lost most of his military importance there and was more occupied with judicial work.

Polis "City," used less often for the geographical entity than for the acropolis* of a town or the whole area controlled by a given state – hence the normal modern translation "city-state." Also used personally to denote the body of citizens.

Polygonal "Many-angled," applied in particular to a form of terrace or fortification walling in frequent use in the Archaic period, where the stones were neither coursed nor squared, but smoothed only on the front face and laid as best fitted with the adjacent pieces. Some work shows greater care and elegance.

Potnia theron "Mistress of the Beasts," used of goddesses depicted holding (often by the tail) a pair of wild animals, frequently birds or lions. A motif borrowed from eastern art and found most often in 7th-century Greek art; the deity seems regularly to be equated with Artemis, while on a number of occasions she is given the face of a Gorgon.

Pronaos "In front of the naos," the porch of a temple.

Prostas "Set in front," the name applied to the porch and, by extension, the whole of a form of house with a main room fronted by a porch, whatever additional rooms were included. Found in particular in Ionia in the Classical period, but traceable back to the early Iron Age* megaron* house.

Protonmagnetometer An electronic instrument used in archaeological survey work. The variation in the magnetic field of the earth in the area is recorded and plotted on a chart from which can be read the possible line of hidden features such as walls and ditches.

Proxenos The representative of one city in another, akin to the modern consul but with the difference that he was a citizen of the place where he lived, and not the place he represented. The role emerges in the 6th century from the deeply rooted custom of guest-friendship (*xenia*) in Greek society.

Prytaneion A building in which the *prytanes* were lodged. At Athens they were the members of the one tribe in the Boule* which was "on call" for one tenth of the year. They lived in or near the Agora in a complex which also housed a number of cults and in which civic dinners were held. The building has not been confidently identified in any excavation.

Punic Derived from the Latin equivalent of "Phoenician" and used to describe aspects of Carthaginian culture, including that of the originally Phoenician colonies in the western Mediterranean.

Pythia Either the priestess who uttered the oracles of Apollo at Delphi, or Apollo's festival and the athletic contests that formed part of it. Named after the slaying of the serpent Pytho by Apollo, for which act he had to undergo a seven-year penance; perhaps an echo of his taking over the cult place of Ge (Earth) at Delphi.

Red-figure A technique of vase decoration in which figures are left in the natural color of the clay while the background is filled in with dark glaze*. Details of the figures are mostly indicated with glaze lines. Light-on-dark decoration is used sporadically in Greece throughout the Iron Age, but the use of the clay ground for this effect first appears in Athens around 530.

Revetments Terracotta sheathing used to protect the exposed timbers of a building, especially in the area of the eaves, where the rafters and ceiling beams terminated. Also used later to clad structural elements of stone, and always painted with lively designs.

Sacral laws Regulations concerning religious affairs, especially behavior in the temenos*, sacrificial procedure and the rights and obligations of priests and officials. Most of the legal texts of the Archaic period preserved on stone or bronze belong to this category.

Sarcophagus "Flesh-eater," an individual burial casket of stone or (more usual in Greece) terracotta. Usually of box-like shape, they were in common use in east Greek states, notably Clazomenae, where fully painted examples were used.

Satyr *or silen* The ass-eared and tailed follower of Dionysus, represented at first on Attic vases of the early 6th century with equine legs as well. By the end of the Archaic period they (or rather actors representing them) appear in satyr plays in Dionysus' honor, in which satyrs caricature heroes and gods. The plays formed part of the same festival as the more serious tragedies.

Sealstones Small semiprecious stones of varying shape (but especially round or ovoid) cut with a design in intaglio on one or both sides. Used originally for placing personal insignia on sealings of documents, jars etc., but found less frequently in the Iron Age★ than in earlier periods. Often worn on a string around the neck. Many Archaic examples have a back carved in imitation of an Egyptian scarab beetle.

Sealstone

Sherd A fragment of a terracotta vase, the regular state of discovery of Greek pots. Also used as a verb – to search an area for surface sherds to discover whether and at what period it may have been inhabited in antiquity.

Sican Belonging to the native culture of central and western Sicily in the Iron Age. Such a culture, distinct from the Elymian★ and Sicel★, can be seen in the archaeological record, but its origins are not clear and are variously guessed at in literary sources.

Sicel Descriptive of the culture of eastern Sicily present before the arrival of the Greeks, although by tradition it was introduced to the island from the Italian mainland only shortly before the Trojan War. Archaeological evidence suggests that the Sicels expanded westwards at the expense of the Sicans★ in the Iron Age★

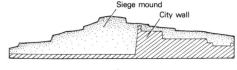

Siege mound

Siege mound An embankment of earth and rubble thrown up against a city wall by an attacker to afford a position of dominance for his weaponry, especially rams. Used in the Archaic period more by eastern kings than Greek states, and exemplified by the Lydian king's mound at Smyrna (c. 610) and that of the Persian commander at Paphos in Cyprus, during the Ionic revolt (498).

Silphium *Ferula tingitana*, a variety of fennel, a plant used by the Greeks for a number of nutritional and medicinal purposes. Produced in large quantities in Cyrenaica, where it becomes the main coin type, but virtually extinct by the 2nd century BC.

Siren The beguiling songstresses of the *Odyssey* whose melody lured sailors to their death. Also the female-headed bird borrowed

by Greek artists from northern Syrian art (a male version was less widely copied) around 700. The original relationship between the two is not clear.

Socle The lowest visible course of masonry in any building or other structure, eg an altar. A stone socle was regularly used by Greeks as a foundation for walls of less durable material, and even in stone buildings the socle was often of larger dimensions than the upper members.

Spartiate A trueborn Spartan – one of the Homoioi ("Equals"). They alone had full citizenship rights in Laconia. They had to be offspring of Spartiate mother and father, and their decrease in numbers over the centuries was a prime factor in the increase of their military preparedness against a helot★ revolt.

Sphinx

Sphinx The winged human-headed lion of Egyptian origin. She retains something of her religious role when adopted by the Greeks, watching over tombs in the form of sculpted monuments; but more often the sphinx appears in Greek art merely as one of the creatures in which artisans in many crafts took so much delight.

Stater A basic measurement of weight, often of about 800 grams. The word means "something balanced out" on a pair of scales, and is therefore confusingly applied both to the single weight and to that of the two objects in the pans. Commonly used of early coins of a much lighter weight (about 8 to 16 grams).

Stater

Stele A stone slab set up as a marker, often over a grave, when it would normally be inscribed and/or decorated, but also used as a boundary stone and in sanctuaries. Often left an irregular shape.

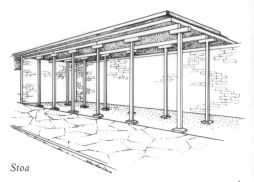

Stoa

Stoa An open-fronted structure akin to the more modern loggia or portico, affording shelter from sun, wind and rain. Found both in sanctuaries and in civic centers. In the course of the 5th century they begin to increase in size, incorporating rooms at the rear and having a second story.

Syssitia Communal male messes, especially in Dorian towns. Each member of a syssition contributed his share, and failure to pay these dues – wine, corn and the like – meant exclusion from the mess and from all concomitant rights and privileges.

Talent A substantial weight, general in the Greek world, amounting in Attica to about 25.5 kilos and composed of 6,000 drachmas. In Homer we hear only of a much smaller talent of gold. The word derived from the Greek for "scales."

Temenos "Allotment," generally used in the Iron Age★ for the god's portion on earth, that is, the area covered by his or her sanctuary. Usually marked off by boundary stones (*horoi*), and sometimes a wall as well; some *horoi* were inscribed with the name of the deity.

Thermoluminescence dating (TL) A method of measuring the time elapsed since a terracotta object was last fired (in most cases therefore since its manufacture). Radioactive particles are absorbed by the clay, and by measuring the infinitesimal glow given off by this absorbed radioactivity the length of time taken to accumulate it since the clay was last made "pure" by a firing can be estimated. Modern copies will therefore include little radioactivity.

Thesmothetai "Law-makers," a board of six officials at Athens charged with the administration of the law, both as keepers of the actual legal codes and as interpreters and judges. Until 461 they retained the right to pronounce justice, though there was right of appeal to the people for convicted persons.

Thespis Traditional "inventor" of tragic plays in Athens during the period 550–530. His major innovation was to transform a simple choral recitation in honor of Dionysus into a "play," by using himself as an individual actor able to converse with the chorus.

Thetes The lowest class in the Athenian state under Solon's income assessment, producing less than 100 measures per annum. Until the 5th century their political role was confined to membership of the general assembly of the people.

Thucydides An Athenian general exiled for a military defeat in northern Greece in 424, better known for his *History of the Peloponnesian War*. He prefaces the first of the eight books with an "Archaeologia" or thumbnail sketch of the major developments in Greek history from the Trojan War to near his own day.

Tondo A round field of decoration on vases, in particular on the inside of cups and plates. The better artists paid close attention to finding satisfactory ways of filling the space with figure decoration.

Tophet The burial area for the cremated bodies of child sacrifices (*see* **Moloch**) in Phoenician colonies. The earliest of these Tophetim is at Carthage, of the late 8th century. There are others at Motya and various sites on Sardinia.

Tragedy Originally a choral celebration in honor of Dionysus performed by competing choirs at his festival in early spring, it gradually developed into more of what we would term a play (*see* **Thespis**). Supposedly named from its being a song (*ode*) in a contest for which a goat (*tragos*) was given as a prize.

Triglyph "Triple carving," the element separating the metopes★ in the frieze of a Doric temple (and used by extension for similar "punctuating" motifs in friezes in the other arts). In origin they were the decorated ends of wooden ceiling beams.

Trireme The standard Greek warship from the later 6th century to the Hellenistic period. Like earlier boats, it relied on oar-power and a reinforced ram for its effect, but the trireme carried three banks of oars instead of the one or two of its predecessors. Thucydides★ says that Ameinocles of Samos introduced the type in the mid-7th century, but there is little evidence of its use before the later 6th century.

Tyrant The name, perhaps of Lydian origin, which the Greeks applied to their own unconstitutional rulers, and which was never in official use. Its modern derogatory aspect

Volutes on an amphora

was acquired when more ruthless dictators came to power.

Tyrtaeus Spartan leader and poet of the mid-7th century, known especially for his partly preserved martial verses, encouraging the Spartans to stand firm against the Messenians in revolt – a war in which he is said to have taken a leading part.

Volute Spiraling decoration, introduced to Greece in the Orientalizing★ period and used very widely in most arts, notably in vase-painting and in architecture, where a pair of volutes are an integral part of the Ionic and Aeolic capital★.

Votive offering Also known as a dedication. An important part of Greek religious practice was the offering of gifts to the gods in their shrines, either to appease or to thank them. The more solid offerings that have been preserved and found in excavation often bear inscriptions naming donor and deity, and sometimes also the reason for the offering. Objects of all kinds and sizes could be offered, and inventory lists of dedications preserved on stone mention perishable commodities such as clothes.

Yoke-man Zeugites, a member of the third class under Solon's income assessment of the Athenian citizenry, producing between 100 and 200 measures per annum. Theoretically each owned a pair of oxen (*zeugos*) and was able to provide his own armor to fight as a hoplite★. They gradually increased their rights, being first able to stand for election as archon★ in 487.

Index